Library of
Davidson College

The Rise and Fall of Project Camelot

*Studies in the Relationship Between
Social Science and Practical Politics*

Revised Edition

edited by
Irving Louis Horowitz

The MIT Press

Massachusetts Institute of Technology
Cambridge, Massachusetts, and London, England

300.72
H816r

Revised edition copyright © 1974 by
The Massachusetts Institute of Technology
First edition 1967

All rights reserved. No part of this book may be reproduced in any form or by any means, electronic or mechanical, including photocopying, recording, or by any information storage and retrieval system, without permission in writing from the publisher.

This book was printed by Halliday Lithograph Corporation
and bound by The Colonial Press, Inc.
in the United States of America

Library of Congress Cataloging in Publication Data

Horowitz, Irving Louis, comp.
  The rise and fall of project Camelot.

  1. Social science research—United States. 2. Social sciences and state —United States. 3. United States relations (general) with Chile. 4. Chile—Relations (general) with the United States. I. Title.
H62.H62   1974   300'.7'2   74-6367
ISBN 0-262-58029-2   79-10047

Contents

Preface to the Revised Edition — vi
Preface to the First Edition — ix

I. THE SETTING

The Rise and Fall of Project Camelot — 3
Irving Louis Horowitz

II. THE DESIGN AND PURPOSE OF PROJECT CAMELOT

Document Number 1 — 47
Document Number 2 — 50
Document Number 3 — 56
Document Number 4 — 60

III. THE ACADEMIC RESPONSE

The Established Order: Do Not Fold, Spindle, or Mutilate — 71
Marshall Sahlins

American Academic Ethics and Social Research Abroad:
The Lesson of Project Camelot — 80
Kalman H. Silvert

Ethics and the Social Scientist   107
Robert Boguslaw

Conflict as Research and Research as Conflict   128
Jessie Bernard

Threats from Agency-Determined Research:
The Case of Camelot   153
Herbert Blumer

IV. THE POLITICAL RESPONSE

Behavioral Sciences and the National Security   177
Dante B. Fascell

America in an Age of Revolution   196
J. W. Fulbright

Project Camelot: An Interim Postlude   203
Theodore R. Vallance

State Department Procedures for Reviewing
Government-Sponsored Foreign Area Research   211
George C. Denney, Jr.

A Socialist Commentary on Camelot   229
Aniceto Rodríguez

A Communist Commentary on Camelot   232
Jorge Montes

V. THE GENERAL IMPLICATIONS

Problems of Government Utilization of
Scholarly Research in International Affairs   239
William R. Polk

CONTENTS

The Necessity for Social Scientists Doing Research for Governments	267
Ithiel de Sola Pool	
After Camelot	281
Johan Galtung	
Project Camelot and the Science of Man	313
Robert A. Nisbet	
Social Science and Public Policy: Implications of Modern Research	339
Irving Louis Horowitz	
The Pentagon Papers and Social Science	377
Irving Louis Horowitz	
Name and Subject Index	401

Preface to the Revised Edition

Few things are more astonishing than the transformation of the newsworthy into the commonplace—which I presume is why we so readily and even eagerly discard old papers, magazines, and yes, even books. But it is perhaps even more unusual, given this phenomenon, when an item in a newspaper, which stimulated an article in a magazine, which in turn provoked this collection of essays in a book, remains valuable and valid enough to be reprinted nearly a decade after the fact. In all fairness it should be reported that the moral thrust rather than the factual content of *The Rise and Fall of Project Camelot* is the key to the success of this collection of papers. In the interest of reflecting the ethical content of social science more fully, it might have been entitled, as one friend suggested, *Foreign Policy, Social Ethics, and Behavioral Science: The Case of Project Camelot*.

For me personally the initial foray into the study of a big money grant run by big-time social scientists carried with it more apparent risks than rewards. That I reaped the benefits of the latter and escaped the penalties of the former I attribute to the helping hand of Providence and not any special talents for avoiding troubles. Indeed, I would say that such talents have not been especially prominent in my professional background or makeup. But all of that is old hat now. What remains are two crucial nuggets, which I impart to the readers of this new edition.

First, studying the powerful is tougher than studying the powerless, but more rewarding. Frankly, the former option is less fraught with moral dilemmas of taking advantage of the weak and disenfranchised. After all, it is one thing to analyze welfare mothers and quite another to take on the Defense Department establishment. But the techniques must be adjusted to the objects of study. The rich and the powerful do not like to be studied any more than the poor and the powerless. But unlike the latter group, it is harder for them to say no. They have much to lose by criticism and exposure—nothing short of their power and their wealth. So the quarry should be relentlessly pursued, without losing sight of the moral aims of the research, and never forgetting that it is very hard for those in power to resist the temptation of being spoken well of. That is why in my own three studies of this type—on Project Camelot in 1965; on Project Themis, or the military uses of social scientists in 1968; and on the crisis in the Institute for Advanced Study in Princeton in 1973—I have had relatively few problems gathering all the data necessary for doing such research.

Second, all such forms of research are in effect studied in the sociology of ethics, that is, in the ongoing enterprise of establishing the empirical coordinates of decision making in a concrete situation. This sort of sociology of situational ethics makes more sense, for me at least, than abstract analysis or reanalysis of Plato's impact on the modern world, or how Wagnerian romanticism affects the course of world empire. It is not that I am belittling such earlier forms of coming to terms with ethical coordinates of behavior; it is simply that they did not represent a real sociological effort to engage moral issues. I think that the area of policy making broadly conceived has permitted the social scientists to evolve a serious sociological vision of the political process—one that starts with situations, not simple electoral head counts or abstract systemic premises in the linkages of figures in the history of ideas.

In this reformation of the tasks of sociological research, I have had the vital assistance of a legion of journalists, lawyers, and other social scientists with a shared vision in the need to develop a sociology of ethics based on situations and cases. The work of David Wise on government secrecy, Alan Westin on government power through information retrieval, Frank Donner on legal incursions on the rights of individuals, Myron Glazer on the methodology of training young social scientists to do research on policy issues; Gideon Sjoberg on showing the moral components in social research, all of these have registered important gains that were both a cause and a consequence of the exposure of Project Camelot to the light of criticism.

My own work and thinking have, I hope, progressed, along with those of my colleagues and coworkers on the issues raised in this volume. But perhaps because Camelot was, for so many of us, the first and still the most dramatic illustration of the confrontation of social science with the agonies of big-time research in a federal context, the statements here possess a directness and crispness that perhaps can no longer be recaptured. This quality was emphasized by the existence of an undeclared war in Vietnam which at the time served to underwrite the moral concerns expressed in the sale of social research to an admittedly unmatched federal sponsor. In any event, with the exception of my essay on the Pentagon Papers —which in their own way represented the final piece of the puzzle of Project Camelot—and a postscript, the book stands as originally published: a memorial to the stupidity and cupidity of *some* social scientists, and an equal reminder of the courage and dignity of *other* social scientists. In short, the Camelot volume once again forcefully brings home a simple paradigm: the struggle between rational and irrational concepts of society goes on among social scientists, no less than between the larger political communities and their hired thinkers. The search for a meaningful social science and that for an empirical social science are thus joined together in concrete terms by searching for the whole truth.

IRVING LOUIS HOROWITZ

Rutgers University
New Brunswick, New Jersey
March 1974

Preface to the First Edition

Etymological research concerning the word "camelot" leads back to that remarkable animal, the camel. It will be noted that this is a composite beast constructed with feet of sponge. Indeed, the name of Project Camelot seems particularly well chosen, since a sponge is a useful physical representation of ambiguity on a scale of firmness. Even in its more prosaic representations, Camelot is shrouded in vagueness. In English folk history, Camelot represents the castle at which the knights of the Round Table in King Arthur's Court held forth in moral splendor; while in French *fin de siècle* political history, the *Camelots du roi* served as bodyguards and secret agents for *La Ligue d'Action Française* — the most extreme royalist and restorationist group of the nation.

This ancestral dilemma has served to keep me from forgetting that most genuine moral struggles are conflicts between competing notions of the good, and only rarely do simplistic good-versus-evil models suffice. Were this not the case, the agony of moral choice would be reduced to an operational decision to do what comes naturally. An additional practical consideration in treating materials in this fashion is that this volume is a reader: a collection of statements intended to represent the widest, wisest, and most exact set of opinions on an issue which is now recognized as a fundamental watershed in the relations between social science and practical politics.

Considering the unusual nature of this study, I should like to make a few claims and disclaimers — as the Camelot documents usually start out — "for the record."

First, this is not sponsored research. I undertook my own part of this study, somewhat reluctantly, to get the complete story concerning the termination of Project Camelot after less than one year in operation. I was initially led to do so by my colleagues at *Trans-action*. There was an editorial consensus that it would be a good idea to get this information first hand so that a magazine of "social science and modern society" could keep its public abreast of the latest happenings. In other words, there was no pressure from anyone, in or out of government circles, to perform either a public relations stunt job or a journalistic smear job.

Second, my main concern in doing this volume was to prepare a statement which went beyond the gossip and simpleminded nonsense which surrounded Project Camelot. I did this by requesting and obtaining direct interviews and firsthand data. This project has had perhaps the worst public relations record of any agency or subagency of the U.S. government. Everyone from right-wing reporters in Washington to left-wing reporters in Santiago had essentially the same negative attitude toward Camelot. It is also clear that such public outcry was ideologically prevented from telling more than one half the story.

Third, I am personally fond of and professionally respectful of many people who either are or were connected with Project Camelot, the Latin American Faculty of Social Sciences in Chile, and the other agencies and institutions which form the fabric and texture of the Camelot story. It might also be said, with some pride on my part, that not a few of those scholars working with or against Project Camelot were former students of mine, while yet others were and remain colleagues and warm acquaintances. The fact that I knew personally so many of the people involved caused me considerable anxiety in undertaking the job of reporting the findings first in an abbreviated form and now in a more extensive version. But something which I know all too well is that there is never a "right person" for any job except the person willing to do the work.

Fourth, I want to make explicit the personal nature of my own appraisal. While I did my best to interview and contact all parties involved in Camelot — critics as well as supporters of the project — and while I worked hard to get all available data, this study still represents a "lone wolf" effort. It is not an official publication of any learned or professional society, nor should it even be viewed as representative of a group sentiment. I welcome the opportunity to put forth this reader, since it enables those observers who came up with a different opinion to make public their own observations. To further assist those interested in additional investigation, I have included a data bank consisting of relevant materials from preliminary designs on Project Camelot.

Fifth, with respect to the selections in this volume, it should be evident that what I have worked for is a *representative* rather than a *definitive* set of papers. With considerable pain and regret, not to mention proper urgings on the part of the publishers, a good number of fine papers have had to be eliminated from the volume. The main criterion for inclusion has been the degree of concreteness manifested. Papers which used the Camelot story as a bridge or jumping-off point for more generic types of analyses have had to be left out. It is possible that a set of papers of this latter type might be organized at a later date. Hopefully, this volume can serve as reference for precisely such wider-ranging examinations.

Sixth, and finally, I want to augment the first point. Not only was this piece of research unsponsored by any governmental or private agency; no individual, acting either on his own or in concert with any federal or private agency, attempted to put intellectual pressure on me. I can record only that once I made clear the aims of my research, everyone connected with (or critical of) Project Camelot was solicitous of my needs — and placed any available information or documents at my disposal. However, in order not to harm anyone inadvertently who told me things in confidence or provided me with essential documents, I shall refrain from the conventional practice of listing the names of those individuals who were most helpful with information and criticism and without which this study could not have been satisfactorily completed. It is to these people that this volume is gratefully dedicated.

IRVING LOUIS HOROWITZ

Washington University
St. Louis, Missouri
February 1967

PART I

THE SETTING

"A new style, less tense with crises, less loaded with statements and declarations, quieter, simpler, closer to the facts, would do much to clear the air of that distrust and that almost despairing scepticism which now obscure it; and it would initiate a much needed recovery of the moral authority of the United States."

Salvador de Madariaga (1962)

Irving Louis Horowitz

Washington University

*The Rise and Fall of Project Camelot**

I. AN INTRODUCTION TO AN ESSAY

American lives have become intertwined with the fate of government contracts. The granting of an award to an aircraft company in California is an occasion for loud newspaper headlines and can create in-migration patterns overnight. By the same token, the cancellation of a contract to a shipbuilder in New York is also an occasion for front-page newspaper stories. In short order, the boomtown can be made into a ghost town. Management and labor, ministers and bankers, Republicans and Democrats, all seem to have a common desire to get hold of government funds irrespective of their private philosophies of government. Academic establishments are no exception, as any investigation of federal aid to education programs will reveal.

With this as a background, the cancellation of a social science contract by an agency of the government can hardly be expected to create a furor among the American people. However, while it might seem that the rise and fall of Project Camelot fits a general government pattern, it has now become

* A much briefer version of this study appeared in *Trans-Action*, Vol. 3, No. 1 (1965). Those portions taken from the original article are reprinted with permission of its editor.

evident that its cancellation by the Defense Department is an event of special meaning and particular consequences for the social science industry. The sound and fury generated by Project Camelot — from Washington to Moscow, involving scholars from Norway to Chile — signify much more than the rise and fall of a single project. Camelot's fate may prove to be the harbinger of vast changes in the structure and function of the social sciences.

The value problems for social scientists are the same whether scholars work for a ten dollar per diem or a one million dollar per annum. What are the vital connections between science and policy, between public findings and secret data, between the myths of society and the facts of sociology, between objectivity and commitment? However, if the "stakes" of a project do not qualitatively alter the value questions, they drastically affect a considerable number of scholars and in so doing alter the practical stakes. A multimillion dollar government "sponsor" has expectations and demands that differ significantly from that of a university bestowing honor or status. The scope of a project therefore decisively influences expectations and outcomes.

These comments introduce a project, the meteoric rise of which is exceeded only by its equally decisive demise. Project Camelot came into being in 1964 as an offspring of the Army's Special Operations Research Office (SORO), with a fanfare befitting the largest single grant ever provided for a social science project. Its termination less than a year later was registered with an official military dispatch that was as lame as it was tame. *What* is the "story" behind Project Camelot? *Who* was in back of it? *How* was it funded? *When* did it start? Above all, *why* did it fail?

Perhaps the best way to begin is with the description of Project Camelot offered in the rather decisive document, dated December 4, 1964, mailed to a select list of scholars around the world:

Project Camelot is a study whose objective is to determine the feasibility of developing a general social systems model which would make it possible to predict and influence politically significant aspects of social change in the developing nations of the world. Somewhat more specifically, its objectives are

First, to devise procedures for assessing the potential for internal war within national societies; *second*, to identify with increased degrees of confidence, those actions which a government might take to relieve conditions which are assessed as giving rise to a potential for internal war; and *finally*, to assess the feasibility of prescribing the characteristics of a system for obtaining and using the essential information needed for doing the above two things. The project is conceived as a three- to four-year effort to be funded at around one and one-half million dollars annually. It is supported by the Army and the Department of Defense, and will be conducted with the cooperation of other agencies of the government. A large amount of primary data collection in the field is planned as well as the extensive utilization of already available data on social, economic and political functions. At this writing, it seems probable that the geographic orientation of the research will be toward Latin American countries. Present plans call for a field office in that region.

An examination shows that the statement of purpose raises as many questions as it resolves. And it should be added that they are not resolved in the more extensive and elaborate documents subsequently published. For to devise procedures for assessing the potential for internal war within national societies, even if it were to answer "feasibility" questions as to whether such internal war is plausible and under what conditions, it does not settle "policy" issues: Would the findings be the same if the "incumbents" are Communists and the "insurgents" are Restorationists? To what extent is the data-gathering process determined by social science needs or by American foreign policy needs? The draft proposals make the assumption that governments are somehow always in the position to take actions to relieve conditions that give rise to a potential for internal war. This philosophical voluntarism goes untested. Thus the *scientific limits* of Project Camelot are never stated.

Obviously, if governments were in a voluntaristic position, there would never be any revolutions, planned or spontaneous. An essential dilemma in Project Camelot, is that it never settled the issue of primary concern: How to assess the characteristics of a social system or evolve instruments for obtaining and using essential information? The problem of the relationship between "pure" and "applied" social science is involved from the outset. The question is how far and with what legitimacy can the social scientist pursue this inquiry. Much more important than responding to every wild allegation about Camelot in the overall picture is to determine the precise character of social science values in a context of extreme political and professional tensions.

II. PROJECT CAMELOT: A COLLECTIVE SELF-PORTRAIT

I would like to offer a collective portrait of how the men working on Project Camelot viewed their own participation and what they felt to be the shortcomings of the project. As a result of data gathered in direct interviews, there appeared to be general consensus on the following six points.

First, men who went to work for Project Camelot felt the need for a more appropriate big-range social science. They wanted to create a social science of contemporary relevance which would not suffer from a parochial narrowness of vision to which their own professional backgrounds (largely in sociology and psychology) had conditioned them. Most of the men viewed Camelot as a bona fide opportunity to do unrestricted fundamental research with relatively unlimited funds at their disposal. Under such optimal conditions, these scholars tended not to look a gift horse in the mouth. As one affiliate indicated: There was no desire to inquire too deeply as to the military source of the funds or the ultimate purpose of the project.

Second, a number of men affiliated with Camelot felt that there was actually more freedom under selective sponsored conditions to do fundamental research in a nonacademic environment than at a university or college. One project member noted that during the fifties there was far more freedom to do fundamental research in the RAND Corporation than in any college or university in America. Indeed, once the protective covering of RAND was adopted, it was almost viewed as a society of Platonists permitted to search for truth on behalf of the powerful. A neoplatonic definition of the situation by the men on Camelot was itself a constant in all of the interviews that were conducted.

Third, a good many of the Camelot affiliates felt distinctly uncomfortable with military sponsorship, especially considering the present U.S. military posture. But their reaction to this discomfort was that "the Army had to be educated." This view was sometimes cast in neo-Freudian terms; namely, that the Army's bent toward violence ought to be sublimated. Underlying this theme was the notion of the armed forces as an agency for potential social good; an enlargement on the idea that the discipline and the order embodied by an army could be channeled into the process of economic and social development in the United States as well as in many parts of the Third World.

Fourth, there was among the Camelot social scientists a profound conviction of the perfectibility of mankind, particularly in the possibility of the military establishment performing a major role in this general process of growth. This perspective was the Enlightenment syndrome. Like the eighteenth century *philosophes*, many members of the Camelot staff shared a belief in the worth of rational persuasion. Just as Voltaire and Diderot thought that they could change the course of universal history by bringing the message of social utility to the monarchs of Europe — to Catherine of Russia, to Emperor Joseph of the Austro-Hungarian Empire, and to King Louis of France — the men of Camelot believed that they too, in some like manner, could affect the course of events. They sought to correct the intellectual paternalism and parochialism under which Pentagon generals, State Department diplomats, and Defense Department planners seemed to operate.

Fifth, one might say that a major long-range purpose of Camelot, at least for some of its policy makers, was to prevent another revolutionary holocaust. At the very least, there was a shared belief that *Pax Americana* was severely threatened and deserved to know its own future. The policy makers of

Project Camelot may be criticized for a certain jejune naïveté on this point; but surely, once Americanism as an ideology is accepted as a basic positive value it is difficult to condemn the policy makers for corruption. The Camelot personnel were upset by those social scientists willing to try nothing and criticize everything, who considered themselves to be in the forefront of applied social science, and saw little difference between scholars engaged in the war against poverty and those directly concerned with the war against violence.

Sixth, what became particularly apparent from speaking with Camelot personnel is that none of them viewed their role on the project as spying for the United States government or for anyone else. The only person who even touched on this discordant note was an assistant professor of anthropology whose connection with the project was from the outset remote and tenuous. So far were Camelot people from thinking of their work in cloak-and-dagger terms that none of them interviewed were even convinced that the armed forces would take their preliminary recommendations seriously (even though that remained their hope). There was perhaps a keener appreciation on the part of the directing members of Camelot neither to "sell out" nor to "cop out" than among scholars with regular academic appointments. This concern with the ethics of social science research seems to result from their confronting, in a daily situation, the problems of betrayal, treason, secrecy, and abuse of data. Even though a university position may ultimately derive from federally sponsored research, the connection is often too remote to cause any steady *crise de conscience*. Another factor seemingly involved is that government work, while well paid, remains professionally marginal. And the sense of marginality undoubtedly causes many federally linked scholars to steadily ponder their policy "roles."

From the outset of their involvement, a number of men had serious doubts about the character of the work they would be doing and about the conditions under which it would be done. But these doubts were more sophisticated than the common garden variety of criticism one might have anticipated.

It was pointed out, for example, that the U.S. Army tends to exercise a far more stringent intellectual control of research findings than does the U.S. Air Force. As evidence for this, it was stated that SORO had fewer "free-wheeling" aspects to its research designs than did RAND. One "inside" critic went so far as to say that he knew of no SORO-sponsored research which had a "playful" or unsponsored quality, such as one finds to be a steady diet at RAND. "It was all grim stuff," I was told by one staff man. And by another, that "the self-conscious seriousness gets to you after a while."

Another line of criticism was that the pressures on the "reformers" (the men engaged in Camelot research often referred to themselves in this way) to effect recommended changes were much stronger than those on the military. The social scientists were expected to be social reformers, while the military was expected to be conservative. What gave an aura of role confusion, no less than role displacement, to several Camelot officials was a vaguely perceived organizational disequilibrium between researchers and sponsors. It was felt that a relationship of equality between sponsors and researchers did not obtain; but rather one of superordinate military needs and subordinate academic roles. On the other hand, some Camelot officials were impressed by the disinterestedness of the military and thought that, far from exercising undue influence, the army personnel were loath to offer opinions even when requested.

Yet another objection made from within was that if one had to work in the policy sciences, if research was to be conducted that would have international ramifications, it might better be performed under the auspices of conventional State Department sponsorship. "After all," I was told, "they are at least nominally committed to civilian political norms." There was a considerable reluctance to believe that the Defense Department, despite its superior organization, greater financial affluence, and executive influence, would actually improve upon State Department styles of work or accept recommendations at variance with Pentagon policies.

There seemed to be few, if any, expressions of disrespect for the work being contemplated by Camelot or a disdain for policy-oriented work in general. This consensus obtained despite the fact that the scholars engaged in the Camelot effort incorporated in their outlook and orientation two rather distinct sets of vocabulary. Their role disorientation led to a scientific eclecticism. The various documents reveal a military vocabulary provided with an array of military justifications, often followed (within the same document) by a social science vocabulary offering social science justifications and rationalizations. The dilemma in the literature emanating from Project Camelot, from the preliminary report issued in August 1964 until the more advanced document issued in April 1965, was the same: an incomplete incorporation of the military and sociological vocabularies.

It might be doubted that a synthesis between military and sociological "styles of work" was possible, given the exclusively heuristic concerns of the Army's interest in the dynamics of insurgency and counterinsurgency and the more general theoretical concerns of the cadre of Camelot in the process of revolution making. If an analogy be permitted, and perhaps forgiven, in the light of the yet-to-be-discussed points, there is a sense in which a criminologist is dedicated to the liquidation of crime and not just to the incarceration of criminals. What was it that the men of Camelot were dedicated to liquidate? Was it conflict in general? Was it counterinsurgent movements? Was it Communist-led revolutions? Was it the social source of discontent? Would any recommendation criticizing the military as a fomenter of discontent (especially in Latin America) be made? In short, the preeminence of a "systems" approach rather than a "problems" approach led to exaggerated model-building techniques that obfuscated rather than clarified major issues. Many Camelot scholars arrived at this recognition also. But unfortunately, it was understood too late; only when the project was declared null and void.

III. THE WEB OF TANGLED EVENTS

As is often the case, the explosion of a big event begins in unpredictable circumstances and in unlikely surroundings. The actual crisis over Camelot came to a boiling point as a result of a congruence of several events. It involves a network spreading from a professor of anthropology at the University of Pittsburgh, to a professor of sociology at the University of Oslo and yet a third professor of sociology at the University of Chile in Santiago de Chile. The "showdown" took place in Chile, first within the confines of the university, next in the popular press of Santiago, and finally, behind U.S. embassy walls. From there on, the Camelot story moved to Washington: demands for a hearing, outcries from congressional figures, pained expressions of grief by State Department officials, revanchist sentiments of anger by Defense Department officials, confusion by military intellectuals, and finally, the official announcement and resolution of the problem by Presidential epistle.

In May 1965, Chile was the scene of wild newspaper tales of spying and academic outrage at being recruited for spying missions. This was high irony, since in the working papers of Project Camelot, it is stated that the criteria for study "should show promise of high payoffs in terms of the kinds of data required," and apparently Chile did not meet these requirements. The "model nations" for the study of Latin American revolutions and coups were to be Argentina, Guatemala, Venezuela, Bolivia, Columbia, Cuba, El Salvador, Dominican Republic, Peru, Brazil, and "special cases," Mexico and Paraguay. In the preliminary design, Chile was not even included among those nations to be given even a casual treatment.

How it was that Chile became involved in Project Camelot's affairs brings us directly to a consideration of Hugo G. Nuttini, Assistant Professor of Anthropology at Pittsburgh, citizen of the United States, and former citizen of the Republic of Chile. From his opening inquiry to the directors of SORO it is clear that Nuttini desired to participate in Project Camelot in whatever capacity was deemed most useful.

The reaction to his desire for participation was extremely cautious and quite restrained. Whatever Mr. Nuttini was or was not, he certainly was not an employee or staff member of Project Camelot. He was finally asked to report on the possibilities of gaining the cooperation of professional personnel with Project Camelot and in general to do the kind of ethnographic survey that has mild results and a modest honorarium of $750. But Mr. Nuttini had an obviously different (and more ambitious) definition of his role; and despite the warnings and precautions that Rex Hopper, then newly appointed head of Project Camelot, placed on his trip (especially Hopper's insistence on its informal nonaligned quality), Nuttini somehow managed to convey the impression of being a direct official of Project Camelot and of having the authority to make proposals to prospective Chilean participants. Here was an opportunity to link the country of his birth with the country of his choice.

At approximately the same time, Johan Galtung was invited to participate in a June conference that would present a preliminary research design for the study of internal war potentials and the effects of government action on such potentials. The proposed plan for the conference had as its basis the December 4th memorandum. The fee for participation of the social scientists attending would be $2,000 for four weeks. Dr. Galtung, who was in Chile at the time and associated with the Latin American Faculty of Social Science (FLACSO) replied in his letter of April 22, saying that he could not accept participation in Project Camelot for several reasons. He could not accept the role of the Army as a sponsoring agent interested in a study of counterinsurgency. He could not accept the notion of the Army as an agency of development rather than as an agency for managing conflict or perhaps even promoting conflict. He could not accept the "imperialist features," as he called them, of the research design. Finally, he could not accept the asymmetry of the project. He found it difficult to understand why it was that just as there were studies of counter-insurgency there should not also be studies of the social effect of counter-intervention, studies of the conditions under which Latin American nations might intervene in the affairs of the United States. Obviously and openly, Dr. Gatlung had spoken to others in Oslo, Santiago, and throughout Latin America about the project. He had clearly shown the memorandum of December 4th to many of his colleagues, and presumably it was from his copy of the memorandum that a Spanish language version was fashioned and circulated.

On the same date as Galtung's letter to Hopper, April 22, Nuttini had a conference with the Vice-Chancellor of the University of Chile for the purpose of discussing at greater length the character of Project Camelot. After half an hour's exposition, Professor Fuenzalida, invited to attend this "briefing session" by the Vice-Chancellor, asked Nuttini point-blank to specify the ultimate aims of the project, its sponsors, and its political implications. Before an answer was forthcoming, Professor Fuenzalida, apparently with considerable drama, pulled a copy of the December 4th circular letter from his briefcase and read a prepared Spanish translation.

At the same time, the authorities at FLACSO turned the matter over to their associates in the Chilean Senate and in the left-wing Chilean press. They blazed forth with banner headlines and with such terms as "intervention," "imperialism," and the "scandal of Project Camelot." This rhetoric was undoubtedly reinforced by the May 1965 events which saw United States troops once more occupy Santo Domingo in the Dominican Republic. After several days of extremely heated University denunciations and a rather complete stand within the Chilean mass communications network against Project Camelot, United States Ambassador to Chile Ralph A. Dungan sent forth his own protest to Washington, which asked for an unconditional cancellation of Project Camelot's Chilean activities.

The public disclosures of the Chilean "situation" heightened the uneasiness over the expansion of Defense Department activities, felt even by those sectors in Chile who were pro-American. Foreign Minister of Chile Miguel Ortiz warned in an interview against allowing the economic and social development plans embodied in the Alliance for Progress to become overshadowed by strategic considerations of fighting nonexistent insurgency movements. By the last week of June, both progovernment Christian Democratic and opposition Left Socialist newspapers throughout Chile condemned the "brazen intervention" by the U.S. Defense Department engaged in the realization of a vast continental spy plan known as "Operation Camelot." The papers, employing strong nationalist language, went on to say "that the worthy and virile reaction of our country to the United States plan to carry out an apparently inoffensive sociological study in our midst is acquiring justified residence." All newspapers agreed that Project Camelot was "intended to investigate the military and political situation prevailing in Chile and to determine the possibility of an antidemocratic coup." After this rather universal Chilean reaction it was clear that Project Camelot could not survive, in Chile at least.

Events from that point on switched to Washington, and under the pressure of State Department officials and the parallel pressure of Congressional reaction Project Camelot was halted in midstream, or more precisely, before it ever really got under way.

There was considerable fortuitousness on the Washington side, no less than on the Santiago side. At the time United States Ambassador to Chile Ralph A. Dungan sent through his telegrams requesting clarification of Project Camelot, what it was and who was sponsoring such operations in Chile. The State Department member of Camelot Core Planning Group, Pio Uliassi, was casting considerable doubt on the Defense Department sponsorship of efforts, which he held more properly belonged to the State Department. As a result of Uliassi's attitude, or rather the negative reaction to his recommendations, there was a steady deterioration of relations between Camelot sponsors and State Department consultants. Indeed, informal charges that the State Department representative on the Core Planning Group amounted to a courier role rather than a creative role, only served to increase mutual suspicion and hostility.

As Camelot became increasingly autonomous, communications between its sponsors and the State Department sharply dwindled. Even before the Chile flare-up, it was clear that State Department officials wished to restore their former control over research projects on foreign areas. The Chile explosion, and the letters from Ambassador Dungan, only permitted what was smoldering behind the scenes to come into the open. The analysis of Project Camelot, issued from what *The Washington Star* mistakenly termed a "low-ranking State aide," formed the basis of a report to State Department officials that underlay later requests to kill Camelot at the earliest possible time. The report mentioned the following points:

a. The Camelot officials considered the State Department official on the Core Planning Group to be an observer rather than a recognized authority able to give counsel.

b. Coordination of Camelot plans for Chile were so lacking that not only was there a breakdown in communication between the State Department and Camelot but also between Army personnel and Camelot officials.

c. Camelot officials, through their participation in a future publication entitled Conflict, would in effect attempt to make political judgments that up to the present were exclusively in the hands of the State Department.

When Ambassador Dungan's communications reached Washington, there was thus already a considerable amount of ferment about Project Camelot. The demands for a Congressional hearing were quick to follow. Senators Fulbright and McCarthy asked for early hearings. And in a private hearing on Camelot held in early July before the House Foreign Affairs Committee, the text of which was not released until December,

Representatives Fraser, Rosenthal, Fascell, and Royball questioned Theodore Vallance on the worth and sponsorship of Camelot. The remarks were cast in terms of military intrusion into foreign policy areas, the lack of coordination between government agencies that leads to dangerous duplication of effort and embarrassing results. Finally, the question of the general allocation of responsibilities was raised. It soon became evident to all interested parties that if SORO as a whole were to be saved, Project Camelot as a part of that whole would have to be sacrificed.

In quick succession, Dean Rusk and Robert S. McNamara, respective heads of the State Department and Defense Department, announced their agreement in principle on future lines of responsibility and communication concerning foreign area research projects. Next, Ambassador Dungan let it be known that Chile would be spared any embarrassment by Project Camelot, regardless of the ultimate outcome of the Project. A week later, announcement was made by the Defense Department that Project Camelot was canceled on the grounds that its original doubt about the practicality of officially sponsored research on other nations had been verified by the reaction in Chile to news of the Project. Shortly after this remarkable case of political clairvoyance, questions were raised, both at the official and journalistic levels, about similar projects sponsored by the Defense Department concerning French Canada (Project Revolt) and rural politics in Colombia (Project Simpático) and Project Michelson, sponsored by the Navy Department, which sought to analyze "goals and goal structures" of the United States, the Soviet Union, and the Chinese People's Republic. In each case, the damage which could be done by "sociological snoopers" was raised. The damage done by journalistic jibing was, however, not mentioned.

While the fate of the various projects ostensibly similar to that of Project Camelot remain to be decided, it is evident that future sponsorship of foreign area research by agencies other than those sanctioned by the State Department is quite unlikely. This is the essence of President Johnson's memorandum to Dean Rusk. The key paragraph in his communication states that "no Government sponsorship of foreign area research should be undertaken which in the judgment of the Secretary of State would adversely affect United States foreign relations." The request for "procedures" to assure this ruling would be carried have already been put into effect. The Special Operations Research Office of American University, while financed by the Defense Department, will in all likelihood become increasingly responsive to State Department needs and wants in the area of foreign nation research or, failing that, return to formalistic information services for the Army. The exact lines of authority are yet to be worked out. But Army officials have already considered this yet one more instance of State Department control of military affairs and Defense Department unresponsiveness to military needs. Thus, in its own way, the termination of Project Camelot contributed in no small measure to the smoldering debate between military and civilian personnel in the Defense Department, no less than to the more generic competition for authority in foreign affairs between State and Defense.

IV. ON THE ADVISABILITY OF PROJECT CAMELOT

The end of Project Camelot does not entail the end of the Special Operations Research Office nor does it imply an end to research designs that are similar in character to Project Camelot. In fact, the termination of the contract does not even imply an intellectual change of heart on the part of the originating sponsors or key figures of the project.

One of the characteristics of Project Camelot was the number of antagonistic forces it set in motion on grounds quite apart from what may be called considerations of scientific principle. The project was criticized and attacked far more in terms of extrinsic issues of strategies and timing than on intrinsic issues of research design. The mystique of social science seemed to have been taken for granted by friends and foes of the Project alike.

1. The State Department grounded its opposition to Camelot on the basis of the ultimate authority it has in the area of foreign affairs. There is no published criticism of the design itself.

2. Congressional opposition seemed to be generated by a concern not to rock any foreign alliances, especially with Latin America. Again, there was no statement about the ineffectiveness of the project on scientific or intellectual grounds.

3. A third group of skeptics, the academic social scientists, thought that Project Camelot and studies of the processes of revolution and war in general were better left in the control of major university centers and in this way kept free of direct military supervision. However, with the subsequent revelations of university participation in far more covert military and paramilitary activities, such criticisms were not militantly pursued.

4. The Army, for its part, while it offered a considerable amount of support at the informal level, did nothing to contradict Secretary McNamara's order canceling Project Camelot. Not simply did military influentials feel that they had to execute the Defense Department's orders, but they themselves were probably dubious of the value of "software" definitions of "hardware" systems.

A number of issues did not so much hinge upon as swim about Project Camelot. In particular, the "jurisdictional" dispute between Defense and State loomed largest. Essentially, the debate between the Defense Department and the State Department is not unlike that which obtains between unions of electricians and bricklayers in the construction of a new apartment house. What union exactly is responsible for which processes? Less generously, the issue is who controls what. The umbrella of responsibility, expertise, and clear lines of authority is at the root a question of power and domination. At the policy level, Camelot was a tool tossed about in a larger power struggle which has been going on in government circles since the end of World War II, or at that historical juncture when the Defense Department emerged as authentic competition for honors as the most powerful bureau of the administrative branch of government.

In some sense too, the divisions between Defense and State are outcomes of the rise of ambiguous politicomilitary conflicts such as Korea and Vietnam, in contrast to the more precise and diplomatically controlled "classical" world wars. What are the lines dividing political policy from military posture? Who is the most important representative of the United States abroad, the ambassador or the military attaché in charge of the military mission? When soldiers from foreign lands are sent to the United States for political orientation, should such orientation be within the province of the State Department or the Defense Department? When undercover activities are conducted, should the direction of such activities belong to military or political authorities? Each of these is a strategic question with little heuristic or historic precedent. Each of these was profoundly entwined in the Project Camelot explosion. It should be plain that the State Department was not simply responding to the recommendations of Chilean left-wingers in urging the cancellation of Camelot. They did employ the Chilean hostility to "interventionist" projects as an opportunity to redefine the ratio of forces and express the lines of power existing at present between the two leading government executive agencies.

Part of the folklore of Washington is that the primacy of the ambassador in foreign countries is a polite fiction. Indeed, the competition he has — from military missions, special roving emissaries sent directly from the presidential office, and from undercover men, sent from the Central Intelligence Agency or the Federal Bureau of Investigation, who often work independently of and even at cross purposes with the ambassador — is not to be dismissed lightly. Perhaps, as a retaliation for these abuses and indignities of his office, the ambassador has sought to reaffirm his own role. And one way has been to control the types of research and investigatory projects planned by itinerant Americans for the nation where he is in residence.

Just why an ambassador should have the right to control scientific research is difficult to appreciate. Such responsibility assumes an intellectual sophistication that is precisely most noticeable by its absence in our Latin American ambassadorial staff. Yet, within a fortnight after Ambassador Ralph Dungan voiced his strong opposition to Project Camelot, the Ambassador to Brazil, Lincoln Gordon, did likewise over a project which was supposedly similar in character but in an earlier stage than Camelot. What seems evident from this resistance to social science projects is not so much a defense of the sovereignty of the nations where ambassadors are stationed as it is a contentment that conventional political channels are sufficient to yield the information desired or deemed necessary on policy grounds. It further reflects a latent State Department preference for politics as an art rather than politics as an object of science. At the theoretical level, this represents the Machiavellian notion that manipulation is the key concept rather than clarification. In any event, this is what Americans stationed abroad often appear to be concerned with. Whatever the proper stance, whether politics is an art rather than a science or whether conventional diplomatic corps members are more likely to garner meaningful information than newly arrived social science researchers, it is evident that a combination of conventional and novel intraservice rivalries played a larger part in the termination of Camelot than objective conditions may have warranted.

Congressional reaction to Project Camelot followed the particular Representative's or Senator's feelings toward military sponsorship of research. Their feelings toward social science involvement in problems of military science and technology were also clearly at stake. From the remarks reported, Congressmen were either positive toward the military and negative toward social science or negative toward the military and positive toward social science. In such instances, what emerged was a cognitive bind. Thus, most members of Congress, when they were informed of the Camelot situation, were pleased at any resolution that would not add stress to their own perceptions. At other times, those negative toward the military used the occasion to criticize the Defense Department's sponsorship of types of research based on intervention into the affairs of other nations, while those negative toward social science used the occasion to note the ineffectual and impotent character of social science vis-à-vis the smooth operations of good diplomats. Project Camelot was thus caught in a pincer maneuver, and it could neither extricate itself nor rely on its associates to "save" itself.

In the main, congressional reaction seems to have been that Project Camelot was bad because it rocked the diplomatic boat in a sensitive geopolitical area. And the first rule of a bureaucratic apparatus is to avoid organizational turmoil, exorcize it before it spreads. Underlying congressional criticism is the plain fact that most Congressmen are more sympathetic to State Department control of foreign affairs than they are to Defense Department control. In other words, despite military sponsored world junkets, National and State Guard pressures from the home state, and military training in the career profiles of many Congressmen, the sentiment for political rather than military control is more agreeable to them. Hence, their negative response to Camelot is perhaps a function of their general sentiments regarding the State and Defense Departments.

One reason for the violent response to Project Camelot is the singular sponsorship of it by the Department of Defense. The fact is that Latin Americans, in particular, have become quite accustomed to and conditioned by State Department approaches and involvements in the internal affairs of various nations. The Defense Department is a newcomer, a dangerous one, inside the Latin American orbit. The train of thought connected to its activities is in terms of international warfare, spying missions, military manipulations, etc. The State Department, for its part, is often a consultative party to shifts in government and has played an enormous part in either fending off or bringing about *coups d'état*. This State Department role has by now been accepted and even internalized by many smaller nations (and some large ones as well) in the Third

World. Not so the Defense Department's image role. The State Department is in Chile; the Defense Department is viewed as an alien force in a country such as Chile — especially since it has such direct ties to the military solution to all political problems — a long-standing anathema to Chilean Christian democracy.

Were Project Camelot to have had State Department sponsorship, it is interesting to conjecture on how matter of fact the reaction to it might have been. The hysteria over Project Camelot is in part due to the popular and diplomatic view that the Defense Department is an alien force in Chile and hence its sponsored activities inherently worse than those initiated by the State Department. But whether this is actually a fault that can properly be placed at the doorstep of Project Camelot is highly conjectural. In point of fact, academic and intellectual criticism of Project Camelot from American colleges and universities, at least, has been sensitive to the complexity of the issues involved. It is true that social scientists of Latin American universities and research centers, notably those of Santiago and Buenos Aires, raised serious ideological objections to the project. But even these remarks are notable for their reserve. It was noted that the "ideological orientation" of Project Camelot was integrated into the research programs in a way which would permit "the generation of hypotheses." It was also noted that the political goals and the military sponsorship of Project Camelot are professionally inadmissible. The questioning of the utility of further collaboration between North American and Latin American social scientists seems to be more rhetorical than threatening. Yet, such doubts rest on criteria that are themselves quite ideological and political. In the main, then, Latin American social scientists, while uniformly negative toward Project Camelot, have not made the kinds of distinctions that would point to a sociologically worthy alternative approach to applied research.

Social scientists in the United States have, for the most part, been reticent to express themselves publicly on the matter of Camelot. The reasons for this are not hard to find. First, many "giants of the field" are involved in government contract work in one capacity or another. And few souls are in a position to tamper with the gods. Second, information on Project Camelot even at this late date has been of a newspaper variety; and professional men are not in a habit of criticizing colleagues on the basis of such information. Third, many social scientists doubtlessly see nothing wrong or immoral in the Project Camelot designs. And they are therefore more likely to be either confused by or angered with the critical Latin American response to the project directors.

There are nonetheless many "informal" and "private" remarks made about Project Camelot that indicate wide discontent with its approach and with the general turn to federally sponsored research involving social scientists. Area specialists in particular have been vociferous in criticizing the "amateurishness" or Camelot's design. Several scholars complained bitterly that it made their task of collecting data on the main social sectors of vital South American nations that much more difficult. One advanced student working on the effects of the Roman Catholic Church on the developmental process of Mexico was told that he could no longer count on Church support since the data would obviously show a left-wing tendency in the Church, and thus anger and perhaps alienate powerful forces in the United States. Perhaps most tragically, there is the case of an advanced doctorate candidate at a West Coast university who had completed his data collection on social stratification in Chile, only to find his materials confiscated by customs authorities. And I am told by another young scholar who just returned from two years in Chile that Camelot "jokes" are now in evidence among the younger Latin American intelligentsia. However, what has to be noted is that serious critical analysis of Project Camelot remains at the private level or at the denunciatory stage. These comments usually concern the way in which the sponsors of Camelot went about their work rather than the contents of their outlook.

One of the cloudiest aspects of Project Camelot is the role of

American University. Its actual supervisory role over the contract appears to have begun and ended with the 20 percent commission a university receives as expense funds on most federal grants. Thus, while there can be no question as to "concern and disappointment" of President Hurst R. Anderson of the American University over the termination of Project Camelot, the reasons for this regret do not seem to extend beyond the formal and the financial. No official at American University appeared to have been willing or capable of making any statement of responsibility, support, chagrin, opposition, or anything else related to the project. The issues are indeed momentous, and must be faced by all universities at which government-sponsored research is conducted: the amount of control a university administration has over contract work; the role of university officials in the distribution of funds from grants; the sort of relationships that ought to be or are expected to be established once a grant is issued; whether project heads should be members of the faculty, and if so, whether they have the necessary teaching responsibility, teaching functions, and opportunities for tenure as do other faculty members.

The difficulty with American University is that it seems to be remarkably unlike most other universities in its permissiveness. The autonomous character of this university is questionable. The Special Operations Research Office received neither guidance nor support from university officials. From the outset, there seems to have been a "gentleman's agreement" not to inquire or interfere in Project Camelot on the part of the University but simply to serve as some sort of camouflage. Such a form of economic opportunism on the part of an institute of higher education can only be considered reprehensible, a symbol of maximum university weakness and disarray. Were the American University genuinely autonomous, it might have been able to lend highly supportive aid to Project Camelot during the crisis months. The fact that American University maintained an official silence preserved it from any Congressional or Executive criticism but at the same time pointed up some serious flaws in its administrative and financial policies.

The relationship between Project Camelot, Special Operations Research Office, and American University reflected shortcomings in lines of organizational authority. When the tail wags the dog, the dog must obviously become an appendage. And this is approximately what happened. American University seems to have been little more than window dressing, a fund repository raking off several hundred thousand dollars for administrative services and having no control over the project and little contact with its directors. The stationery itself would indicate what the lines of power are, since the *Special Operations Research Office* was originally set in larger type than the *American University*. The relationship of Camelot to SORO as a whole presented a similarly muddled organizational picture. The Director of Project Camelot was nominally autonomous, and in charge of an organization rivaling in size and importance the over-all SORO operation. Yet, at the critical point the decision taken on the part of SORO was ultimately to project itself by sacrificing what nominally was its limb. That this part happened to be a vital organ may have hurt, but the loss of the organ was considered scarcely fatal. In fact, the issue of SORO's strategy of yielding up Camelot as a sacrifice to the pagan gods remains a continually debated issue.

Under such circumstances, many social science institutes throughout the major university centers in the United States wondered out loud why the work of Project Camelot was not allocated to them on the basis of competitive bidding or simply awarded to the capable institutes outright. While social scientists in American academic life are increasingly well funded in their research projects, it is nonetheless the case that they badly lag behind their colleagues in the natural sciences both in the amount of monies received from the government for research purposes and in the conditions under which these funds can be manipulated. The huge amounts, relatively speaking, put at the disposal of Project Camelot were considered another effort to prevent social scientists at major universities from partaking of these funds. It was said, and not denied by the relevant officials, that the Defense Department felt more comfortable in a controlled research situation than they might have in a free research situation. The retort of university-oriented social scientists has been that it is precisely the mistakes made by Project Camelot directors that are best avoided by the kind of atmosphere present in universities rather than in "think tanks" provided by the armed forces.

The directors of Project Camelot tried to meet such objections by not "classifying" any of its research materials, so that there would be no stigma of secrecy. It also tried to hire, and even hire away from academic positions, people well known and respected for their independence of mind. The difficulty is that even though the stigma of secrecy was formally erased, it remained in the attitudes of many of the employees and would-be employees of Project Camelot. Many of the middle-echelon, less-sophisticated personnel unfortunately thought in terms of secrecy, clearance, missions, and the rest of the bureaucratic ethos that powerfully afflicts the Washington scientific as well as political environment.

It is apparent then that Project Camelot had much greater difficulty hiring a full-time staff of high professional competence than in getting part-time, summertime, weekend, and sundry assistance. Few established figures in academic life were willing to surrender the advantages of their tenured positions for the risks of a project.

Military opposition to Project Camelot was either nonexistent or confined to doubts about the general worth of social science projects. Those men in the armed forces who have a positive orientation toward social science — having worked with social scientists and social materials in the preparation of foreign-area handbooks or having utilized the valuable armed forces organizational and communication studies made by social scientists — were of course dismayed by the cancellation of Project Camelot. In addition, there was a group of military officers who were themselves trained in various social sciences and hence, saw in the attack on Camelot a double attack — upon their role as officers and their professional competence. But the Army was so clearly treading in new territory that it could scarcely jeopardize the entire structure of military research to preserve one project.

It can be argued that this very inability to preserve Camelot, threatening other governmental contracts with social scientists, no doubt impressed a number of armed forces officers. But this consideration had to be weighed against the over-all dangers to military policy. And there is an old military adage that where possible the fight be conducted on grounds and in terms chosen by the attacking force.

The claim is made by the Camelot staff and various aides that the civilian critics of the project played into the hands of those sections of the military predisposed to veto any social science recommendations. The claim that "software" can never assist "hardware" has indeed been made more than once. But it will be said, if this is the case, why did the military offer such a huge support to the social science project to begin with. The answer to this is easier to find than might first be imagined. Four million or seven million dollars is actually a trifling sum for the military in an age of a multibillion dollar military establishment. The amount is significantly more important for the social sciences where such contract awards remain relatively scarce. Thus, a set of differing perceptions arose as to the importance of Camelot: an Army view that considers a four-to-seven million dollar grant as one of many forms of "software" investment and, in contrast, a social science perception of Project Camelot as the equivalent of the Manhattan Project, which led to the manufacture of the atomic bomb.

V. THE FEASIBILITY OF PROJECT CAMELOT

While most public opposition to Project Camelot centered on its advisability, a considerable amount of scientific opposition centered on its feasibility. This contrasted with the stated attitudes expressed by most of the men I contacted who were involved with Project Camelot. For them, the issues generated were not so much technical as ideological. A curious linguistic dimension frequently cropped up: Camelot personnel would speak of the "Chilean mess" rather than the "Camelot mess" as the outsiders held. Nor should this perspectival distinction be lightly dismissed. In fact, no public document issued by the Camelot directors contested the possibility that, considering the successful completion of the data-gathering stage of the project, Camelot personnel could indeed establish basic criteria for measuring the level and potential for internal war in a given nation. Thus by never challenging the feasibility of the work, the political critics of Project Camelot were providing backhanded compliments to the efficacy of the project design.

From a social scientific viewpoint, however, more than political considerations are involved. It is clear that for social scientists, particularly those not directly connected with Project Camelot but having a shared interest in problems of the military, revolutions, the developing regions and their potencies, the critical problems presented by Project Camelot are scientific. In what follows, I shall attempt to summarize what were the most frequently expressed objections to the research design and those that I, in particular, consider to be most relevant.

Earlier, it was pointed out that the research design of Camelot was from the outset plagued by ambiguities. The documents never quite settle on whether the purpose of the contract was to study counterinsurgency possiblities or the revolutionary process as a natural event. Similarly, it was difficult to determine whether this was to be a study of comparative social structures, a study of a single nation "in depth," or a study of over-all social structures with a particular emphasis on military possibilities. While many factors were included for future study, no assignment of relative weight was given. In this way, the methodological relativism of the design contributed to heightening the ambiguity. The organizational support for such ambiguity stemmed from the different perspectives expressed by senior Camelot scientists.

In the four parts of the "master publication" there seems to be at least four different methodologies employed: a social systems design; a design based on analytic case study materials; a study of internal conflict by means of manual and machine simulation; and an ethnographic report on internal war potentials, which in turn incorporates an appendix attempting to link the report to mathematical functions of authority and competition. Clearly, in a project of this size there was room for different methodological approaches. However, it is not clear just what the relationships were between the individual parts of the project and between each part and the whole. While no one was able to explain these discrepancies, there was a candid admission that they did indeed exist but would have been "worked out" during the life of the project. In other words, though it was the case that most criticisms leading to the termination of Project Camelot were unconcerned with its intellectual potential, it was especially at the latter level that Camelot personnel thought there was a great deal to be desired. Indeed, a considerable internal opposition (especially on the part of Camelot's advisory committees) to the program was grounded in just these questions of methodology.

An aspect of the research design that unquestionably gave rise to serious criticism and skepticism about Project Camelot was the platitudinous and programmatic content of the original research proposals. An "orientation" that is "scientific," offering a "balanced course between theoretical and empirical work," bringing to bear "all the relevant disciplines and talents required," will obviously raise doubts as to the viability of the methodology. Further, the "over-all outline," while spoken of, failed to materialize in the documents. They are highly eclectic, drawing upon theoretical design effort, analytic case studies, survey research, and "comparative analysis." Many methods, disciplines, outlooks seem to be represented. The only criticism in the documents is reserved for the efforts of "an individual scholar with limited resources." While this may have been useful to stimulating federal financial support, the fact is that the encouragement of "lone wolf" attitudes, of separate research by individuals on their own, may have considerably reduced the suspicion held that Project Camelot was, in Johan Galtung's words, an example of "managerial sociology" or some sort of medieval Jesuitical collectivity.

Eclecticism damaged the scientific aims of the Camelot research. What took place, as illustrated in the main summary, is that the four different research associates of the working group presented an outline in four parts, in a manner which by no means made it evident that unified results were either anticipated or even plausibly to be expected. Had the four sets of working papers been presented as just that — four sets of papers — instead of a "unified front" of ideas and attitudes, the scientific character would have been enhanced, and the policy-oriented aspects could have been placed in a larger perspective of social science scholarship. This said, it must also be noted that the many people who had the opportunity to make criticism were quite reticent to express themselves. The Project Camelot working groups, when they did make criticisms, found a ready response from the Project directors. Also, the first year on any project of such a scale cannot be expected to have sophisticated conclusions.

There was a noticeable tendency toward the use of hygienic and sanitized language in the descriptions of the project. We are told about a "precipitant" of internal war as being an "event which actually starts the war." Whereas "preconditions" are "circumstances which make it possible for the precipitants to bring about political violence." Obviously, "events" never started wars, only *people* do. "Precipitants" never bring about political violence, only *participants* do.

This is followed by a general critique of social science for failing to deal with social conflict and social control. And while this in itself represents an admirable recognition, the tenor and context of the design makes it plain that a "stable society" is the considered norm no less than the desired outcome. The "breakdown of social order" is spoken of accusatively. Stabilizing agencies in developing areas are not so much criticized as presumed to be absent. A critique of U.S. Army policy is absent because the Army is presumed to be a stabilizing agency. Rather than reflecting love for the Army, the formulations simply assume the legitimacy of the Army tasks. "If the U.S. Army is to perform effectively its part in the U.S. mission of counterinsurgency it must recognize that insurgency represents a breakdown of social order. . . ." But such a proposition has never been doubted—by Army officials or anyone else. The issue is whether such breakdowns are in the nature of the existing system or a product of conspiratorial movements. Here the hygienic language disguises the antirevolutionary assumptions under a cloud of powder puff declarations.

Sanitary terminology is also evident in describing political regimes and in determining nations to be studied. Studies of Paraguay are recommended "because trends in this situation (the Stroessner regime) may also render it 'unique' when analyzed in terms of the transition from 'dictatorship' to political stability." What "transition"? Since when have social scientists perceived dictatorship and political stability as occupying the same level of meaning? No dictatorship has ever been more "stable" than Hitlerism. One might speak of the transition from dictatorship to democracy or from totalitarianism to authoritarianism. But to speak about changes from dictatorship to stability is an obvious rubric. In this case, it is a tactic to disguise the fact that Paraguay is one of the most vicious, undemocratic (*and stable*) societies in the Western Hemisphere.

These typify the sorts of hygienic sociological premises that have extrascientific purposes. They illustrate the confusion of commitments among Project Camelot spokesmen. The very absence of ideological terms such as "revolutionary masses," communism, socialism, capitalism, et cetera intensifies the discomfort one must feel on examination, since the abstract vocabulary disguises rather than resolves the problems of international revolution. It does not proceed beyond U.S. Army vocabulary, not because this vocabulary is superior to the revolutionary vocabulary, but simply because it is the language of the donor. To have used clearly political rather than military language would not "justify" governmental support. Futhermore, shabby assumptions of academic respectability replaced innovative orientations. In fact, by adopting a systems approach, the problematic, open-ended, and practical aspects of the study of revolutions were largely omitted; and the design of the system became an oppressive curb on the contents of the problems inspected.

This points up a critical inplication of the Camelot affair. The importance of the subject being researched does not uniquely determine the importance of the project per se. A sociology of large-scale relevance and reference is all to the good. It is important that scholars be willing to risk something of their reputations in helping to resolve major world social problems. But it is no less important that in the process of addressing their attention to major international problems the autonomous character of the social science disciplines, their own criteria of worthwhile scholarship, not be abandoned. It is my opinion that the ambiguity, asymmetry, and eclecticism of the fragmented and programmatic nature of even the most advanced documents circulated by Project Camelot lost sight of this "autonomous" social science character in the pursuit of the larger demands of society.

It never seemed to occur to the Camelot directorship to inquire into the chances and desirability for successful revolution. This is just as solid a line of inquiry as that which was emphasized: Namely, under what conditions will revolutionary movements be able to overthrow a government? Furthermore, they seem not to have thought about inquiring into the role of the United States in these countries. This points up the lack of symmetry. The project need not have focused exclusively on the North American presence. However, the problem should have been phrased to include the study of "us" as well as "them." It is not possible to make a decent analysis of a situation unless one takes into account the role of the different people and major groups involved. In its initial stage at least, there was no room in the design of Camelot for such contingency analysis.

This one-sidedness is not unusual in sociology. As a result, shortcomings in this approach did not glare up at any of the key participants to the project. Camelot did not seem sufficiently different from ordinary sociological practices to warrant any special precautionary measures. And the precedents relied upon were indeed of a reassuring variety.

An early example was industrial sociology, where many people worked for many years on essentially managerial problems. But there were some sociologists with an affinity for labor who saw through the business bias and began to complain about a sociology that simply performs the dirty work of industrial management. An even stronger case is medical sociology. In that field, almost everyone took (and still takes) for granted the proposition that what the doctors want and think is good for everyone. Until *Boys In White,* it never occurred to anyone to ask how things might be from the patient's point of view. Later, there were other exceptions, research that insisted on treating doctors just like anyone else. The nature of the asymmetry in Project Camelot is two-fold. First, it failed to ask *all* the questions that need to be asked. Second, it did not open to investigation the motives and bias of the sponsoring agencies.

In short, many sociologists are used to asking their questions improperly simply because to do so may serve heuristic ends in a marketable way. When they are presented with the opportunity to influence policy makers as in the case of Project Camelot, they can do little better than puffing up stale methodological forms for new use. There are also the primitive substantive guidelines used. The Enlightenment assumption that people in power need only to be shown the truth in order to do the right thing is unacceptable. Nevertheless, it is clear that some well-intentioned people have accepted elitism as an exclusive framework. They need to be reminded that this is by no means the only possible position.

In discussing the policy impact on a social science research project, we should not overlook the difference between "contract" work and "grants." Project Camelot began with the U.S. Army, that is to say, it was initiated for a practical purpose determined by the client. This differs markedly from the typical academic grant in that military sponsorship is distinctive for its "built-in" ends. The scholar seeks the grant, whereas this donor stipulated projected aims. In some measure, the hostility for Project Camelot may be an unconscious reflection of this distinction between grants and contracts, a dim feeling that there was something "nonacademic," and certainly not disinterested, about Project Camelot irrespective of the quality of the scholars associated with it.

This raises the yet deeper issue: Are social scientists to approach contract work in the same spirit as they approach grant work? Does contract work, once accepted, signify broad acceptance of the terms of the contract, or is it simply a formalism, a cover-all enabling the scholar to proceed at his will to do as he wishes. The originating statements about the nature of Project Camelot are ambiguous on this point. They promote contractual obligations of working within the Army's project design and yet indicate the free-funding characteristics of the grant. In all likelihood, contributing scholars viewed Camelot funds much as they would any other funds received from a private donor.

Project Camelot documents suffered greatly from the sin of pride. They made a fine show of incorporating many social scientists and diverse points of view. There was no effort to impose ironbound a priori theoretical outcomes. However, the assumption that Project Camelot was somehow essential and vital to the national interests went undisputed. All available scientific thought was to be fed into Project Camelot, while the utilization of all this input was left unexplained. This assumption of critical importance was undoubtedly a primary factor in why the men of Camelot were shaken when the Chilean story became public knowledge. It brought home the fact that what is essential for some may be insignificant for others.

Characteristic of all research projects is an inflated sense of self-importance. This is necessary if for no other reason than it would be hard to generate enthusiasm and self-sacrificing work without the myth that what one does is potentially earth-shattering. This very impulse toward self-importance on the part of Camelot returns us to the basic verities of the relationship between things that are scientifically valid and things that are socially important.

VI. THE ETHICS OF POLICY RESEARCH

Just what are the limits and obligations, no less than the rights, to investigate the viscera of another society on behalf of a government foreign to that society? This question, which in effect is nothing short of the nature and limits of sovereignty and legitimacy, can perhaps be more readily understood by reference to an example from "middle-range" research. By placing secret recording devices in a juryroom in order to study its decision-making process, have sociologists not also violated the basis of jury procedures by tampering with their sovereignty as such? Is the information yielded worth the costs involved? The same question must be raised in connection with Camelot and the study of a foreign nation in depth.

The issue of "scientific rights" versus "social myths" is perennial. Some maintain that the scientist ought not penetrate beyond legally or morally sanctioned limits and others argue that such limits cannot exist for science — at least not for an applied science. In treading on the sensitive issue of national sovereignty, Project Camelot reflected and became subject to the generalized dilemma. For this matter of the legitimate rights of the army, of scientists, of the sovereignty of the national entities chosen for scrutiny, was bound to be felt as well as stated with some indignation. In sheer deference to the scientific researcher, in recognition of him as a scholar, he should have been invited to air his misgivings and qualms about government and especially army-sponsored research, to declare his moral conscience. Social scientists were mistakenly approached as skillful, useful potential employees of a "higher" body, subject to an authority greater than their scientific calling.

What is central is not the political motives of the sponsor. For social scientists were not being enlisted by Camelot in an intelligence system for "spying" purposes. But given the social scientist's professional standing, his great sense of intellectual honor and pride in his subtle and far-reaching capacities, he could not be "employed" without damaging his self-image and stature. His professional authority should have prevailed from beginning to end with complete command of the right to thrash out the moral and political dilemmas as he viewed them. The Army, however respectful and protective of free expression at the formal level, was "hiring help" and not openly submitting military problems to the *higher* professional and scientific authority of social science.

To be a servant of power is distinct from being a wielder of power. The relationship of a professional savant to a policy maker is different from that of the psychoanalyst to a patient. Not only does the psychoanalyst exercise a legitimate form of superordination; but such a role dominance derives from a public acceptance of his intellectual skills. In the case of the social and political scientists on Project Camelot, this was never made clear. Had the Army approached the problem the way a patient going to an analyst might, namely, that something was chronically wrong and it ought to be repaired if repairable, some balance might have been maintained. But the right of the armed forces to cancel its contract with Camelot was never placed in question. This relationship of inequality at the informal level at least corrupted the lines of authority and profoundly limited the autonomy of the social scientists involved.

The social scientists on Camelot contributed to this imbalance by an ingenuous eagerness to adopt or incorporate an alien vocabulary no less than an alien set of sociological assumptions. It became clear that the social scientist servant was not so much functioning as an applied social scientists as he was performing the role of supplying information to a powerful client. What happened in Project Camelot is that values and heuristics were linked in an illicit alliance. The uniform assumption made by Camelot personnel was that the scientific worth of the project was uniquely determined by the scope and social significance of the project, thus ignoring the important function of independent criteria in measuring scientific research.

What is at stake in a practical way is the extent to which the social importance of a work can justify its scientific character. Project Camelot failed to respond to this problem of linking importance to quality. The question of who sponsors research is not nearly as decisive as the question of ultimate use of such information. The sponsorship of a project, whether by the U.S. Army or by the Boy Scouts of America, is by itself neither good or bad. Sponsorship is a factor for consideration only insofar as the intended outcomes can be predetermined and the parameters of those intended outcomes tailored to the sponsor's expectations. The defenders of Camelot failed to penetrate to the nature of objections because the formulations made by its spokesmen were in terms of the independence and freedom of the project, whereas the critics of the project never really denied this freedom and independence but questioned instead the purpose and character of these intended results.

The sensitivities of the project to political issues are an independent dimension. It is not simply a question of the character of the project but the political atmosphere in which a project is placed on the marketplace.

At the time of Camelot, there was the American intervention in the Dominican Republic. The occupation by United States troops had a catalyzing effect on the rest of Latin America, particularly a country such as Chile, which did not go along with various rulings of the Organization of American States. Chile thus became acutely sensitized to the possibilities of the overthrow of its own regime. One accusation went so far as to say that the purpose of Camelot was the overthrow of the constituted Chilean government, much as the government of Brazil was overthrown a year earlier for its own intransigence to earlier O.A.S. efforts with respect to Cuba. However groundless such accusations against Camelot may be, the failure of the project directors to take the political situation into account led them to make assumptions about foreign receptivity to its design that simply were unreal and insensitive. It may be that the very multitude of purposes leads to a gigantic problem. Be that as it may, men continue to seek out the purpose of life; and research projects which fail to address themselves to the fact that nations like persons are jealous of their rights — real or presumed — cannot help but lead to disastrous consequences.

It would be a gross oversimplification, if not an outright error, to assume that the theoretical problems of Project Camelot derive from the reactionary character of the project's designers. As has been indicated, the director went far and wide to select men for the advisory board, the core planning group, the summer study group, and the various conference groupings who were in fact more liberal in their orientations than any random sampling of the sociological profession would likely turn up. But in a sense this search for broad representation was itself a problem rather than a solution. To choose a panel of experts with the deliberate aim of assembling representatives of particular approaches — from believers in maximum usage of counterinsurgency techniques to believers in the utter inefficacy of counterrevolutionary tactics and from advocates of massive deterrence to adherents in civil disobedience — is not fallacious in itself as it is in its expectations. It is fanciful to expect such people to adjudicate their differences by analogy with the committee procedure of a bureaucratic organization. It should surprise no one that the result is more often than not a common denominator than a well-rounded position or design. The premium on accommodation is great enough so that the April 1, 1965, Report suffers at once from four weakened formulations without arriving at the much vaunted well-rounded position.

The representation of this confusion between science and policy is made often and in a way which is often self-contradictory. For instance, in his reply to the Argentine sociologists' declaration, Professor Hopper says that "there is no ideological orientation of the project beyond the conviction that the scientific method is useful and therefore ought to be applied to the research objectives of the project." However, in nearly every page of the various working papers, there are assertions that clearly derive from American military policy objectives rather than the scientific method. The steady assumption that internal warfare is damaging and is a status in which "a government might take [steps] to relieve conditions which are assessed as giving rise to a potential for internal war" itself disregards the possibility that a government may not be in a position to take actions either to relieve or improve mass conditions, or that such actions as are contemplated may be more concerned with reducing conflict than with improving conditions. The added statements about the U.S. Army and its "important mission in the positive and constructive aspects of nation building . . ." assumes the reality of such a function in an utterly unquestioning and unconvincing form. The idea of an applied science, of a selective program of assistance to some social forces at the expense of others, should not be taken as a mandate for disregarding the rules of the scientific game. And the first rule is not to make assumptions about friends and enemies in such a way as to promote the use of different criteria for the former and the latter.

The many and diverse studies being conducted of foreign nations will continue. The military will press on for more exact information, particularly in areas close to the military buffering point, and finally the social scientists will press on in their search for a policy-oriented El Dorado. They are no more likely to give up the search for policy relatedness than the military is willing to give up the search for scientific information. So all of the questions raised by the birth and death of Camelot only push on in a more agonizing way the problems long raised by Kant in philosophy and Weber in sociology, and which continue to plague the social science world.

The story of Project Camelot was not a confrontation of good versus evil. Not that all men behaved with equal fidelity or with equal civility — that obviously was not the case. Some men were weaker than others; some more callous and some more stupid. But all of this is extrinsic to the problem of Camelot. The heart of the question must always be, What are and are not the legitimate functions of a scientist?

One interesting sidelight is how little the question of communism came into focus, and yet it is clear that one's attitude toward Left and Right, toward social reform and social change, toward Americanism or anti-Americanism, form the warp and woof of the attitudes expressed on the project. In some sense, this is an ultimate vindication of social science as a human science, since the ideological goals sought are clearly fused to the organizational instruments used.

In conclusion, two important points must be kept clearly in mind and clearly apart. First, Project Camelot was intellectually and from my own perspective ideologically unsound. However, and more significantly, Camelot was not canceled because of its faulty intellectual approaches. Instead, its cancellation came as an act of government censorship and an expression of the contempt for social science so prevalent among those who need it most. Thus it was political expedience, rather than Camelot's lack of scientific merit that led to its termination: it threatened to rock State Department relations with Latin America.

Second, giving the State Department the right to screen and approve government-funded social science research projects on other countries, as the President has ordered, is a supreme act of censorship. Among the agencies that grant funds for such research are the National Institutes of Health, the National Science Foundation, the National Aeronautics and Space Agency, and the Office of Education. Why should the State

Department have veto power over the scientific pursuits of men and projects funded by these and other agencies in order to satisfy the policy needs — or policy failures — of the moment? President Johnson's directive is thus a gross violation of the autonomous nature of science, even though the project itself may well have been a gross violation of sound canons of morals and methodology.

We must be careful not to allow social science projects with which we may vociferously disagree on political and ideological grounds to be decimated or dismantled by government fiat. Across the ideological divide is a common social science understanding that the contemporary expression of reason in politics is applied social science, and that the cancellation of Camelot, however pleasing it may be on political grounds to advocates of a civilian solution to Latin American affairs, represents a decisive setback for social science research.

VII. PROJECT CAMELOT: A RETROSPECTIVE EVALUATION

As in all major events, the passage of time does not so much diminish interests as it alters perspectives. Issues have arisen that will occupy and preoccupy the attention of social scientists and policy makers for years to come. Here, we can only allude to some of the new perspectives that have emerged in the wake of Project Camelot.

We shall now concentrate on three points — each of which has come up quite frequently in correspondence and conversations on Project Camelot. These may not be the central issues for the public at large, but they certainly appear to be central for the social science community.

First, a big issue is whether the social scientist should work for the government (or at least for certain agencies within the government). In our terms, this is the conflict between "selling out" on one side and "copping out" on the other. This conflict can only be resolved by a firm concept of *autonomy* — both organizational and ideological. In a world of power, it seems to be more sober to develop countervailing modalities of power than to huff and puff at the walls of the national sovereignty. At this level, the trouble has been that social science organizations too often are used as clearing houses for "trustworthy" scholars, while these same organizations make far too few demands upon federal agencies. At times, it appears as if the leadership of social scientific organizations still does not believe that the successes of the social sciences are yet real. Having been reared in a period of relative deprivation for the social sciences, the social scientists view all funds as big and all projects as wonderful. Perhaps if we were to realize that the social sciences are no longer at the stage of primitive accumulation, we might be able to resolve this dilemma of selling out versus copping out.

Second, some critics of Camelot are vigorous in affirming the right of the State Department to censor projects of a social science nature. They say that the problem is not one of substance but of subjects; that is, Who is in charge of these programs? I believe this to be an irrelevant consideration. The need of the moment is not for more liberal-minded censors (although it may be for more liberal attitudes in general) but for an end to censorship as such — benign or malignant. To borrow a thought from the late Bernard Shaw: censorship, mild or severe, is severe. The problems presented in the design of Project Camelot cannot be resolved by presidential fiat or administrative edict but only by the constant checking and cross checking that define the methods of social science research.

Third, other critics of Camelot wish to place a moratorium on social science work for or under federal sponsorship. It is my view that a less drastic, but perhaps far more effective, way of gaining respect for the social sciences would be an across-the-board change in the format of the higher arts of grantsmanship:

a. The need for more grants (scientifically initiated research) and fewer contracts (agency initiated research).

b. The need for a financial pool arrangement, that is, on every grant received there should be a portion set aside (preferably under the supervision of either the university or the social science institute processing grants) for *free research* unconnected with the grant — and disbursed without regard to either the disbursor or recipient of the grant.

c. The need for more emphasis on individuals and less on collectivities. The big whooping grants given to terms may have so many dysfunctional byproducts (the creation of new bureaucratic substructures, the mediocrity of the finished product, etc.) that it may be time for the social science agencies themselves to begin researching the shortcomings in team efforts (as in the past they did of individual efforts) and request, even demand, of federal and private agencies more concern and attention to the needs of the individual scholar.

Equation of policy research with applied social science in general is perhaps summed up by the word "instrumental." The assumption of those who argue on heuristic grounds appears to be as follows: *If all research conducted by scholars for the government is operational and if such operational research is subject to some form of control then any research done for the government is subject to control.* We should deny the premise and therefore the logic of the conclusion as well. The somber implication that work done for the government is something other than scholarship raises doubts as to the credibility of social science research in area studies. Precisely this recourse to operational definitions of government-sponsored work may stimulate, rather than curb, subterfuge in assignment of funds and create a broad-scale suspicion (among Latin Americans at least) that even university-based research is not necessarily liberated from government-determined operational needs.

It is perfectly fair to expect that the division of Federal agencies responsible for sensitive work be made as crystal clear as possible and with a minimum of embarrassment to our own personnel — researchers and diplomats alike. It is also the responsibility of the State Department to conduct foreign affairs in a way that will neither discredit our own people nor outrage the people of the host countries. It is also fair to expect the State Department to prevent the kind of executive agency rivalries that would lead to chaos and competition rather than useful information. But the terms of the presidential mandate under which the review board has been set up are frighteningly extensive. They are likely to inhibit not only the operational research represented by Camelot but also the kind of independent research — let us say on the consequences of United States intervention in the Dominican Republic — that may be either noninstrumental or downright counterinstrumental in character.

The problem with Project Camelot is not exclusively political but methodological as well. The identification of revolution and radical social change with a social pathology is the final proof, if such were necessary, that the functionalist credo of order, stability, pattern maintenance, stress management, and so forth does indeed reveal strong conservative drives. However, a cautious note should be added: The fact that certain functionalists and systems designers employ their method for conservative goals does not mean that all functional or structural social scientists are conservative — or for that matter, that the goals of Project Camelot created a need for such a strict methodology. Examination of the documents shows that there is scant evidence of a direct linkage between functional analysis and ideological faith. Some men connected to the Project even revealed a somewhat Marxian methodological preference.

If Project Camelot has served to focus the attention of social science on the acute problems of the interconnections between organization and research, ideology and science, then its "unanticipated consequences" will have by far outweighed the discomforts and even the agonies of the present moment.

Clearly, Project Camelot, by raising in the sharpest way the question of the *credibility* of American social science precisely at that point in time when the problem of data reliability seems to have been resolved, is an issue of paramount significance. The coming of age of American social science has been a painful experience. But could it have been otherwise?

PART II

THE DESIGN AND PURPOSE OF PROJECT CAMELOT

Document Number 1

The following description of Project Camelot was released on December 4, 1964, through the Office of the Director of the Special Operations Research Office (SORO) of the American University in Washington, D. C. It was sent to scholars who were presumed interested in the study of internal war potentials and who might be willing to assemble at a four-week conference at the Airlie House in Virginia in August 1965. This release, dated December 4, 1964, is a summary version of a larger set of documents made available in August 1964 and in December 1964 [I.L.H.].

Project CAMELOT is a study whose objective is to determine the feasibility of developing a general social systems model which would make it possible to predict and influence politically significant aspects of social change in the developing nations of the world. Somewhat more specifically, its objectives are:

First, to devise procedures for assessing the potential for internal war within national societies;

Second, to identify with increased degrees of confidence those actions which a government might take to relieve conditions which are assessed as giving rise to a potential for internal war; and

Finally, to assess the feasibility of prescribing the characteristics of a system for obtaining and using the essential information needed for doing the above two things.

The project is conceived as a three to four-year effort to be funded at around one and one-half million dollars annually. It is supported by the Army and the Department of Defense, and will be conducted with the cooperation of other agencies of the government. A large amount of primary data collection in the field is planned as well as the extensive utilization of already available data on social, economic and political functions. At this writing, it seems probable that the geographic orientation of the research will be toward Latin American countries. Present plans call for a field office in that region.

By way of background: Project CAMELOT is an outgrowth of the interplay of many factors and forces. Among these is the assignment in recent years of much additional emphasis to the U.S. Army's role in the over-all U.S. policy of encouraging steady growth and change in the less developed countries in the world. The many programs of the U.S. Government directed toward this objective are often grouped under the sometimes misleading label of counterinsurgency (some pronounceable term standing for insurgency prophylaxis would be better). This places great importance on positive actions designed to reduce the sources of disaffection which often give rise to more conspicuous and violent activities disruptive in nature. The U.S. Army has an important mission in the positive and constructive aspects of nation building as well as a responsibility to assist friendly governments in dealing with active insurgency problems.

Another major factor is the recognition at the highest levels of the defense establishment of the fact that relatively little is known, with a high degree of surety, about the social processes which must be understood in order to deal effectively with problems of insurgency. Within the Army there is especially ready acceptance of the need to improve the general understanding of the processes of social change if the Army is to discharge its responsibilities in the over-all counterinsurgency program of the U.S. Government. Of considerable relevance here is a series of recent reports dealing with the problems of national security and the potential contributions that social science might make to solving these problems. One such report was published by a committee of the Smithsonian Institution's research group under the title, "Social Science Research and National Security," edited by Ithiel de Sola Pool. Another is a volume of the proceedings of a symposium, "The U.S. Army's Limited-War Mission and Social Science Research." These proceedings were published in 1962 by the Special Operations Research Office of the American University.

Project CAMELOT will be a multidisciplinary effort. It will be conducted both within the SORO organization and in close collaboration with universities and other research institutions within the United States and overseas. The first several months of work will be devoted to the refinement of the research design and to the identification of problems of research methodology as well as of substance. This will contribute to the important articulation of all component studies of the project toward the stated objectives. Early participants in the project will thus have an unusual opportunity to contribute to the shaping of the research program and also to take part in a seminar planned for the summer of 1965. The seminar, to be attended by leading behavioral scientists of the country, will be concerned with reviewing plans for the immediate future and further analyzing the long-run goals and plans for the project.

Document Number 2

This is an extract from the "Working Paper" issued by Project Camelot on December 5, 1964. It was prepared at the request of the Office of the Chief of Research and Development, Department of the Army. It was to serve as a basis for briefings and discussions within the Army staff. Part One, the section reproduced here, is intended to orient military readers [I.L.H.].

In July of 1964, the Chief of Research and Development, Department of the Army, requested that Special Operations Research Office (SORO) of the American University develop a plan under the terms of its contract ARO-7 for research "to test the feasibility of developing a social systems model which will give the following capabilities:

1. Measurement of internal war potential: a means for identifying, measuring and forecasting the potential for internal war.
2. Estimation of reaction effects: a means for estimating the relative effectiveness of various military and quasi-military postures, practices, and levels of military involvement over a wide range of environmental conditions.
3. Information collection and handling systems: means and

procedures for rapid collection, storage and retrieval of data on internal war potential and effects of governmental action, with appropriate consideration of existing and likely future facilities for processing and analysis."

The present document gives a summary of actions taken since that request and provides a plan for the accomplishment of the research.

REQUIREMENT FOR PROJECT CAMELOT

A. The U.S. Army counterinsurgency mission places broad responsibilities on the Army for planning and conducting operations involving a wide spectrum of sociopolitical problems which are integral parts of counterinsurgency operations. The Army must, therefore, develop doctrines based on sound knowledge of the problem areas.

The problem of insurgency is an integral part of the larger problem of the emergence of the developing countries and their transition toward modernization. Some of these countries are just emerging into a new era of economic and social development; some are ruled or controlled by oligarchies which, in order to maintain their own favored positions, resist popular social and political movements toward economic or social betterment and removal of frustrations; still others have only recently obtained political independence. In the past, an insurgency has been perceived primarily, if not entirely, as a matter of internal security in the nation concerned to be countered when it became overt by military and police actions. In the present framework of modernization, however, the indicated approach is to try to obviate the need for insurgency through programs for political, economic, social, and psychological development. Military support of such programs can be a significant factor in the nation-building process.

Responsibility for conducting counterinsurgency operations must rest with the indigenous government. Carefully applied assistance and advice by U.S. governmental agencies can, however, materially influence the outcome. U.S. Government agencies abroad coordinate their activities through the country team which in many countries concentrates on providing assistance in developing plans and programs for preventing or countering insurgency. The programs recommended to the indigenous government may include advice on (1) the use of military force, (2) police activities, (3) educational programs, (4) social improvement programs, et cetera. The U.S. military must be prepared to participate in developing these plans and programs.

The most fruitful efforts would be those designed to achieve early detection and prevention of the predisposing conditions. Responsibility for planning such efforts should be shared by all governmental agencies. The exclusive responsibilities of the Army as a part of the military component of the country team planning committee must be considered in the context of the over-all counterinsurgency problem.

In this context, counterinsurgency operations seek to create an environment of security and popular trust which will promote orderly progress toward achieving national and popular goals. It is far more effective and economical to avoid insurgency through essentially constructive efforts than to counter it after it has grown into a full-scale movement requiring drastically greater effort.

Although U.S. counterinsurgency doctrine during the past few years has stressed preventive measures, the scientific knowledge on which to base such doctrine has been weak. Questions and answers about causes of insurgency have frequently been stated in terms unrelated to the way in which social groups and forces interact in determining the capability of the society to exist as a reasonably integrated whole.

That there is a poverty of knowledge in this area is understandable. Social science resources have not yet been adequately mobilized to study social conflict and control. A recent survey indicated that less than 1% of social scientists listed social conflict as their primary area of interest and less than 2% listed social control. The amount of research in this area sponsored by the military has been relatively insignificant.

Projects have often been in the form of discrete studies focused on some problems that have been sharpened by recent operational failures. There has been no large-scale attempt to analyze comprehensively the interrelated processes of social conflict and social control.

If the U.S. Army is to perform effectively its part in the U.S. mission of counterinsurgency it must recognize that insurgency represents a breakdown of social order and that the social processes involved must be understood. Conversely, the processes which produce a stable society must also be understood. Indeed, the study of insurgency should encompass the whole social process.

B. Throughout, the work of Project Camelot will be characterized by an orientation which views a country and its problems as a complex social system.

A country, viewed as a social system, is made up of many different and interdependent groups of people in pursuit of various goals. When groups fail to function so as to provide for the needs of the people that make up these groups, there is a tendency for them to break down and for their symbols to change meaning or lose value. People then tend to become involved in other lines of action which they perceive to be leading to a change for the better. Such actions may include sabotage, wildcat strikes, shootings and other acts of violence which, when continued, lead to a breakdown of law and order, to an inability of the economy to provide regularly for minimum essential needs and services, and to a further discrediting of the holders of political power. Much of this sort of action comes under the label of insurgency. There are many "explanations" of insurgency and prescriptions for dealing with it and its precursors. Many of these explanations and prescriptions derive from good but limited information and analysis and often reflect a specific point of view, such as economic or psychological, to the exclusion of others.

This project will differ from other efforts to study the symptoms and causes of insurgency, and methods of dealing with it and its preconditions, not only in size and scope but in insisting from the start upon a careful analysis of all components of the problem, and in bringing to bear in a coordinated effort the research talents of the relevant disciplines. This means calling on the resources of sociologists, psychologists, anthropologists, mathematicians, economists, political scientists, and military men.

The end product and other outputs of the project may be specified as follows:

1. Project Camelot has as its main objective an evaluation of the feasibility of developing and implementing a dynamic social systems model to:
   a. Identify indicators of conditions and trends which, if continued, would probably lead to the outbreak of internal war.
   b. Determine the probable effects of various courses of action by the indigenous government upon the social processes in the indigenous culture.
   c. Maintain information on the conditions referred to in *a.* and *b.* above in such a way, including the specifying of dynamic interrelationships among classes of information and the societal elements represented thereby) as to provide a timely and reliable basis for planning and policy guidance.

2. In the course of the project, intensive analysis of a single country will be made as a part of the effort to ascertain the feasibility of conducting similar studies on a continuing basis.

3. The main objective (1 above) will be sought through the pursuit of a number of other objectives instrumental to it. This will consist mainly in the development and testing of models of social processes and subsystems which are believed to be essential components of the processes and problems of internal war. Such model development will have three major advantages:
   a. It will provide guidance to the research.
   b. It will provide a framework of relationships which will

serve to integrate findings and translate data into a form which may have operational utility.

c. It will serve as a protection against the distinct possibility that no all-encompassing model of a dynamic social system can be achieved in the course of this project.

4. The project will also produce conceptual and theoretical papers and reports of specific studies conducted during the course of the project. Many of these will be of immediate interest or educational value within and without the Army. A large number will be important as contributions to scientific literature and as resources which will facilitate the work of this project. These intermediate research products are discussed later.

Document Number 3

This document is also from the December 5, 1964, Working Paper. Its particular importance results from the fact that the "story" of Project Camelot broke in Chile, which, as the reader will see, is not one of the nations recommended for examination. The broader importance of this document concerns the legitimacy of this form of investigation, that is, whether such in-country efforts represent ethnography or espionage [I.L.H.].

SELECTION OF COUNTRIES FOR STUDY

I. CRITERIA FOR SELECTION

The following seem to be the essential criteria for selecting countries to be studied in the course of Project CAMELOT:

1. *Information already available.* This refers to (*a*) data and facts which have been collected by various social scientists in the past and (*b*) data which are normally developed by various agencies of the indigenous government or by indigenous economic interests.

2. *Accumulated knowledge and understanding about the country.* This refers to historical, economic, anthropological, sociological, and other *understanding* of the country and its society that has grown up during the relatively recent past.

3. *Accessibility of the society for further study.* Here the considerations are mainly political and will hinge upon the degree to which the research objectives can be made to comport with the interest of the local government and the ongoing programs sponsored by U.S. agencies represented in the U.S. country team.

4. *Research talent available.* It would be obviously unwise to attempt to study countries for which few specialists exist with a basic knowledge of the institutions and languages of the countries.

5. *Cost.* Admittedly, dollar cost is a secondary consideration but one which could easily become primary if the countries are widely separated and distant from the U.S. base of operations. Additionally, cost in time would be incurred and increased if highly dissimilar countries are chosen since this would require considerable investment in standardizing field research instruments for purposes of comparative analysis.

6. Finally and most significantly is the relevance of selected countries to U.S. foreign policy interests. It is by no means essential that all countries studied be among those listed as critical by the special precedence groups for counterinsurgency. However, early and highly probable utility of the findings of our project would require choice of countries of current and lasting concern for U.S. interest.

II. COUNTRIES RECOMMENDED

A review of geographical areas and countries world-wide against the criteria enumerated above, leads to the recommendation that studies be undertaken in these countries.

A. For Comparative Historical Studies

In Latin America: Argentina, Bolivia, Brazil, Colombia, Cuba, Dominican Republic, El Salvador, Guatemala, Mexico, Paraguay, Peru, Venezuela.

In Middle East: Egypt, Iran, Turkey.

In Far East: Korea, Indonesia, Malaysia, Thailand.

Other Countries: France, Greece, Nigeria.

B. For Survey Research and Other Field Studies: Bolivia, Colombia, Ecuador, Paraguay, Peru, Venezuela, Iran, Thailand.

By definition field work will be required in the countries where surveys are run. Additionally, field work will be necessary in certain countries in order to generate data on currently critical situations therein. Therefore, to the countries where surveys will be done there should be added Argentina and Brazil from the list of countries where historical studies are programmed.

The above paragraphs are not intended to exclude visits to other countries. Such visits may be necessary for purposes of document tracing and collating of existent data on recent revolutionary trends and on economic and social developments bearing on variables important to hypotheses being tested in Project CAMELOT.

Finally, it is recommended that selection — from the above list — of a country for the final phase of intensive study be deferred until experience of the first year provides improved criteria for such selection.

III. ACCESS REQUIREMENTS

It is not possible to specify exactly the extent of access necessary for the historical studies since this will be a function of the amount of data currently available and the particular requirements of each study. It is possible to say, however, that it is not likely that more than three man months would be necessary. In addition, the local interaction will be minimal with most of the research being conducted in archives.

The survey research, on the other hand, will require approximately six man months of access for each study undertaken. Since local survey organizations, or at a minimum local interviewers, will be used, the amount of interaction with the local population will not be extensive.

The effort at the single country analysis in the third year of the study will require more extensive field work. Thus it is programmed that approximately six research personnel will be required in a country for a period of nine months to a year. This results in 54 to 72 man months in the field. While these estimates cannot be taken as formally programmed, they do represent an indication of the level of in-country effort contemplated.

Document Number 4

The following "Brief Description" of Project Camelot was made public on June 15, 1965, when it became clear that serious criticism of both its methods and purposes were forthcoming from the scholarly community abroad and the military establishment at home. It was designed as a "press package" [I.L.H.].

I. INTRODUCTION

Project CAMELOT is a large-scale study concerned with understanding the development of preconditions and precipitants of internal conflict and the effects of indigenous government actions on those verbalizing conditions. The study involves the refinement of social conflict theory through use of a research design which integrates data from analytic case studies, social system studies, and manual and machine simulation.

The need for a study such as CAMELOT has existed for several years. The advances in the behavioral sciences in the last five to ten years suggest there is a basis for a project directed at analyzing low level conflict in its early stages. Project CAMELOT represents an attempt to apply and extend this work to the problem area of internal conflict.

CAMELOT proposes to identify the dynamics of indigenous government action with respect to the preconditions and precipitants of internal conflict. The project assumes, therefore, that there is a regularity to human relationships and that predictability rests on a continuance or ordered patterns of interaction. It further assures that it is possible to devise methods for identifying these patterns of interaction as they relate both to the development of social strains and to the effectiveness of indigenous government action in dealing with those strains.

As a research project in the social sciences, CAMELOT is unprecedented in scope and intensity. The several million dollars committed to the project for a three and a half year period permit CAMELOT to utilize and integrate the skills of competent scholars in numerous fields. The project is being carefully planned in close consultation with outstanding research scientists and will involve an effort of an estimated 140 professional man years.

A preliminary project design for CAMELOT, completed April 1, 1965, extends the study efforts described in this paper. The over-all project design provides guidelines for developing a model of social conflict and a model of a social system. The project design is constructed in accordance with recent developments in the social sciences, including increased understanding about the nature of conflict. The analytic methods envisioned as end-products will be refined through the process of analyzing some twenty case studies on internal conflict, through five studies of contemporary social systems, and from the result of manual and machine simulation. A one-country, in-depth study, the final test of the analytic methods is scheduled for 1968.

One of the implicit objectives of CAMELOT is to test whether such a large-scale, closely integrated project has a higher probability of payoff than a series of small, loosely related investigations in the general area of concern. Similarly, CAMELOT will investigate the comparative value of data gathered by survey research, content analysis, expert opinion, and participant observation as well as through library research.

Project CAMELOT is no small task. In comparison to other problem areas, little study has been conducted on social conflict. One recent survey of social scientists in the United States revealed that less than one percent considered their primary field to be social conflict. The challenge to the research community is great, but the responses of social scientists to CAMELOT thus far have been enthusiastic.

II. PROJECT ORIENTATION

It is desirable at this point to make explicit several assumptions that have guided the development of plans for Project CAMELOT. These orienting guidelines set the tone for the type of research contemplated.

First, Project CAMELOT will employ a scientific approach, that is to say, it is an objective, fact-finding study concerned with *what is* and not with what *ought to be*. It will not formulate value statements concerning the adoption of any particular policy but will provide a possible basis for policy.

Secondly, CAMELOT will pursue a balanced course between theoretical and empirical work. It will not become solely involved with theoretical considerations which, however intriguing, may lie beyond the realm of test and verification; nor will it be so blind to a theoretical underpinning as to wander aimlessly into indiscriminate research areas, exposed to the danger of finding itself at its conclusion with a sizable but shapeless mass of data.

Thirdly, CAMELOT, in the pursuit of its objectives, will bring to bear all the relevant disciplines and talents required, whether they be drawn from the fields of sociology, psychology, anthropology, mathematics, economics, political science, or operations research. Project CAMELOT will assemble and direct these various research talents in a coordinated study of the problem of internal war potential and the effects of alternate government actions.

Fourthly, CAMELOT is a unclassified, open project the results of which will be made available through normal scholarly channels. In addition it is anticipated that all the data will be made available to other scholars, in the United States and abroad, for their analysis.

III. RESEARCH DESIGN

A. OVER-ALL OUTLINE

In the context of the above orientation, the over-all outline of the research design is along the following lines. The research objectives have been translated into what are being called research foci, or areas of substantive research. The *theoretical design effort* is primarily charged with development of a model* of a social system and a model of internal conflict to be used to guide further research.

The second research foci is called *analytic case studies*. This research will involve the detailed examination of some twenty historical instances in countries in which there have been severe internal strains — many involving internal conflict — since World War II. The specific research design for these case studies will be derived from the models resulting from the theoretical design work.

The third research foci will involve systematic study of socioeconomic conditions in *five contemporary societies* again using, as the basis for study design, the model of a social system. The fourth area of research will be a *comparative analysis* of the case studies of internal conflict and the social system studies. Manual and machine simulation make up the last research foci. Research in these two areas will be designed to supplement the other research derived from the models.

* The term model is used to mean an explicit set of assumptions, definitions, and propositions regarding the functioning of a social system and the development of internal conflict. These assumptions, definitions, and propositions must be logically consistent and descriptive of the system under study. This work will be largely drawn from existing social theory and specify the information requirements for the later studies. The models will be so designed as to provide information for testing many relevant theories and propositions and not just a single one.

B. DISCUSSION

The concepts of a model of a social system and a model of social conflict are central to the conception of the research. The initial models, developed largely from the body of work that has been done previously on social systems and social conflict, will be used as the theoretical structures for the analytic case studies and the social system studies. The results of the comparative analyses of the individual studies of internal conflict and ongoing social systems will be used to refine the models for an in-depth study of a single country. The data from the single country study will then be used for a final revision of the model to be used for a possible replication of the study to test the feasibility of estimating internal conflict potential in a given country and measuring the effects of various indigenous government actions on the preconditions or problems which may lead to internal war.

There is an important need for the pretheoretical processing of data. The data on incidents of internal conflict just do not exist in adequate form for comparative analysis. The work to date has been largely qualitative in nature and lacking in the type and amount of quantification that is required.

It is therefore necessary for case studies to be carried out in order to generate the type of data that will allow quantitative comparative analysis. In any scientific attempt at generalization there must be a body of adequate data. Since it is not possible to specify *a priori* the exact form of all possible models that might be useful, it is necessary to develop a broad range of information requirements for the case studies so that many types of models can be developed and later tested with the data.

Therefore, the initial social conflict and social systems models developed will have as a primary objective the specification of the types of other models that may prove valuable to the project. Thus communications models, power models, economic models, decision-making models, developmental models, and others will be explored for information requirements. The research design for the individual analytic case studies and the individual social systems studies will be planned to include the information requirements for all of the *various* models.

One weakness of previous research in this area is that an individual scholar with limited resources has collected only that information relevant to his particular theoretical orientation or model. Thus the data have been of limited use for testing other ideas. CAMELOT will attempt a major contribution to social science by collecting data so that the many models, theories, and ideas of individual scholars can be evaluated. The social systems studies and the analytic case studies will provide the bulk of the data for the comparative analyses. This latter effort will result in a refinement of the initial models for both the social system and the development of internal conflict. These refined analytic models will be then used as the framework for the in-depth, one-country study.

Many approaches will be used for the comparative analyses. These will range from (*a*) factor analysis type of data reduction searching for critical variables (with multiple regression analysis of the critical factors on the actual occurrences of internal conflict) to (*b*) content analysis (possibly with machine help) of the shifts in the use of political symbols, to (*c*) a more qualitative review of the significance of institutional and structural aspects of the societies in question and their relationship to the outbreak of internal conflict. These examples are illustrative of the types of analysis that are appropriate and have proved to be heuristic in previous efforts in social analysis.

As stated above, feedback from the comparative analyses will be used to refine the analytic models, thus providing for accumulation of knowledge. In the development of scientific knowledge, this process of theory building is critical. Unfortunately, in the area of social conflict there has been little such development. This project will utilize the best of previous work as the foundation for an explicit attempt to improve understanding cumulatively.

The one country in-depth study will test the models which were refined with the comparative data. This one country study will provide the basis for testing the feasibility of developing a system to obtain, store, and retrieve data on the preconditions of internal conflict and the effects of indigenous governmental actions vis-à-vis these underlying strains.

The main loop of the research effort involves the elements discussed above. Ancillary to this main loop, but by no means unimportant, are studies involving manual and machine simulation, including mathematical modelling and small-group experimentation. They are not included in the main stream of the design because mathematical modelling is a young, unproven technique in social science and small group experimentation is concerned with different types of theory building and data collection than large-scale social analysis.

Mathematical modelling has been eminently successful in dealing with a certain class of specific problems as best exemplified by developments in the field of operations research. In large-scale social analysis, however, the results have been less successful. The opportunity exists with this project to generate data in such a form that the techniques associated with mathematical modelling may in the end prove to be highly profitable.

Small-group experimentation, particularly when concerned with concepts such as cohesion, socialization, goal development, and motivation in primary groups, contains a body of theory and methods that cannot be overlooked. Many have suggested that much of the fabric of a society is shaped, changed, and controlled in primary groups as the first level of social integration Again as in the case of mathematical modelling, this level of analysis is differentiated from the societal analysis undertaken in the primary loop of the research design. The extent to which resources are expanded in this area will be a function of the further refinement of the research design in the Spring of 1965 and the results of the review of the design by a Summer 1965 Seminar.

IV. SUMMARY

CAMELOT is approaching the problem of internal conflict from the standpoint of developing an explicit framework for the extensive collection of historical and contemporary data necessary to scientifically and systematically analyze the processes by which strains and tensions in a society may lead to internal conflict. This study will approach the problem comparatively to develop and refine models that can be tested in a given country. CAMELOT's basic objective is to test the feasibility of developing an analytic methodology for analyzing the underlying causes of internal conflict in any given country and to measure the effects of various indigenous governmental actions vis-à-vis the underlying problems.

PART III

THE ACADEMIC RESPONSE

Marshall Sahlins

University of Michigan

The Established Order:
*Do Not Fold, Spindle, or Mutilate**

We all know what the right to investigate freely, to think freely, and to write freely means to our field and ourselves, and what the loss of these would mean. Mr. Chairman, I am concerned that our involvement in cold war projects such as Camelot does jeopardize these freedoms. Of course I speak for myself; but the sentiments are not entirely my own. I have had a chance to discuss these matters with colleagues from several universities. Without presuming to represent them, I am trying here to formulate concerns many have expressed.

The following, Mr. Chairman, constitute grounds for apprehension:

1. The scale and character of government interest in Strategic Social Science. In the nature of things, this is seen only through a glass darkly. We do know the six-million dollars allotted to Camelot was merely for a "feasibility" study (3 and one-half years). An ultimate investment of several times that per annum was contemplated — one ex-Camelot scholar told me the talk was of 50 million a year. Meanwhile

* Previously unpublished. Delivered first at the November 1965 Meetings of the American Anthropological Association in Denver, Colorado.

Problem Camelot goes on, with the aid of some anthropologists, in Africa as well as Latin America, New Guinea as well as Southeast Asia. And on the home front, intelligence agencies erect concealed bases of support: sundry "front" foundations or "pass-throughs" created with covert government funds. These funds dispense "grants" for certain "academic" research and travel. There are grounds to suspect the CIA fronts are camouflaged by names closely approximating those of listed and legitimate private foundations.

2. Mr. Chairman, there is a serious possibility that such tactics will become our tactics. It is already a minimum demand of internal vigilance that everyone investigate the source of funds he is offered for foreign-area research, conferences on field work needs, or the like. I understand that in at least one instance anthropologists have been invited by colleagues to attend a conference subsidized by the Defense Department without however being informed in advance of this sponsorship. Here is an example of the corrosion of integrity that must accompany an enlistment of scholars in a *gendarmerie* relation to the Third World. Subversion of the mutual trust between field worker and informant is the predictable next step. The relativism we hold necessary to ethnography can be replaced by cynicism, and the quest for objective knowledge of other peoples replaced by a probe for their political weaknesses.

3. The State Department announces it will create a board of review for government-sponsored external research, with the aim of blocking investigations not in the nation's best interests. This is a clear threat to free inquiry. I realize the purpose of the broadly worded presidential directive was to prevent repetitions of Camelot. But directives outlive the intentions of those who issue them and ought to reckon with those who implement them; so that directives wrong in principle must be opposed on principle. Nor is the theory of good people administering bad laws a proper philosophy of American democracy.

4. As it is, we cannot get into half the world; as scholars-in-

armor we would soon not be on speaking terms with the other half.

I refer to the call to this meeting:

Some field work already in progress in various parts of the world, particularly in Latin America, has already suffered adversely, being forced to curtail or even suspend operations. Reports have been received and verified about the investigation and embarrassment by their governments of foreign scholars who have been actively helping United States social scientists. This, in turn, rapidly erodes the resources of goodwill upon which we can draw and militates against the conduct of adequately staffed and assisted field work.

The New York Times foresaw just this predicament in September 1964, in commenting on the disclosure by a congressional subcommittee of a CIA front foundation: "What evidence," *The Times* asked, "can American professors or field workers present to prove they are not engaged in underground activities when it is known that the CIA is using its money to subsidize existing foundations, or is creating fictitious ones?"

This harassment falls on everyone, just or unjust: independent scholar or academic cold warrior, foreign intellectuals as well as the Americans with whom they work. In some sense it is not our fault. It is not our fault that America appears to many people an interventionist and counterrevolutionary power. And it is not our fault that American agents, whose relations to progressive movements seem instinctively hostile, operate under cover in the Third World. But the least we can do is protect the anthropologist's relation to the Third World, which is a scholarly relation. Field work under contract to the U.S. Army is no way to protect that relation.

Perhaps it was Camelot's greatest irony that it forgot to program itself into the project. As a tactic of fomenting Latin American unrest and anti-North American sentiment, Camelot would be the envy of any Communist conspiracy. We have heard of the self-fulfilling prophecy; here was the self-fulfilling research proposal.

5. Strategic research raises serious issues of classification

and clearance. Scientifically, the relevant concerns are the right to freely communicate one's experiences to colleagues at home and abroad and the right to participate in research according to one's merit and promise — without regard to the FBI's understanding of patriotism. Here we should take into account a distinction much favored by the Camelot scientists: that it *is* research, not intelligence. Participating scholars conceived the project to be a fine opportunity to develop knowledge useful, even critical, to social science. It was a chance, too, to advance the frontiers of research technique. The project design of April 1, 1965, indeed opens new vistas on the study of revolution and counterrevolution, such as "operations research techniques, manual and machine simulation, machine content analysis, and new types of analysis of survey data" — which is perhaps why one friend, an unautomated anthropologist of decided views, suggested that the most heartening thing about Camelot was its intellectual prognosis.

For Project Camelot, the DOD gave assurance that findings would not be classified and clearance would not be necessary. In fact, there are no ironclad guarantees. The government has the power; in this respect the scholar is in very unequal relation to Defense, State, or the CIA. And what will the ruling be on Project Kula-Ring, Operation Leopard-Skin Chief, and other future scientific investigations of the CIA or DOD? Moreover, it is difficult to conceive that classification would not have eventually occurred in Camelot. A working paper of December 5, 1964, stipulates as the most significant criterion for inclusion in the study the relevance of the country to U.S. foreign policy interests. The program for historic studies (April 1) asks investigators to probe official corruption, the strength of insurgent parties, and the measures taken to cut off external aid to insurgents; to determine the effectiveness of the established government's intelligence service; to give approximate numbers of forces available for counterinsurgency; to say whether the regime fomented foreign wars or "black" coups to suppress internal unrest; to determine whether the government permitted Communist infiltration of itself or radical movements; to name names, note groups, and identify leaders. All sorts of questions such as these were deemed important in the preliminary archival studies. Suppose the answers proved important and informed the field worker's check lists. Can you now suppose these field reports would be published?

(In connection with the assurances about classification, I understand that when Camelot was summarily cancelled the DOD asked participants not to publicly discuss the project, and this request was respected. That the DOD's request was prompted by the international repercussions of Camelot's premature disclosure is better understood as an augury than a mitigating circumstance, and as a reflection on the character of the project.)

6. The idea that Strategic Social Science will liberalize strategy as it advances science seems to me a snare and a delusion.

I form the impression that good and conscientious Camelot scientists thought they might put something over on the Defense Department. They were going to get in some good research, whatever the U.S. Army's objectives. Besides, if somebody's going to do this sort of thing, better it be sensible and humane people. Here was a chance to educate the military to foreign realities, an opportunity to reconstruct American attitudes and policies. And with this hope went the perception that the Defense Department is divisible into "good guys" and "bad guys"; and the former, although a minority, managed to get this "software" research through and ought to be encouraged.

I think this all unnecessarily naïve, a failure to analyze the structure of the Establishment, the relation of the sword to the pen, the strengths of the cold war demonology, and the present foreign-political position of this country. The quixotic scholar enters the agreement in the belief that knowledge breeds power; his military counterpart, in the assurance that power breeds knowledge. The level of innocence is best documented by ethnography, although the point appears also in Camelot documents. I asked a Camelot psychologist who was pleased to expound this distinction between black knights and white knights, what was the content of the progressives' program. He said, in the first place, that enlightened Pentagon officers see the military of Latin America — acting in concert with the U.S. Army — as the best available vehicle for reform: they are organized, efficient, intelligent, and have the social machinery. That is what he said. So help me.

7. The cold war researcher is potentially a servant of power, placed in a sycophantic relation to the state unbefitting science or citizenship. The scholar sells his services to a military, intelligence or foreign policy client, who has certain plans for the product. Although formal clearance requirements may be suspended, it is only artless to claim there is no informal selection of academic personnel on the basis of agreement in cold war principle — if not tactic — or no penalty to outspoken public criticism. Academicians who have demonstrated creative support are at least differentially favored for higher appointments in the existing scheme of things; those who cannot agree run some risk of being shut out, unless they shut up. If this is important research, carried out as it may be under institutional contract, the government agency is in a position to make one's commitment to prevailing policy a condition of professional opportunity and success. On the other side, one's freedom as a citizen to dissent is constrained, on pain of antagonizing the employers-that-be. This fate can be predicted even for those first engaged by the agency on research of their own choosing, "basic research": they are equally retainers, mortgaged to past and future favors. Clearly, neither science nor democracy can function in such an atmosphere.

The science and government question is delicate, complicated, and perennial. But now that it has come to us, perhaps we can add an understanding of the sociology in it that betrays all good intentions. Even the military or intelligence agency may have good intentions about academic independence; yet informal screening and watchful discretion will go on. For the agreement between cold war scholar and government bureau is largely self-policing. "Cameloticians" themselves understood the principle and wrote it into their project. In the checklist for case studies appears a section titled "Government Control of Scientific Institutions." It aims to assess the power of the established regime and the loyalties it could command in a crisis. There is a subhead called "Scientists." It asks only this: "What percentage of scientists work for Government and for private organizations? Of those who work for private organizations, such as universities, what percentage supplement their income through Government contracts, extra jobs, consultations?"

8. The scientific status of cold war research is equivocal. Camelot documents bear out Senator Fulbright's suspicions: "Implicit in Camelot," he said, "as in the concept of 'counter-insurgency' is an assumption that revolutionary movements are dangerous to the interest of the United States and that the United States must be prepared to assist, if not actually to participate in, measures to repress them." Consider this example of "scientific" question from the project design: "Was the Government guilty of excessive toleration of alienated, insurgent, or potentially insurgent groups?"

But most clearly in its characterizations of revolutionary unrest does Camelot reveal its basic valuations. I am not speaking of personal biases or construing anything about motivations. It seems a better — and sufficient — interpretation that what had been for some time a cultural common-law marriage between scientific functionalism and the natural interest of a leading world power in the status quo became under the aegis of Project Camelot an explicit and legitimate union. In any event, revolutionary movements are described in Camelot documents as "antisystem activities," indications of "severe disintegration," varieties of "destabilizing processes," threats to "legitimate control of the means of coercion within the society," facilitated by "administrative errors." Movements for radical change are in Camelot's view a disease, and a society so infected is sick. Here was a program for diagnosing social illness, a study in "epidemiology," called just that by a senior researcher. Another consistently refers to revolutionary movements as "social pathology," though disclaiming in footnote that they are necessarily to be avoided. A third conceives the growth of demands for change as "contagion." "Did the government," he proposes to determine, "couple limited and managed reforms with repressive measures to prevent the contagion and spread of social unrest?" Of course, waiting on call is the doctor, the U.S. Army, fully prepared for its self-appointed "important mission in the positive and constructive aspects of nation-building." The indicated treatment is "insurgency prophylaxis."

If Camelot had been given a title more appropriate to its "scientific" character, it might have been, "The Established Order: Do Not Fold, Spindle or Mutilate." But aside from President Kennedy's fondness for the musical comedy, "Camelot" was apparently for the Army happily symbolic of the knight in shining armor come to slay the dragon of disorder — and so gain half the kingdom. Social scientists, however, might have reflected on the deeper medieval connotation: their recruitment as the scholastics of cold war theology.

Every citizen has the right to engage in counterinsurgency research and practice. But in my opinion none of us has leave, as scholar or citizen, to so delude himself and others about the scientific legitimacy and disinterested objectivity of this work. Here certain distinctions must be made. Just because the subject of research is intellectually important, it does not mean that the research proposal is important, or even any good. And just because the people involved in a bureaucratic operation are honest and conscientious — as every Camelot scholar I know is — does not mean that what they are engaged in has these qualities. This last sad fact all recent history teaches us.

Mr. Chairman, I have tried to formulate colleagues' opinions I have heard and which I share. For each and all the reasons stated I object to any further engagement in strategic research by American anthropologists working under contract to defense, foreign policy, or intelligence agencies of the U.S. government. I happen to believe it is no good for the country or the peoples among whom we have lived. I am convinced it is no good for our discipline or our mortal selves. I frame no resolutions, however, because I am undecided on the value of doing so. It would be an advantage to make clear to our government and the world that we are autonomous scientists concerned in our studies with a rational inquiry into man and his works. As against this, tedious debate and discussions of wording would probably not enhance solidarity nor produce a resolution of moral strength. More critical, we have no sanctions and cannot legislate ethics, and perhaps we should not try. For the moment, I favor the principle of letting each man learn to live with himself.

Kalman H. Silvert

Dartmouth College

*American Academic Ethics and Social Research Abroad: The Lesson of Project Camelot**

American social science is in a crisis of ethics. Certainly, however, "American social science" — whatever that amorphous corporation may be — is not broadly aware of any particular problem, or that its motives, techniques, and practitioners are falling into disrepute in many parts of the emergent world. Latin America, the most developed of the underdeveloped, is appropriately the scene of a confrontation putting into question the honesty, decency, and even simple competence not only of all of us engaged in that area but also of students of all our disciplines wherever they may work. The crisis, long recognized as latent by sensitive observers, has now passed into an acute stage. At this moment, not a single survey research study can be done in Chile. Throughout Latin America, quantitative studies have halted or been impeded, and all scholars, whether in teaching or research, find their actions questioned in direct correlation with the sophistication of the persons with whom they deal.

* *Reprinted from American Universities Field Staff Reports* (West Coast South American Series), Vol. 12, No. 3 (July 1965), with the permission of the director.

These statements are not an exaggeration. Nor can they be dismissed by patronizing references to the sensitivity of Latin Americans, the harassment by leftist intellectuals, or the hostility of persons with inferiority feelings. The primary responsibility for the present state of affairs rests with Americans despite the obvious complications induced by the nature of Latin Americans, who in this case are merely reacting to misbehavior. The immediate cause of the present contretemps is the attempt of the Special Operations Research Office of American University to launch a large-scale sociopolitical study of internal warfare in Latin America with funds provided by the Department of the Army. The extremely noisy debacle that ensued almost immediately cannot be explained in the narrow terms of a few bungling individuals or even of misguided policy; the ground for today's disgrace was well prepared by the ethical incomprehension, cavalier attitudes, and tolerance of ignorance manifested by American universities and scholars for many years. The sum of these saddening shortcomings bore heavily on Latin America as it became a lucrative and thus intellectually attractive field after the Cold War came to the Caribbean, producing a crisis far surpassing the immediate circumstances.

Such charges are serious indeed. They reflect on the personal work morality of scholars. They question the manner in which universities have chosen their priorities for foreign-area studies. They raise doubts concerning foundation activities, the sponsorship of research, the proper relationship between government and the scientific community. These matters are already being considered by two Chilean investigative committees. They will soon be treated in the Congress of the United States, and some stir of reaction is finally beginning in academia.

Let me make it entirely clear that in this matter I am what an anthropologist would call a participant observer. I was in Chile at the time the present crisis erupted and discussed the matter with some, though not all, of the principal actors. One of my own research undertakings is paralyzed. I have an investment spanning 25 years, as student and professional, in Latin America. I have also been pained with the low prestige accorded scholarly work on Latin America and have both welcomed and been fearful of the present coming of the prestigious folk to the area. I make these statements, and put them in the first person singular, so that the reader may be fully aware that I consider myself an engaged scholar. By "engaged," I mean that I am personally concerned about the course of social events; by "scholar," I mean that I attempt not only to use objective procedures but also to take care that the specific questions I ask are theoretically determined and not the fruit of passion. I also presume that to be a scholar means to assume the rights and duties of freedom of inquiry and communication, accepting no covert sponsorship, being ridden by as few hidden motives as may be consistent with the dignity of personal privacy, and taking intellectual risks. Elementary as these remarks may be, they seem to need repetition at this particular time and especially as prelude to my attempt to present a subject that makes so much personal difference to me.

PROJECT CAMELOT

The Special Operations Research Office labeled its proposed research Project Camelot. It was supported with an initial $6,000,000 for three to four years by the Department of the Army. These particular plans came to fruition in 1964, although for many years previously SORO has worked under much smaller contracts involving secondary research largely carried out within the United States. But the unfortunately titled Camelot[1] projected an extremely broad look into at least half a dozen Latin American countries toward the end of isolating the conditions leading to internal revolt and

---

[1] In colloquial Spanish, *camelo* means joke or jest; hence, Project Camelot is often spoken of as Project Camelo(t). *Camelo* is also close to *camello*, or "camel," a notoriously nasty beast.

deriving a set of conclusions indicating what could be done to contain or channel the effects of revolutionary disturbance. Historical as well as quantitative techniques were to be employed, and all sectors of society from schools to court systems and from paupers to presidents were to be analyzed. The directors of the undertaking sought advice from leading social scientists and attempted to recruit as stellar a force of scholars as would lend themselves to research so sponsored and focused.

The enthusiasm of the interested persons in the Defense Department and of the academicians involved is easy to understand, as are their administrative procedures. The military have become increasingly concerned with counterinsurgency and antiguerrilla techniques because of the Southeast Asian situation, as well as the manner in which Castroism triumphed in Cuba. From counterinsurgency to the employment of soldiers in civic action programs is but a short step, for everyone knows that the sympathy of the peasant is a requirement of insurgents who seek to live off the land. A military force expecting to face many years of bush wars overseas has a legitimate interest in wanting to learn as much as it can about the conditions which spawn various types of revolution, the measures taken to combat "internal wars" in other countries, and in general the politics of modernization which are the backdrop for so much revolutionary disturbance. The question is not at all whether concerned military officers should know of these matters; it is instead how the knowledge should be accumulated and presented in the first place and then what conclusions should be drawn and who should determine the action appropriate to these conclusions.

Likewise, the enthusiasm of the social scientists involved is easily understood. The opportunity existed for a massive, richly supported, highly detailed study into the conditions for social change in general as well as into the more specific subject of revolution. The study of modernization as well as of comparative societies has become of increasing academic concern in the past decade; indeed, there is probably more solid theorizing and competent field work going into these problem areas than into any others in the social sciences. In addition, the policy implications of this work are clear; and for those intellectuals who "want to make a difference," the combination between heavily endowed academic research and immediate access to the instruments of powerful implementation can prove irresistible.

It should also be understood that Camelot represents no new departure, that the actors might well have felt no need to consult the academic community concerning the ethics of the matter because so much similar work has already been done and is still being done. A difference in scale is not necessarily a difference in type. In any event, to what formalized academic bodies could the Camelot directors have turned for an advisory opinion on the ethics of their undertaking? How many scholars who knew of this widely publicized project actually wrote to SORO questioning the wisdom and ethics of the matter?[2]

So, Camelot began its short run. Chile was selected as the first country for study. Given the subject of the research, I am not sure why Chile was considered. Once past its postindependence trauma, the country has suffered only one massively violent episode (in 1891). Since that time, normal constitutional procedures in changing governments have been interrupted only once (from 1925 to 1932). With respect to civil violence as such, its history as an independent nation presents a better record than that of the United States. Its very peacefulness and commitment to civil liberties and democratic procedures have made Chile highly attractive to scholars as a safe training ground for other, more risky, places. Thus it may well be that the Camelot researchers were think-

---

[2] This question, though unanswerable fully by anyone outside American University, can be answered in tiny part here. The writer was requested to join in Project Camelot last year. He declined but raised no troubling questions.

ing of Chile so that they might learn how recurrent revolutions are avoided in at least one Latin American country.

The person who made the first contact in Chile for Camelot was Dr. Hugo Nuttini,[3] an ex-Chilean, now an American citizen and an associate professor at the University of Pittsburgh, according to Chilean press reports. After making some initial contacts in December 1964, he returned to the United States, following up with letters and a second trip in April 1965. The report of the affair in *Ercilla*, a Chilean news magazine, contains details exactly as they were told to me by some of the major participants:[4]

He [Nuttini] spoke with Urzúa [a sociologist at the Catholic University who had studied with Nuttini at UCLA], explaining that [the study] would cover "a series of aspects of the Chilean social system," and that it would be backed by "several million dollars" granted by the National Science Foundation. He added, by way of bait, that among the directors of the project there figured distinguished North American social science personalities, citing names of such prestige as Kingsley Davis, Seymour Lipset, and Robert K. Merton.

In March he began the final offensive. He wrote exploratory letters to Raúl Urzúa and Álvaro Bunster, Secretary General of the University of Chile, dated the 22nd and 30th respectively, telling them of the matter in very similar terms.

"The project in question," read the letter to Álvaro Bunster, "is a kind of pilot study in which will participate sociologists, anthropologists, economists, psychologists, geographers and other specialists in the social sciences, and which will be supported by various scientific and governmental organizations in the United States. The researchers are all members of the most prestigious universities in this country, such as Pennsylvania, Yale, California, Columbia, Chicago, etc. . . ."

Not once — not during his later trip to Santiago, either — did he mention which were the "governmental institutions" supporting the project, nor did he again mention the names of the participating scientists.

[3] Ironically, in view of events, Dr. Nuttini was not a regular member of the Project Camelot staff. He was in Chile for a survey into the suitability of the country as a case.

[4] *Ercilla*, July 7, 1965, p. 20.

The April trip was the beginning of the end. Nuttini ran across a Norwegian sociologist, Dr. Johan Galtung, teaching at UNESCO's Latin American Faculty of Social Sciences, a two-year school attended by students from throughout Latin America. Galtung, deeply dedicated to his task and profoundly loyal to his students, had been invited to attend a Camelot planning session during the month of August in the Washington area. He was thus fully informed concerning the nature of the project, which was never handled with any duplicity at all in the United States. Nuttini, confronted by Galtung with documentary evidence (the completely open and frank letter of invitation to the conference), persisted in proclaiming his ignorance of the Department of the Army connection. In *Ercilla's* words, the same as those told me by Galtung, the end of Nuttini was as follows:

The upshot of the story was the unmasking in both universities of the agent, and his simultaneous protestations of innocence, alleging that he "had been fooled," that he would "immediately abandon the project," that he would call Washington to settle accounts. The indignation of the Chilean scientists was rooted in a double reason: one of them patriotic, that of being used as tools in an espionage plan; and another professional, the betrayal to which their own North American colleagues wished to induce them.

Until this moment, the affair had not gone far beyond university circles. But then came the American intervention in the Dominican Republic. This action was widely interpreted in Latin America as signaling the political end of the Alliance for Progress and a regression to support right-wing military governments throughout Latin America as the best insurance against Castroism. This conclusion was reached not only by civilians but also by many military groups, which began immediate agitation of both an internal and external nature, leading to the mobilization of at least two armies in South America. Project Camelot then snapped into another focus: It became intimately laced in public opinion with interventionism and militarism, with the image of the United States as a power dedicated to the throttling of any revolutionary movements of whatever Center-to-Left stripe. The often-repeated statements by very high American officials that Communists tend naturally to rise to the top in any conditions of social turmoil led to immediate charges that American foreign policy was, in effect, *macartista* or McCarthyite in refusing any longer to differentiate among progressive parties. Wrapped into already grave suspicions of antiguerrilla programs, it was only natural that Camelot should be seen as part of a carefully planned policy instead of merely a project whose research design was still far from being complete.

Another circumstance not only increased the confusion but also deepened Chilean suspicions of the nature of the enterprise. Before the outburst, the American Embassy knew nothing of Project Camelot or the coming of Nuttini. In addition, it became obvious with the passage of time that the State Department was most unhappy with the entire undertaking. It was the diplomatic protest of the Chilean government against Project Camelot that precipitated the revelation of these discrepancies among official American agencies. In answering the official protest of the government of President Eduardo Frei, the Embassy was forced to make clear its lack of prior knowledge and its embarrassment at the entire situation. This event served further to convince many Chileans that the United States' Latin American policy was really being made in "The Pentagon." The impression was not lightened when the Chilean Minister of the Interior goodheartedly but innocently absolved the American "government" from blame, making the standard Latin American discrimination between the armed forces and the civil authorities.

The Chilean government subsequently established a committee of the Ministry of the Interior to investigate the case, and the Congress has launched its own investigation with a special *ad hoc* committee. *El Siglo,* the Communist daily, has of course been playing the matter for all it is worth, running a long series featuring photostatic copies of Camelot's long and involved research plan. The terminology has been allowed to slip also: "Project Camelot" has become "Plan Camelot," the word espionage has been accepted by most political shades as appropriate to the incident (as *Ercilla's* ready acceptance indicates), and even such conservative papers as *El Mercurio* employ these words in description of the matter.

SOME IMMEDIATE IMPLICATIONS

Whether social science research with large groups is presently impossible in Chile and many other countries is not known. Even if survey work is officially permitted and even if respondents agree to answer, it cannot be known whether the answers will be a reasonably valid statement of attitude. A friend from the Catholic University, writing to advise me to halt my own field work, said:

With all this, our research at the School is halting all field interviewing until the "water passes." Not only for the problems which may arise, but very importantly because we feel that the validity of the studies is in peril due to the great "sensibilización" [sensitizing] that is taking place. To give just one example: one of our colleagues worked very hard and came forth with a very good research design for a study paid by the Chilean government, for the Chilean government and intended to benefit all Chileans. The field work is scheduled for next week, but even in this case it is problematic that it will take place.

After indicating some of the unknowns in the situation, he concluded with the sober note, "One thing is already done: research in sociology has been hurt and what's more, this affair has severely damaged the future of Chilean-American cooperation in scientific and other endeavors."

Certain easy excuses will undoubtedly be used to back away from the full implications of the incident, which in my opinion are more profound than friendly Chileans, hurt as they are, would themselves be willing to admit. One of these bromidic explanations I have already indicated: putting the blame on the emotionality or ideological bents of the Chileans. Another, even nastier and more demeaning, is of the type to be whispered about. It is that American University is really a low-grade institution, that the scientists employed in Camelot were just second-raters and not representative of the most honest of American intellectuals, and that even the Army itself has long played second fiddle to the Navy and Air Force with their long histories of support of academic research. This explanation is already being advanced by Chileans friendly to American social science. Álvaro Bunster, the University of Chile's secretary general mentioned in the *Ercilla* article, is quoted in the same source as saying, ". . . the entity charged with coordinating its (Camelot's) execution was the American University in Washington, with which I became acquainted during my visit to the United States in 1959, which enjoys no academic prestige either in the United States or abroad, and which is located in the same city as the national government . . . ."

It is true that American University is not Harvard; it is also true that Dr. Rex Hopper, academic director of Project Camelot, is not Talcott Parsons; and it is also true that the Department of the Army does not have its prestige counterpart of the Navy's Office of Naval Research or the Air Force's RAND Corporation. But it is not true that other universities and other scholars have not crossed into the same shadowy area of ethics entered into by Camelot, that other universities and other scholars have not committed grave tactical errors in Latin America, or that other militarily sponsored social research has not been carried out in Latin America.

The academic problems sharpened, but not invented, by Project Camelot can be expressed in three relationships: the first, between social science and the government; the second, between professional competence and integrity; and the third, between Latin American studies as such and the general performance of the American academic community.

The least difficult to discuss is the nature of the proper ties between the political and academic worlds. The trail has already been blazed by the physical scientists, and formalized procedures and institutions exist in all fields clearly defining the relationship of the scientist to his task, to the public, and to his profession. Legitimate differences of opinion exist, of course, concerning whether a scientist working on The Bomb has a special citizenship duty, for example. But the public identification of interest is plain, and the set relationships to the policy process into which any physical scientist may wish to place himself are also evident.

No such clarity exists in the social sciences. We have no National Science Foundation discharging a brokerage function between the two worlds. We have had no such consistent public debates on academic objectivity and public commitment as have, say, the atomic physicists. No broadly accepted statement of ethics has come from our professional associations, and very few university administrations have concerned themselves with the problem.[5] The result has been that social scientists have generally crossed and recrossed the lines separating their functions from governmental policy making, the only inhibitions being their personally held standards of conduct.

No problem of integrity exists for two polar groups of social scientists: those who work inside governments on a long-term basis and those who because of their disciplines, research interests, or convictions stay entirely inside the university world. (A third group, the commercial contract scholar, sells his services where he wishes. His product is sometimes of very high quality. In any event, he does not concern us here because he has neither the pretensions nor the security of the academic scholar.) It is the social scientist working both fields who is in danger of betraying both of his masters through the loss of his powers of independent analysis. And he adds to his other academic difficulties a partial silence imposed by his access to classified materials, so that para-

---

[5] There are a few exceptions, of course—among them Harvard University. The AUFS has always been highly sensitive to the problem, and throughout its existence has exercised extreme caution to remain entirely private and unencumbered.

doxically he is often able to muster fewer data for his students than his uncompromised colleagues.

A serious question exists whether social scientists under certain kinds of government contract should continue to have the protection of academic tenure. As is well known, the purpose of tenure provisions is to assure academic freedom. But sometimes the exercise of such freedom is in conflict with necessary security provisions. More subtly, how does a scholar under contract know that he is adopting one hypothesis instead of another for truly scientific reasons rather than because of a particular applied interest or even political prejudice? How can the persons reading the published work of this scholar know that he may have a personal, nonacademic involvement in the research? Recently many academicians have been pronouncing themselves on the international politics of Southeast Asia. A letter to the editor of a major newspaper signed by a series of university professors may lead the unwary reader to think that a neutral, objective, academic opinion is being expressed. The wary reader and the uncommonly informed one will note that many of these letters are signed by persons who have been deeply involved in making the very policies they pretend to defend as objective scholars. Do these scholars think themselves beyond the lures of money, prestige, and personal political passion? If so, do they seriously expect the public at large to accept this self-estimation unquestioningly?

By no means am I suggesting that social scientists should turn their backs on policy questions, that governments should refrain from employing social scientists or using social science materials. What I am suggesting is that the peculiar attribute and unique scientific virtue of the university-affiliated social scientist is his freedom. Once abridged, for whatever reason, then the people relying on his objectivity are in serious danger of accepting a misrepresented product, as many government agencies have learned.

I am fully aware that individual personality factors may prevent a professor from benefiting from the security given him by tenure. I suggest, however, that institutionalized temptation to the voluntary relinquishment of freedom be avoided, in the expectation that personal idiosyncracy will be cancelled out of the final product by the numbers of persons engaged in the social sciences, as well as by the free exchanges in our increasingly numerous journals.

Let me add, too, that I do not believe that our present state of ethical disarray has created a Frankenstein's monster rapidly conducing us to the socially engineered society. It is this possibility which has frightened some Chileans inordinately. *Ercilla* concludes the article from which I have been citing as follows:

In spite of the scant publicity which the "affaire" has received, in Latin America various conjectures are being spun about the discovery. It is being seen that many at times incomprehensible speeches made by President Johnson himself as well as by other American officials have a firm theoretical basis, translated into a well defined international policy which, with the passage of time, will be made concrete in very real measures tending to reinforce "tranquility" — that is to say, North American superiority — in the underdeveloped countries of the world.
In this way the North American and Brazilian pronouncement that now there are no national wars, only international ones, can eventuate in the death of the concept of sovereignty. The social sciences put at the service of intervention in the internal affairs of a country would do the rest.

The writer of the article need not be so pessimistic optimistic about the social sciences. American economists do not know how to halt inflation in Latin American countries. American political scientists do not know how to help Latin American governments collect taxes. American anthropologists do not know what to do about the swamping of Indian cultures by national communities. Few American psychologists know that Latin America exists outside the pages of *The Times* or *The Monitor*. American sociologists have no theory of social change adequate to explain Latin American cases. Social scientists working in the government cannot protect the image of the United States in Latin America, and even the election pollsters have been surpassed by some of their Latin American colleagues.

Latin Americans can relax on the issue of the magical effectiveness of the social sciences. But when they say they can no longer accept individual American social scientists at face value, they are correct. The solution for Latin America, however, is not to close the doors to all foreign-conducted or -sponsored research and teaching. It is rather to insist upon clean credentials and academic competence — just as should we.

SCHOLARLY COMPETENCE AND INTEGRITY

The statements I have made about what social science cannot do anywhere, let alone in Latin America, are not to be taken to mean that I think we are in a hopelessly low estate. To the contrary, we are increasingly masters of our disciplines; our grossest failures stem from our being willing to try what we are not peculiarly competent to do. The economists cannot effectively stop inflation in Latin America because some of the measures necessary to the task are political. Public administration men cannot make income tax collection easy because certain legitimacy and consensus patterns are necessary before the payment of such imposts becomes in large part a voluntary, individual act. The protection of certain segments of Indian culture before the tidal wave of national society is much more a function of ideological choice and public will than of anthropological writings about acculturation. To expect such macrosocial problems to submit themselves to mere social scientific manipulation or to think that the policy advice of social scientists is magically efficacious is a denial of the statesman's art and a burdening of the social scientist with what he is incompetent to handle.

Under the very best of conditions, the social scientist can do the following for governments with his special skills:

a. He can generate and make available new data.
b. He can order these data to permit informed guessing about the nature of the lacunae.

c. He can indicate relevant theoretical patterns for the interpretation of the data.
d. He can — explaining himself carefully — indicate the probabilities of effectiveness of various selected courses of action.
e. He can indicate which choices are foreclosed by the adoption of given courses of action.
f. He can indicate which new choices will be made available by the adoption of given courses of action.

Needless to say, very few if any scholarly documents submitted to any government have satisfied these difficult requirements. The temptation to take the easy path straight from description to prescription is great. But to go past these limits is to assume a vested interest in the ensuing policy itself, thereby rendering the scholar suspect in further objective analysis. Of course, I also continue to insist he is not peculiarly competent to make such value judgments. There is, however, always one overriding value decision the social scientists must make; that is, whether he will lend his talents to any government seeking them. I should suggest that if the government asking assistance is likely to use its powers to restrict that very freedom of inquiry essential to the academic task, then the social scientist is committing professional suicide, not to speak of what else he may be helping to do to existing or possible democratic institutions.

The point I am seeking to underline is that the social scientist should be given deference only when he is working in the peculiar area of his competence. To the extent to which he is incompetent but pretends to competence, he fails of professional integrity. Most unhappily. incompetence has manifested itself not only when academicians get out of their fields but even within them. Recent academic research and teaching by Americans in Latin America is heavily studded by examples of persons simply unequipped to do that to which they pretend. The Camelot fiasco, for example, could at least have been mitigated — if not totally avoided — if greater skill had been used in organization and administration. Professor Nuttini's conduct in Chile is a lesson in how not to do such things; the inattention in Washington to timing and to other people's views is a product of faulty technique as well as insensitivity, and the carelessness in the wording of documents and their distribution reveals methodological innocence as well as contempt for one's research subjects. Once again, however, the Camelot directors are not alone.

On my recent visit to Chile, I was asked if I, too, was "an exporter of data," a kind of academic copper company engaged in mining attitudes and carrying away the profits, never to be seen again in the country. Puzzled, I asked the why of the question. It seems that a very prestigious American professor, a faculty member of one of this country's most prestigious universities, had recently finished a study with the assistance of a local UNESCO agency. Asked to leave his code books and IBM cards, he refused, clearly wanting to publish before letting anyone else in on his act. My guess is that in the future he will certainly send the materials. But the reaction in Chile among local scholars as well as international civil servants was that this person had violated the essential conditions of his agreement as well as the canons of academic openness. This kind of misunderstanding is needless and of course disturbs the work of everyone else. Unhappily, this particular professor had had no previous Latin American experience, and although he valiantly learned the language quite well, he still did not succeed in leaving the field clean after his departure so that his American colleagues would not be forced into easily avoided difficulties.

A full awareness of the terms of the responsibilities one accepts in a foreign area can also be included as part of the baggage of the competent scholar. Another internationally famous scholar, one of those allegedly named by Nuttini as an adviser to Camelot, despatched a letter of denial to the Communist newspaper which had named him as a participant. In strict fact the letter was, of course, entirely honest. The trouble is that this person is working in Latin America supported by funds from other government agencies. Because there is no secret about the matter, interested professionals throughout the area are fully aware of these financial ties.

If his letter of denial was to be honest in broad as well as strict fact, should it not have mentioned this connection and sought to inform Latin Americans as to the difference between, say, AID money and Department of Defense money for the social sciences? Certainly the difference between "clean" and "dirty" money, as the slang words go, is difficult enough for North Americans to determine. Why should Latin Americans be more aware and tolerant of the differences than anybody else? If social scientific research is to have a cumulative history in Latin America, instead of being the casual and accidental fruit of scholars of widely varying skills tapping funds which gush and dry up with the political seasons, then we had better start worrying immediately about the fate of our colleagues of the moment and of the future. The first step toward rebuilding the consciously extended confidence of Latin American scholars and governments is to be willing to reveal the sources of our funds, the premises of our studies, the nature of our data, and the bases of our conclusions. We should also make every effort to go beyond making data and findings available; we must help to make effective the ability of trained Latin Americans to use those materials, for clearly simple revelation is not enough. The skill to understand is also required.

The incrusted mistakes of a decade of amateurism are behind the disgust directed at Camelot. That ten-year period is the one of mounting United States interest in Latin American affairs, of an increasing flow of Fulbright scholars as well as otherwise highly trained and mature specialists, many of whom have not bothered to learn the specific conditions pertaining to Latin America. Some have never learned the requisite languages, hardly any one has studied the cultures in depth. How they expect to teach well or to analyze their data with subtlety, let alone design appropriate research instruments in the first instance, I cannot say. But now the entire world knows that their technical shortcomings have an effect beyond their articles and books: they prevent other articles and books from being written, they bring disrepute on American academic life in general, and they mislead policy makers thirsty for reliable information and imaginative analysis.

The most pathetic result, however, is political. Many independent but sympathetic Latin Americans who have been distinguishing between United States policy and other sectors of American life are now becoming convinced that they were wrong. In effect, they understand American scholars as refusing to accept the responsibilities of a plural, democratic society.

COMPETENCE, THE ACADEMIC WORLD, AND INTEGRITY

The academic slippage which has become so apparent in our Latin American activities is one of the possible (though not necessary) costs of a free and largely self-regulating academic community. As I have said before, truly professional research is the return legitimately to be expected by the society at large for respecting academic freedom. The full assumption of professional responsibility also involves projection and prediction in order to create a stock of ideas for future choice as well as to provide a test of present ideas. Institutionalized anticipation is the fruit of the relatively sanctionless risk taking made possible by real academic freedom. Our present frenetic concern with "catching up" in Latin America is an unmistakable indication that American higher education, seen as a total institution, has not paid for its freedom by anticipating needs in this respect, at least. The lack of ethical definition can also be taken as a failure to build into our several social science disciplines those standards which, carried by individuals, would have obviated the mistakes now a national concern in Latin America.

My point now transcends the individuals of whom I have been so far speaking and poses the question of whether there has been a lack of integrity at the institutional level, the product of the failure to assume a patent obligation. For long it has been the conventional wisdom — repeated *ad nausaum* without ever an attempt at careful empirical demonstration — that the quality of Latin American studies is the lowest of all area scholarship. This judgment is clearly false for anthropology, history, and language and literature. How true is it for political science, one of the most maligned of the disciplines?

Merle Kling, in a devastating analysis of the shortcomings of American political scientists specializing in Latin America, writes,

> Little capital (funds, talent, or organizational experience) has been invested in political studies of Latin America, and as a result the returns have been relatively meager. Personnel with adequate training and appropriate technical competence have been in scarce supply, research techniques adapted to Latin American studies have been of a relatively primitive nature, and the level of productivity has been low. Political scientists conducting research on Latin America, like some landowners, have been reluctant to introduce advanced tools and machinery and to extend the intellectual acreage under cultivation — that is, to acquire new skills, to accept technical assistance, to encourage methods designed to diversify the crop of research findings, and to consider a redistribution of disciplinary properties. Political scientists specializing in Latin America have not reached, to borrow Rostow's familiar metaphor, the take-off stage . . . .[6]

Let us accept this evaluation just for the sake of argument. Is the prestige of this field so low because the practitioners are so poor? Or are the practitioners so poor because the prestige is so low? These factors certainly interact to ratify the continued existence of an unhappy situation. I am afraid that no beginning of an explanation of this phenomenon is possible without turning to the disagreeable question of academic stratification — the professorial class system, if you will. Here is a list of the universities having the eleven top prestige

[6] "The State of Research on Latin America," in Charles Wagley (ed.), *Social Science Research on Latin America* (New York: Columbia University Press, 1964), p. 168.

departments of political science, in order, chosen by a recent nationwide poll of political scientists.[7] I will add statements concerning their politics and government professors who also are engaged in Latin American studies:

Harvard	None.
Yale	A junior professor with a Harvard degree.
California (Berk.)	Junior professors in a state of turnover.
Chicago	No regular professor.
Princeton	None. Hiring an Africanist for retooling.
Columbia	Nontenured associate professor.
Michigan	Nontenured junior professor. A long history of course offerings.
Wisconsin	Nontenured junior professor.
Stanford	Nontenured junior professor.
California (UCLA)	Searching. Using *ad hoc* professors.
Cornell	None. Searching.

In sum, there is not one senior professor of Latin American politics in any one of the major departments. If this list were to be published as of ten years ago, we would find only two or three of these institutions even as far along the road as they are now. A little over half of all American doctorates in political science are produced by these departments; but, "Taking the latest (1962 – 1963) faculty rosters, we find that perhaps 4 per cent of the political scientists teaching at the leading eleven schools come from nonprestige institutions — and that these exceptions are found largely in the lower half of the group."[8] Aside from the basic academic question of whether Latin America offers any intrinsically important data for political science, ambitious students have not studied Latin American politics in the past because, among other possible reasons, it was simply impossible to do so in most of the academically politic institutions. Worse, top job opportunities were nonexistent. Thus the best Latin Ameri-

---

[7] Albert Somit and Joseph Tanenhaus, "Trends in American Political Science: Some Analytical Notes," *The American Political Science Review*, Vol. 57, No. 4 (December 1963), p. 936.

[8] *Ibid.*, p. 937.

can offerings are generally in universities such as Texas and North Carolina which do not attract the best graduate students — or at least those destined for the prestige departments.

Kling, in the article to which I have already referred, states that few Latin American examples are used in comparative government texts. He is correct. But is his implication that it is the fault of the Latin Americanist correct? The evidence is that scholars outside of the area have not bothered to read what literature is available. Their absolute certainty that they are dealing with an intellectual desert is another element in the massive self-fulfilling prophecy of which we have been speaking. Let us take some examples. Because I shall have to cite, thus revealing names, I will quote only two persons both of whom have reputations so secure that nothing I might say could damage them.

Bibliographies and bibliographical articles would seem an apt place to look for an answer to the question of whether anybody is reading. Hans J. Morgenthau, in an article, "International Relations, 1960 – 1964,"[9] assesses the current state of his field. Of 135 footnotes, 48 refer to specific countries or regions; two of this number are books on Latin America. "The literature on foreign policy," writes Professor Morgenthau in this section, "especially that of the United States, is of course, particularly abundant and unequal in quality. Here are some books which are likely to have a more than ephemeral importance." His Latin American listings are Adolf A. Berle, *Latin America: Diplomacy and Reality*. New York: Harper & Row, 1962; and Salvador de Madariaga, *Latin America Between the Eagle and the Bear,* New York: Frederick A. Praeger, 1962. These choices are incredible, as I am sure the two authors would agree. The Berle book is a short and glittering statement of his personal appreciations of Latin America, suggestive of policy premises and applications. The

[9] *The Annals of the American Academy of Political and Social Science*, Vol. 360 (July 1965), pp. 163 – 171.

Madariaga book does no credit to its author's distinguished life; it is an often inaccurate survey of Latin America, informed by a Hispanophile racism of no analytical value and in questionable taste. At least half a dozen journalistic surveys are much more reliable, better informed, and even better written.

If Dr. Morgenthau wanted to cite just two or three books on inter-American policy, he might have mentioned such works as Bryce Wood, *The Making of the Good Neighbor Policy*, New York: Columbia University Press, 1961; J. Lloyd Mecham, *The United States and Inter-American Security: 1889-1960*, Austin: University of Texas Press, 1961; or perhaps even a historical work with contemporary relevance like Dana G. Munro, *Intervention and Dollar Diplomacy in the Caribbean, 1900-1921*, Princeton: Princeton University Press, 1964. Certainly anyone taking Dr. Morgenthau's suggestions about Latin American readings would find his every prejudice about the field confirmed if he thought those two the best available.

Dr. Morgenthau is not alone in his disregard. For many years journals have listed Latin American materials out of alphabetical order, invariably at the end. Until the January 1964 issue of *Foreign Affairs*, for example, "Latin America and the Caribbean" was the last bibliographical entry. Since that issue, Latin America has moved into a section entitled "The Western Hemisphere," immediately following "The United States." Poor Africa has been relegated to the caboose. Alphabetical order may mean little. But when the Ford Foundation gets to Latin America only after Asia, the Middle East, and Africa, we have the operationalization of the *Foreign Affairs* bibliography.

Even when Latin America gets out of the book citation stage and into the analytical reference level, the specialist may feel it had been better neglected. Consider the following rather subtle reference by sociologist Edward Shils: "In Latin America, the armed forces historically have played a role similar to that of the military in many of the new states of Asia and Africa."[10] It may take a moment to recognize that that sentence is backwards and should read, "In many of the new states of Asia and Africa, the armed forces are playing a role historically similar to that of the military in Latin America." After all, the Latin Americans have been at it since 1810, and the military of the "new states" only during the past twenty years. It is more than passing strange to attempt to draw a baseline from twenty years of historical experience when a variegated set of experiences in twenty republics exists for periods of up to 155 years.

There is no need to belabor this point with multiple examples. I suggest merely that it is time for rigorous and realistic thinking about Latin American studies instead of the unprofessional surrender to stereotypes and status that has helped to hinder the growth of research as well as the reading and evaluation of what already exists.

The present state of emergency is a direct product of the insufficiencies of our major universities and scholars, just as it is of the persons in the field, as well as all the other factors I have mentioned. This background to the situation should not be neglected lest we expend our expiatory energies in beating only on the scapegoat in Washington.

SOME PERSPECTIVE

To put an analysis into perspective is all too often to dilute it with the tepid water of sweet unreasonableness. If the chances are that the punishment for our academic sins will not be overly harsh, the reasons are implicit in the general conditions and not in the promise of any dramatic change toward virtuous behavior. It is very probable that, after the passage of a little time, American social scientists will once again be able to work with relative ease in Latin America.

[10] "The Military in the Political Development of the New States," in John J. Johnson (ed.), *The Role of the Military in Underdeveloped Countries* (Princeton, N.J.: Princeton University Press, 1962), p. 8.

Greater care will be taken to maintain respectable appearances on our side; Latin American social scientists and government officials will be more cautious in extending us their assistance; and that small part of the public which is informed will maintain a reserve affecting the nature of their participation in ways nobody will ever measure. Camelot has dissolved, a few other projects sponsored by agencies of the armed forces will be cancelled or camouflaged, and greater care will be exercised to inform American ambassadors in Latin American countries of academic activities in their bailiwicks. A foundation or two will sponsor meetings on the coordination of overseas projects and the proper nature of government-sponsored academic research. In a year from now, everything else being equal, an occasional wry remark will be heard at a cocktail party by way of memoriam.

Matters will follow this slow course because in neither Latin America nor the United States can radical change occur. The Latin Americans may extend their gaze to include a sharper perception of Europe, but they cannot blind themselves to the United States. The reasons are not by any means only political or economic. The enormous cultural weight of the United States in Latin America is a fact as obvious as the Andes. More pointedly, the contemporary revolution in the social sciences is a North American product, and whether Latin Americans go to Great Britain, France, Germany, or Italy, they will still return with one or another version of modern American social scientific empiricism. They can also put to good use foundation assistance and interchanges with American educational institutions. It is not that they could not get along somehow without us, but rather that most Latin American intellectuals — including highly nationalistic ones — would prefer not to be forced to so long as their continued collaboration with American scientific institutions does not imply a narrow political subservience. What Camelot surely has done is to speed the Latin American desire to diversify academic contacts. As there is already Soviet university work stirring in such countries as Chile and El Salvador, we may expect more elsewhere in the normal course of events. It is for the French and British, however, that major room will have to be made, a tendency being promoted for the past several years by the Department of State and American foundations as well as by some Latin American universities.

American reactions inside the universities will be even slower and more difficult to recognize. The reason is that professors and professorships cannot be made overnight, that good research takes time to produce, and that the decentralized nature of American higher education creates subtle eddies among the stimuli of communications, the sorting of responses, and the flexing of implementation. We may expect a bit more care in the foundations and some discussion, as I have said, but we shall still have to wait for the maturing of the current vastly expanded crop of scholars in training. We shall also have to wait for the social science "community" to attend seriously to the idea that there are ethical questions involved in policy studies, that ethics and technique are not to be separated under certain conditions, and that institutional snobbery is as testable for its validity as are election predictions.

For a while it was thought — and is still thought by some — that "retooling" was the answer to the problem of Latin American studies. All we had to do was take an expert from another field, let him turn the cyclopean eye of his genius on Latin America, and the deficiencies of the field would rapidly be dissipated. The grotesque mistakes already made by some of these persons show that, even in Latin American studies, the price of admission has to be paid. A highly trained specialist in Indian politics will find his Hindi — if he has any — of rather little use in Quito. And unless he is more theoretically gifted than most persons writing in the field of development, he will also find that his hypotheses may have little relevance to the only major underdeveloped part of the Western cultural world. It really will not do to have an internationally famous American scholar declare at an international meeting that it is a shame that there is so much more documentary material available on Africa than on Latin America. It really will not do to have as the only political scientist sitting on a major committee dispensing fellowships for Latin American studies an excellent scholar in another area who has never done research in Latin America, cannot speak either Spanish or Portuguese, and has so far made only academic touristic trips to the region. To be a violin virtuoso is not to be a pianist.

The reasons for a past lack of interest in Latin American politics are now fairly clear: the countries have little power; they pose — or until recently posed — no cold war threat; they are Catholic countries traditionally looked down on by Protestant ones; they have little prestige among the ivied universities who have followed the area leads of Oxford, Cambridge, the Sorbonne, and Berlin first into Africa, Egypt, the Middle East, and China, and then the realpolitik leads of international affairs into Soviet studies. I should like to suggest a reason now not for the lack of interest, but for the lack of success in most of what political research has been done. It is that Latin America is a very difficult area to fit into extant theory. The range of cases is immense: twenty different republics with increasingly different histories are also characterized by vastly varied internal conditions. We must study migratory Indians and megalopolis, village economies and machine-tool industries, constitutional democracies and populist falangisms and mercantilistic dictatorships as well as village gerontocracies and institutionalized lawlessness. Latin America is the graveyard of simplistic and deterministic theories, of those schemes which hold that a nation which has "taken off" will automatically reach self-sustaining flight. Latin American societies will not submit to simple notions derived without an adequate knowledge of the area's amazing store of data.

Let all who can revel in this potential richness. El Dorado

can become real for the talented and dedicated social scientist. The mine will contain only fool's gold for the lazy and the self-seeking. But, as usual, the fool's gold will drive out the good metal if we are thoughtless enough to allow it currency in the marketplace.

Robert Boguslaw

Washington University

Ethics and the Social Scientist*

Problems of ethics arising in the everyday situations faced by social scientists create enormous difficulties for analysis because of the often-conflicting sets of principles that shape the behavior of individuals. These reflect legitimate but real differences in their separate *valued* objectives. Variations occur both in the perception of relevant facts necessary to describe the situation and in the hierarchy of principles or heuristics internally consistent for a given social scientist.

WHAT IS IMPORTANT TO ME AS ONE HUMAN BEING

As I think about the things that I find important, I find it difficult to sort out my own feelings. I have always felt that "earning a living" was not enough — that somehow I would

* *Editor's note:* This is an abbreviated version of a paper prepared at the invitation of the Department of Political Science, Northwestern University, for delivery at the Conference on Normative Analysis of Political Life sponsored by that department in the Spring of 1966. The author is one of the senior social scientists recruited by Dr. Rex Hopper to work on the Camelot project. However, he did not join the Special Operations Research Office until early in June 1965. The project was cancelled before he had an opportunity to make any substantive contribution either to its basic orientation or its research design. Dr. Boguslaw is now Professor of Sociology at Washington University, St. Louis [I.L.H.].

like to leave the world a better place than it was when I found it. This generalized concern has always been important to me. Presumably a depth psychologist could trace its source to some combination of events occurring in my early childhood — but the fact remains that it is a feeling I have had for a long time and have no wish to change. Since it is an important part of me, I choose to treat it as a prime datum and not as a manifestation of neuroticism.

MY UNDERSTANDING OF OUR SITUATION

As a boy, I became very much aware of the existence and consequences of poverty. My early professional goals included the study of economics because I felt that this would help me understand how I could help do something about poverty. Hitler, Mussolini, and four years of war convinced me that economics, at least as I had understood it, was not enough. I now felt that the essentially simple puzzle of how to devise a poverty-free economic system was not the prime issue but rather the problem of understanding the apparent irrationalities of people. I focused on the study of sociology and became thoroughly familiar with small-group research. I wanted to understand the processes of authoritarianism and cooperation in human affairs. How could one deal with the apparent gross irrationalities that seemed to shape so much of group behavior?

It developed that RAND, a large nonprofit corporation established by the United States Air Force to do research in a variety of areas, asked me to participate in a project described as essentially a small-group study to be conducted in a laboratory with what appeared to be unlimited resources. I had a decision to make. Should I or should I not enter this situation? What indeed was the nature of the situation?

On the most obvious level, it was a unique professional opportunity. It seemed clear that I could learn more about small-group behavior in this situation than I might in any other I could envisage. I talked to many colleagues, former professors, and friends. In the course of these discussions and in the course of my own soul-searching, I began to have some serious misgivings. I felt and feel complete antipathy to the Air Force as a specialized institution for mass violence. As such it represents something utterly contrary to everything I have ever stood for. On the other hand, it was this same Air Force that had played an important part in bringing about the defeat of Hitler and Mussolini. Obviously, there existed some high-ranking officers within it who were every bit as authoritarian, ruthless, and reactionary as any Nazi or Fascist could possibly be. But then, I suppose, one could say the same for some academicians as well.

This institution had agreed to what I understood to be a "hands off" policy with respect to the research. The RAND project seemed to offer an opportunity to study people with "real" problems as contrasted to the interminable studies of college students on which I had been weaned in graduate school. In addition, I wanted to become more familiar with the newer methods and techniques of research that held so much promise for social science. What could one do with computers? What were the possibilities of research within laboratory settings using the most sophisticated tools available from the physical sciences? Why was the Air Force interested in supporting such studies? Because it was interested in learning how to help people work more effectively with each other. What people? Crews manning air defense stations around the perimeter of the United States. I learned an enormous amount about research technology. And I still feel that as a result of that research and the System Training Program that stemmed from it, thousands of Air Force officers and enlisted men have learned something about the alternatives to authoritarianism and the use of cooperation as a positive force in human affairs.

During the last dozen years, I have become aware of the fact that much of the public discussion and technical analyses of the nuclear arms race is not merely uninformed but based upon a detachment from reality that is frightening. For some years now I have been deeply concerned with problems of nuclear disarmament and the domestic barriers to disarmament. My interest in Project Camelot was a direct outgrowth of these interests in the context of issues raised in the developing countries. Now these may not have been the objectives of the sponsors; they were, however, mine — and, I know, of some others as well.

I was quite familiar with the reputation of the Army Research Office among knowledgeable social scientists. This reputation was one of maintaining close scrutiny and direction over the design, content, and course of research conducted under its sponsorship. I finally became convinced, however, that Camelot was accepted as a bona fide departure from this policy — that it was indeed to provide an opportunity for social scientists to conduct an unprecedented and enormously significant study in the field of social change. That the preliminary documents prepared with a skeleton staff needed much work and possibly complete redirection was clear. But it was equally clear that this completely unclassified study represented a challenge worthy of the best people in the social science profession. And, indeed, the roster of persons associated with the project in one capacity or another did resemble a respectable portion of a Who's Who of American social science.

SOCIAL SCIENTISTS

To discuss the value alternatives available to social scientists and the implications of choosing among these alternatives, I should make it clear who it is I am talking about when I use the term social scientist.

I know many persons who call themselves and are called social scientists. For purposes of normative analysis in social science, however, it seems clear that they do not constitute a single identifiable unit.

In the first place, they are members of professional associations — the American Political Science Association, the American Sociological Association, et cetera. Not all social scientists derive their legitimacy from membership in a professional society. I can think of several well-known social scientists who, as a matter of principle, refuse to maintain membership in their apparent major professional society. Are these not social scientists? I am quite certain they are, but I am not the Board of Examiners of the U.S. Civil Service Commission or the editor of a professional journal or the consulting editor of a publishing firm. All of these can, at some level, affect the career opportunities of professional social scientists and in turn can be influenced by a professional society. In one sense, then, the professional society can serve as a trade union on behalf of the professional interests of its members. It can also provide a common framework of rules to regulate behavior of its members and of other persons who wish to identify themselves as professionals. The degree of potential control it exercises over professional careers provides many temptations to use it as a vehicle for exercising control on behalf of special interests in or outside the ranks of its members — witness the behavior of the American Medical Association vis-à-vis the issue of Medicare, et cetera.

Another way of explaining what it is to be a social scientist is to focus on the word science. The scientist is a person who searches for wisdom. The scientist has an ethical duty to pursue knowledge. But he must be free. If not, he is in danger of being used for ends that are unethical, that is, that inhibit the search for knowledge. The search for truth, one might argue, requires the right to dissent from existing dogma. But scientific societies and scientific journals are notorious for their insistence upon dogmas of all kinds: the dogma of acceptable methodology, the dogma of report format, the implicit dogma of acceptable areas for investigation — are all more or less prevalent in various fields of the physical sciences. When it comes to the social sciences, the potential limitations on freedom of inquiry are virtually limitless.

Frequently, these limitations have nothing at all to do with professional societies as such. Thus Professor Kalman Silvert, a highly competent and deeply concerned political scientist, has described two "polar groups" of social scientists. One type consists of those who work inside government on a long-term basis. The second type consists of those who stay entirely inside the university world. For neither of these two polar types, Professor Silvert asserts, does the problem of integrity exist. It is the social scientist "working both fields who is in danger of betraying both of his masters through the loss of his powers of independent analysis."[1]

For me, this dichotomy comes as something of a shock. For Professor Silvert, the government is contrasted sharply with the university. If I were to propose some dichotomy along similar lines, my instinctive reaction would probably have been to oppose private industry with the university. Professor Silvert makes no mention of social scientists working for major oil, automobile, or advertising companies. He implicitly gives his blessing to academicians who accept support from foundations established by the wealth of such persons as Henry Ford, John D. Rockefeller, and Andrew Carnegie.

I am not aware of any studies sponsored by the Ford Foundation reporting on safety features in American automobiles or the lack thereof. In an area where there clearly exists a public interest but where additional research may well prove to be unprofitable for a given firm or industry, is there not a legitimate justification for government research sponsorship? Are the major foundations the best source of support in this kind of situation? I can also think of studies like Ferdinand Lundberg's classic *America's Sixty Families*, whose findings might well be embarrassing to the families identified with these and other major foundations. Indeed, I find it difficult to imagine any serious study of American

[1] Kalman H. Silvert, "American Academic Ethics and Social Research Abroad, Lesson of Project CAMELOT," *American Universities Field Staff Reports* (West Coast South America Series), Vol. 12, No. 3 (July 1965), p. 9.

economic and political life which would not as a matter of course be required to deal with facts relating to foundation families and individuals. Must we then insist that university professors not accept foundation grants? This is a meaningless form in which to pose the question. The critical question is not necessarily the source of financial support but rather the nature of the conditions associated with any form of financial support. To what extent do these conditions require that the research be confined to trivial aspects of political and social life? On a broader level, to what extent can the trivialization of so much of American social science be explained by the publish or perish tradition found almost universally in American universities? Is a social scientist one who has published a given number of sanitized papers in sanitized professional journals? Or is he, on the other hand, someone who has attempted to come to grips with significant social problems? One might well make a case for either definition. But it is not at all clear that the dogmas appropriate for one are at all relevant for the other.

It has been suggested that "the academic institutions of the twentieth century often provide formidable obstacles to the pursuit of science. This is particularly true in the United States, where the governing boards of these institutions are made up of businessmen and similar lay groups."[2]

Thus, Professor Silvert seems to have completely forgotten the work of such men as Thorstein Veblen — "only one of the many social scientists who have found it difficult at times to carry on the proper business of posing embarrassing questions about the social order, but . . . the first to thoroughly scrutinize the American university as itself a source of bias in scientific research."[3]

Less than a decade ago, a comprehensive study of personnel practices in American universities concluded that "The typical professor, if such there be, suffers from his acceptance

[2] Bernard Rosenberg, Israel Gerver, and F. William Howton, *Mass Society in Crisis* (New York: Macmillan, 1964), p. 486.
[3] *Ibid.*

of an ideology which is incongruous with his situation. He tends to see himself as a free member of an autonomous company of scholars, subject to no evaluation but the judgment of his peers. But he is likely to find himself under the sway of a chairman or dean or president whose authority is personal and arbitrary . . . academic authority is exercised largely by means of the personal control which the administrator has over the salary, rank, and prerogatives of the working professor."[4]

It is obvious that not all universities and not all departments are identical in this regard. But, it should be equally obvious that neither are all government agencies identical in the amount of control they seek to exert over contractees or grantees.

It is undeniably true, as William R. Polk has pointed out,[5] that one of the most sensitive problems in governmental use of scholarly research can be found in the simple human fact that we all like to use ideas and concepts that bolster our previous commitments. Offices dealing with problems develop vested interest and invest prestige in them.

All this is undeniably true — to some extent. As Polk himself previously points out, however, "A large government, like a great university, is a congeries of institutions. Generalization is almost as difficult about the one as about the other."[6]

And it is undeniably true that there exist within our own government and other governments individuals whose actions are not completely determined by the apparent logic of their bureaucratic roles. An enlightened social science community would perhaps be prompted to encourage such individuals in their efforts to provide support for research that has been given explicit freedom from bureaucratic con-

[4] Theodore Caplow, and Reece J. McGee, *The Academic Marketplace* (New York: Basic Books, 1968), p. 228.

[5] William R. Polk, "Problems of Government Utilization of Scholarly Research in Internal Affairs," paper delivered at 1965 Annual Meeting of the American Political Science Association, Washington, D. C., p. 13 [see pp. 239–266 in this volume — I.L.H.].

[6] *Ibid.*, p. 2.

trol. My own understanding of Project Camelot, for example, was that it was intended precisely as such a project — that is, one that would *not* be operational in character; that *would* be addressed to the study of fundamental problems of social change. That it received widespread support from some parts of the academic social scientific community and widespread condemnation from other parts is, I believe, in part attributable to its own potentially innovating character. It has become virtually a cliché to charge American social science with obsessively pursuing trivia and rigorously avoiding analysis of critical social and political issues. That the charge has become familiar does not make it any the less true. The prestige of physical sciences in this country has probably encouraged the trend toward social science gadgetry and methodological gimmickry; the perish or publish tradition in universities has probably enforced an excessive concern with what is "publishable" in the correct journals; institutional pressures discouraging close examination of fundamental social and political processes have unquestionably made an important contribution to the glamorization of trivia.

Social scientists who wish to reverse this tendency face many obstacles. In the first place support from familiar funding sources is characteristically not available. Secondly, attacks can be launched against the proposed work not only from colleagues who have other research fish to fry but from various elements outside the social scientific community who feel threatened by some part of the work.

Now this is not to imply, of course, that all deviant work in the social sciences is competent by virtue of its deviance alone. Obviously, third- and fourth-rate social scientists can and do use these conditions as a rationalization for their own ineptness. But neither is the converse true. There is increasing evidence that not only the predictable malcontents but some of the best minds in our field are becoming impatient with the familiar tradition of American social science research and wish to do something about it. The sad fact is that we have probably forgotten or perhaps have never learned to do effective work in the nontrivial areas. The temptation to cast such work in the mold of more familiar efforts is almost overpowering. "What is the research design," we ask. And, "What are your variables?" And, "What are your hypotheses?" and, "What is the population from which you will draw your sample?" And, "Where are your research instruments?" And, "What are the previous studies in this area?"

And so it goes through the long litany of established research practice. Questions like, "Who can or might distort the purposes of this research for his own political ends?" "Which interest groups can be made to see this research as in their own interest?" "To what extent can one risk acceptance of their support without destroying the basis of the research itself?" "How are the researchers to balance their own sense of traditional scientific morality against the tactics of those who will see this morality as a weakness and exploit it to the limits dictated by their own political purposes?" "Is it at all possible to conduct even the most 'basic' and 'non-applied' research using real world events as data without *some* risk of the results being taken over and used by 'bad guys'?" Such questions seldom, if ever, get asked. It is tempting to speculate about the extent to which the Camelot difficulties were ultimately attributable to the lack of a sophisticated social science tradition in these areas.

To be a social scientist under these conditions requires something more than graduate school expertise searching for a likely place to try out a new research technique. And the problem of ethical considerations gets inextricably tied to more fundamental problems of individual morality. It is not to be found in the cant of the unsophisticated innocent, the rationalizations of established researchers, or the caustic ironies of unsuccessful competitors.

ACTION PRINCIPLES AND SITUATIONS

I believe I have made much of my own priority system of action principles clear in what I have said. Perhaps the best way to further explicate them is to react to what I perceive to be the action principles and definitions of others.

George Lundberg states what social scientists are for and what they should be able to do in the following classic terms:

. . . it is the business of social scientists to be able to predict the social weather, just as meteorologists predict sunshine and storm. More specifically, social scientists should be able to say what is likely to happen socially under stated conditions. A competent economist or political scientist should be able to devise for example, a tax program for a given country which will fall in whatever desired degrees upon each of the income groups of the area concerned. Social scientists should be able to state also what will be the effect of the application of this program upon income, investments, consumption, production, and the outcome of the next election. Having devised such a tax program and clearly specified what it is to do, it is not the business of the social scientists any more than it is the business of any other citizens to secure the adoption or defeat of such a program. In the same way, competent sociologists, educators or psychologists should be able to advise a parent as to the most convenient way of converting a son into an Al Capone or into an approved citizen, according to what is desired.[7]

I have no quarrel with Lundberg's desire to predict social weather or to assess the impact of various tax programs. I do, however, take issue with his concept of social science as an activity that can be pursued in a value vacuum. The notion of science as a means for providing an exhaustive analysis of all possible alternatives from which the nonscientist can select is simply not viable for the world I know — given the level of research technology available in the foreseeable future. I share Lundberg's desire for increased sophistication in research instrumentation, but I am not willing to concede that the critical decisions of our times must be made without reference to the disciplined intelligence that comes within my own meaning of science. To use terms I

[7] George A. Lundberg, *Can Science Save Us?* (New York: Longman's, Green, 1947), pp. 30–31.

have explained more fully elsewhere,[8,9] Lundberg's concept of science is one that postulates only established situations. He implicitly omits consideration of the possibility of an emergent situation science. Such a view permits the social scientist to avoid responsibility for policy guidance and as such it is certainly a safe procedure to follow. But values play an important role implicitly (though characteristically not explicitly) in the formulation of research projects. The selection of "safe" areas for investigation specifically introduces a biasing factor into the range of scientifically established alternatives available to policy makers. It introduces a similar bias into the character of scientific information and analyzed situations available in the chronicles of social science. This is a responsibility and a risk that every social scientist must take every time he formulates, conducts, or interprets the results of his studies.

Charles Tilly observed recently, in reference to Project Camelot, "Where the sponsor has a visible interest in the outcome and a significant likelihood of acting on the findings, any one of us takes on a measure of responsibility by accepting his support."[10]

Tilly apparently saw Project Camelot as a high-risk situation. There existed the risk of failure, the risk of becoming embroiled in the public relations problems of the sponsor, the risk of taking on some of the "taint" and troubles of the sponsor, the risk that the sponsor's own desire to thrive might affect the research itself. The implications one may draw from his view is that the social scientist should avoid risks. For a person with essentially a problem-solving interest in public affairs and an observer's interest in them, this is certainly good advice. I have indicated what my own priorities are.

[8] Robert Boguslaw, "Situation Analysis and the Problem of Action," *Social Problems*, Vol. 8, No. 3 (Winter 1961), pp. 212–219.

[9] _____, *The New Utopians: A Study of System Design and Social Change* (Englewood Cliffs, N.J.: Prentice-Hall, 1965).

[10] Charles Tilly, "Communication to the Editor," *The American Sociologist*, Vol. 1, No. 2 (February 1966), p. 84.

ATTITUDES AND ETHICS

Attitudinal sets inevitably shape ethical judgments — no matter how much we might wish this were not true. Attitudes become organized around either objects or situations. Milton Rokeach, for example, distinguishes between an attitude object (person, group institution issue, et cetera) and a specific situation (an ongoing event or activity) around which a person organizes a set of interrelated beliefs about how to behave.[11] He cites several studies to demonstrate that attitude objects may activate relatively more powerful beliefs than those activated by the situation. Similarly, the situation may generate more powerful beliefs. Thus it has been shown that the threshold of discrimination toward Chinese seeking overnight lodging and restaurants is without exception lower in non-face-to-face situations than in face-to-face situations. Again, the threshold of discrimination toward Negro miners by white miners is always lower in town than in the mines.[12]

For anyone who likes to trace his attitudinal sets neatly, the Camelot controversy is an exercise in frustration. Rightists, leftists, and in-betweeners seem to be lined up indiscriminately on all sides of the major issues raised and the ethical judgments involved become unaccountably fuzzy.

One way of finding a path through this morass of ignorance, malice, naïveté and sheer conceptual fuzziness is to attempt to sort out some object attitudes from some situation attitudes.

It is clear that many Latin American social scientists and liberal social scientists in this country possess very negatively charged attitudes whose object is any military organization and especially the U.S. Army. This, of course, has been exacerbated by feelings toward the foreign policy of the United States and the use of American military forces in such places as the Dominican Republic and Vietnam. In addition, there

[11] Milton Rokeach, "The Nature of Attitudes," Mimeographed, p. 6 (to be published in the *International Encyclopedia of the Social Sciences*).

[12] *Ibid.*, p. 12.

is virtually world-wide hostility directed toward such covert agencies as the American Central Intelligence Agency for the role it played in the abortive invasion of Cuba and for what is suspected to be its role in propping up or helping to oust governments throughout the world. I personally do not approve of recent U.S. foreign policy; I share many of these attitudes directed toward military organizations; I share all of them directed toward covert agencies. My view of the Camelot situation serves, however, to change some of these attitudes. I *know* that the purpose of the social scientists involved in Camelot was quite different from those attributable to stereotyped caricatures of the Military Race. I *know* that the driving force behind many of the intellectuals and some policy makers involved in Camelot stemmed precisely from a dissatisfaction with American foreign policy and represented an attempt to find nonmilitary and nonviolent solutions to international problems. I feel certain that the CIA had nothing whatever to do with the project and indeed that the unclassified nature of the project and its social science orientation may well have presented a serious threat to some bureaucrats within that agency and, of course, in other agencies.

The ethical questions arising for me in connection with this affair stem from the unthinking behavior of social scientists who unquestioningly accepted distorted newspaper versions of the "facts" and use this shabby evidence to launch pious tirades against professional colleagues.

I have no wish to defend the good judgment of the anthropologist who apparently thought it expedient to deny the source of sponsorship of the study. I personally would not have behaved in this fashion. Copies of the preliminary drafts of the research plan were widely distributed in this country and abroad in an effort to obtain the comments of competent social scientists of every methodological bent and political orientation. But neither do I wish to defend the judgment of those social scientists who seized upon this lapse to help crucify a research project with potentially enormously important implications both for social science and foreign policy.

The danger in failing to discriminate between attitudes toward objects and those held with reference to situations, may well be thought of as one measure of simple prejudice. We have all become familiar with the many forms of prejudice directed at objects with dark skins or long noses. A central concern of the bigot is to define appropriate terms of belongingness. In the hands of a pious academician, invocation of ethical rules can become directly comparable to the informal rules for admission to a country club. Obviously, all this is not to argue for an ethics-free scientific community but rather one which has developed the competence to apply rules relevant to varying situational contexts.

ETHICS AND VALUES

Each of them begins with some notion of objective fact. The psychologist has a theory of individual behavior and sees the Camelot situation a typical for the application of this theory. The political scientist has a different kind of theory — accounting for group behavior in the context of a struggle for power. Without necessarily disputing the facts implicitly used by the psychologist, he focuses on a different set of apparent facts and finds he can explain the situation by using his theory. The businessman focuses upon a third set of data, empathizes with the research entrepreneur who lost a multi-million dollar contract, and projects his own evaluation through a "Whew!" If he were someone who felt the federal budget was too high, he might be happy about the situation; if he were a creditor of someone working on the project, he might be unhappy.

In each case however, there is (1) an assumption about a set of facts held to be true about a situation and (2) a set of personal or professional objectives (presumably the psychologist and political scientist wish to *understand*, the businessman wants to *profit*).

Now (1) if the situations faced by individuals or groups

of human beings could be defined (either stochastically or absolutely) in terms of prototypical situations, and (2) if social scientists had conducted sufficient research to classify each situation as it arose, and (3) if they could account for behavior in each situation, then we would be faced with a world filled with what I have called *established* situations. One could then sort through every conceivable objective and prescribe the most effective set of actions to achieve that objective.

But many and perhaps all of the significant situations occurring in the everyday world of political and social reality are not established but rather *emergent;* that is, the situation has not previously been coded; or it is not classifiable given the present level of scientific knowledge; or if it has been coded, the research necessary to specify effective behavior has not been accomplished; or the characteristics of the individuals or groups involved in the situation have not been adequately determined.

One way to deal with emergent situations is to invoke the use of heuristics or principles. But there are many pitfalls surrounding the use of heuristics. In the first place, they may be stated in form of a desired objective; for example, I want to solve puzzles or I want to help make this world a better place in which to live. Second, they may be stated as guides for action: for instance, to solve puzzles effectively I must not have a vested economic or emotional interest in any particular solution, or if I see another social scientist doing things that make the world a worse place in which to live, I ought to stop him somehow.

Now the *real* reason I spend so much time talking about Camelot is that I know something about it as a situation and can assess, at least to my own satisfaction, some of the conflicting heuristics utilized by other social scientists who discuss it. I would like to review some of these assessments.

1. Professor Silvert — whom I respect as a scholar and as a human being seems to use a heuristic which might be stated as follows: "A scholar must be free from outside coercion; he is

free when working for a university but not free when accepting money from the government — therefore he must avoid working for the government."

Stated in these terms the heuristic is not dissimilar from one used by contemporary Radical Rightists. This might be stated as, "It is important for the individual to be free; government restricts individual freedom — therefore one should try to minimize or eliminate the role of government in the affairs of men."

The difficulty with this latter, essentially anarchistic, perspective of political life is simply that it completely ignores the situational context in which the heuristic is applied. Thus, in the face of oligopolistic or monopolistic control of specific market areas, a government responsive to consumer needs for moderate prices and minimal quality standards can take steps to increase the freedom of individuals by government controls. Similarly, it is certainly *possible* for a government to be responsive to something more than the narrowly defined specialized interests of its operating bureaucracies and to sponsor social science research that is indeed responsive to the broader needs of its population and to the requirements of peace in a nuclear age.

Defining the role of government as Professor Silvert does can well result not only in lack of improvement in the current situation but in deterioration of the quality of government-supported research through the mechanism of a self-fulfilling prophecy — especially if Professor Silvert is joined in his view by other social scientists of his caliber.

2. Professor Tilly — his letter seems to reflect a genuine concern for a heuristic which might be stated as follows: "Social scientists should solve problems." Corollaries to this might read (a) "Having demonstrated a capacity to solve problems in certain more or less prototype situations, a social scientist may agree to apply this capacity to the 'real world,'" and (b) "A social scientist should not accept support from the government since the government has a vested interest in certain solutions. This interest will make the research ineffective."

Professor Tilly does, however, acknowledge that he has

"drawn financial support from several research centers and foundations, including the National Science Foundation, but has not conducted any of the research on government contract." This passage does not make clear whether Professor Tilly is ignorant of the fact that the National Science Foundation is an agency of the government or whether he is finding refuge in the word "contract" as opposed perhaps to some such word as "grant." If the latter is true, then he is presumably discussing the *terms* of arrangement with a sponsor rather than the sponsor himself. But then we might inquire into the terms of his arrangements with his other sponsors. To what extent does the price of these arrangements involve a more or less conscious "trivialization?" His statement on ethics would apply equally to situations he admits being in himself and to situations he is disturbed about. ". . . the researcher takes on willy-nilly some of the taint and the troubles of the sponsor. He cannot ignore the probable uses of his findings, the ways the sponsor's own desire to thrive may affect the research, or the claims he makes to the sponsor on behalf of his field of knowledge. These issues lie at the heart of professional ethics."[13]

In a larger sense, what Professor Tilly raises is the client relationship involved in subsidized research. What is the payoff to any client who supports research? For many it is the public relations value of having publications appear reflecting the source of support. Here, the canon of *respectability* may well be invoked as a criterion. Thus Tilly seems to be less consistent than Lundberg for whom it is perfectly ethical to "advise a parent as to the most convenient way of converting a son into an Al Capone." For Lundberg, the ethics of social science are related to his concept of an appropriate motive for a scientist, "to find an answer that meets the requirements of a scientific answer."[14]

Certainly such a sponsor's "desire to thrive" may affect the research. In all probability, a sponsor who wanted his son con-

---

[13] Tilly, *op. cit.*, p. 84.
[14] Lundberg, *op. cit.*, p. 20.

verted into an Al Capone would himself have some taint and troubles. And if the social scientist made inappropriate claims on behalf of his discipline, presumably the father-sponsor would have somewhat less ability to verify these claims than the federal government of the United States.

For many Camelot critics, a prime concern seemed to be, "One should do only those things that make it possible for social scientists to continue doing work." There is an expression of faith in the positive value of doing work by social scientists. It says nothing about the nature of this work except perhaps that it not rock any boats. One might formulate other principles: one such principle might read, "Never engage in a study which deals with nontrivial aspects of social and political life" or "Before engaging in a study, be certain you have the active support of a powerful and authoritarian government within the country to insure that no unfavorable criticism of social science can be expressed," or, "make certain you engage in significant research surreptiously — to avoid possible criticism of the social science profession," and so forth.

4. Camelot — a fact about Project Camelot that continually seems to be forgotten in the popular discussion surrounding it is the simple truth that no data collection was ever begun on the project and that the final research design had not been completed. The discussions leading to the public furor were all held with social scientists — not a naïve public. The popular outcries against the research concept and the preliminary research plans were at least in some measure based upon an ignorance of the nature of social science research and how it differs from the more familiar intelligence activities of the James Bonds among us. One might well raise the issue of the "ethical" responsibility of social scientists to await the receipt of verified information before joining in the uninformed popular furor. This principle that might say, "Be sufficiently informed about social science methodology and social science problems so that you can explain research projects and research findings to non-social scientists. Feel free to indicate how your

own judgment and/or your own value structure is different from that of another scientist." Of course, even such an apparently safe rule might lead to difficulties. Well-meaning social scientists might be quoted out of context to serve someone's political end; too much information about the characteristics of some research instruments might make them invalid with some populations, et cetera.

CONCLUSION

I began this paper by suggesting that social scientists in the situations they face in everyday life encounter enormous difficulties dealing with ethical dilemmas because of conflicting sets of principles that shape their individual and group behavior. I have tried to show how these problems stem not only from conflicts in the rankings assigned to valued objectives but from difficulties in recognizing what action in a given situation will most effectively achieve a specific objective. Further complications arise from the difficulties involved in obtaining accurate, unbiased and complete information about the details of situations in which these actions occur. As a result, considerable confusion may be experienced and expressed. As we have seen, otherwise scrupulously careful and responsible members of the profession are led to engage in recriminations and poorly thought through accusations that can readily become malicious in their effects, if not necessarily in their intent.

As social science begins to emerge from the morass of inconsequentiality in which so much of it has for so long been embedded, its obligation to develop more sophisticated methods for normative analysis becomes urgent. It can no longer afford to relegate this subject to the obscurity of philosophy texts or to the sporadic emotional outbursts of its practitioners. In the absence of progress in normative analysis, the efforts of social scientists and the content of social science research will increasingly be shaped by the subtle controls implicit in a "value-free" ideology. And even for those who reject this ideology, well-motivated but misdirected attacks on colleagues and nontrivial research efforts will continue to occur as they have occurred in the past. This is part of the tragedy of a profession and a world in which it is becoming increasingly more difficult to distinguish the good guys from the bad guys without a value program.

Jessie Bernard

American University

*Conflict as Research and Research as Conflict**

RESEARCH, REPORTING, INVESTIGATION, AND ESPIONAGE

Among the many lessons learned from Project Camelot was the fact that there is still so much confusion in the mind of the public with respect to the nature of research. Even a knowledgeable columnist like John Chamberlain wrote as if Project Camelot were an intelligence operation.[1] And even among those who recognize the distinction between research and intelligence operations, there was some confusion with respect to research which, while it uses scientific techniques, is primarily fact finding or descriptive in nature and research which, like Project Camelot, is aimed at theoretical rather than at immediately practical goals. Thus there was, for example, some disparagement of fact-finding research of the survey type, such as that engaged in by the United States Information Agency, because it was slow when compared

* Working Paper for World Congress of Sociology, Evian, France, September 1966. Reprinted with the permission of the Center for Research in Social Systems, American University, Washington, D.C.

[1] John Chamberlain, column in *The Washington Post*, August 14, 1965.

with a competent reporter who could arrive at a picture of the situation faster and perhaps even more accurately than pollsters or surveyors. Project Camelot itself foundered in part because of confusion with respect to the differences among scientific data, news, information, and intelligence.

Not all research is scientific in process or in purpose. The product of research may be news, information, or intelligence, as well as descriptive facts or scientific generalizations, according to the processes involved. For even the application of scientific techniques does not necessarily mean that the product is itself a contribution to science. Any gathering of facts for whatever end may use scientific techniques: the detective, for example, may use a wide variety of laboratory tests in his investigation of suspects. And we are told that espionage consists increasingly of the study of scientific reports.

Even within the category of research in which both the purpose and the process are scientific, a distinction has to be made between descriptive research and pure or basic research. In descriptive research, the substantive data are themselves intrinsically important; in basic research, data about the specific subjects who happen to constitute the sample are not in themselves important.[2] The anthropologist studying a particular tribe may apply a wide array of scientific techniques to his project; the results he achieves may be intrinsically important. They tell the colonial administrator concrete facts about the people he is dealing with. On the other hand, they may be intrinsically unimportant but theoretically extremely important for testing a hypothesis. It may make no difference at all to the administrator whether a certain rite takes one form or another; it may make a

[2] Since Project Camelot was designed as a scientific research project, it made no difference which specific "subjects," that is, countries, were selected for study. The major criteria for selection were not to be the importance of any specific data about them. It would certainly have been laughable to set up an unclassified project to secure intelligence. The criteria for selection of its sample of social systems for study were related only to their representativeness of the phenomena.

great deal of difference to a theory of social structure on diffusion or change or what-have-you. Almost any kind of survey can yield intrinsically important substantive information whether it contributes to a science or not.

Basic or theoretical research uses subjects only to test or to determine relationships. The subjects are themselves quite secondary. No one cares what they really think or do; the main objective is to determine how what they think or do is related to something else, as consequence or as antecedent.

Reporting is subject oriented. Facts are the purpose and the facts are themselves important. So, too, with investigation. Investigation is practical. It seeks specific facts and figures. It wants information that is concrete, specific, applicable, and, if possible, that will, so to speak, "stand up in court." It has an immediate purpose. And espionage, of course, which is secret and often illegal, is even more specific and concrete; it seeks to ferret out exactly what the plans and accomplishments and resources, for example, of an opponent are. It is omnivorous: science, rumor, news, anything — may be grist for its mill.

In the United States, these distinctions are becoming clarified; but they are still not understood by everyone, as John Chamberlain's comments show. It is apparently difficult for some people to believe the disinterested claims of the science model. It is inconceivable to them that data should be sought that are not immediately applicable. Still successful research in the area of conflict depends in part on making the distinctions clear. Without such clarification, so-called "access problems," which are difficult at best, may become insuperable. For research itself may involve conflict.

RESEARCH AS CONFLICT: "ACCESS PROBLEMS"

The research process which produces the data with which sciences — physical or social — are built is not itself a science nor even necessarily scientific. Like any other creative enterprise, it is an art.[3] It involves hunches, insights, intuitive leaps, and the like. In the social sciences, in addition, it often involves interpersonal skills. It is, as Leighton Van Nort has commented, a diplomatic as well as a scientific enterprise. For both researcher and researched are human beings and their relationship itself is involved in the research process. In the study of conflict, therefore, whether in the laboratory[4] or in the field, it may make a difference who does the research.

Sometimes the process of scientific research in the social sciences is itself a conflict situation. The researcher in such cases is trying to get responses from subjects who, for whatever reasons, do not wish to give them. In the case of some psychological research, for example, complete candor on the part of the researcher with respect to what he is after would nullify his results. The subject would not reply correctly. Community researchers sometimes face the same hazard or "access problems." If the subjects knew the purpose of the researches, replies would be prejudiced. Vague and misleading reasons are sometimes given to justify the questions asked. Tests have sophisticated checks built into them to trap the suspicious and wary. There is sometimes a veritable "battle of wits" between researcher and subjects.[5] The scientific researcher feels justified in his efforts because he knows the subjects' fears are groundless; he knows that all individual

[3] Robert Redfield, "The Art of Science," *American Journal of Sociology*, Vol. 54, No. 3 (November 1948), 185–190; Jessie Bernard, "The Art of Science: A reply to Redfield," *ibid.*, 55 (July 1949), pp. 1–9. The point of the second article was not that science was not an art, but that both physical and social sciences were, the first no less than the second.

[4] Jessie Bernard, "Some Current Conceptualizations in the Field of Conflict," *American Journal of Sociology*, Vol. 70, No. 4 (January 1965), pp. 453–454.

[5] On the practical, not scientific, plane, rules for "beating the tests" have even been formulated. See, for example, William H. Whyte's *The Organization Man* (New York: Simon and Schuster, 1956).

data will become unidentifiable in the data hopper, hard as it is to convince the subjects.[6]

This particular "access problem" has become attenuated in the United States. A generation has grown up so accustomed to research that it thinks nothing of filling in a dozen questionnaires a month or replying to a score of pollsters a year on any topic from their most intimate sex life to their most public voting behavior. Refusals are remarkably rare. People have become accustomed to the idea that individuals are lost in the statistical pool. And so also, presumably, more and more people in other countries are becoming accustomed to research; more and more accept questionnaires, tests, forms of one kind or another.[7] Polling agencies flourish in many countries. Young people are increasingly socialized into a world with almost insatiable needs for information about people.

Not everyone, however, even today, accedes. Some people still resist. They reject the idea of being studied; they do not like to be observed. They refuse to fill in questionnaires, they slam the door in the pollster's face, they do not show up in laboratory experiments. They are "anal" types. They are secretive by temperament or by training.[8] They represent the perennial "refusals" whose existence is the bane of the statisticians' existence. Their absence in the sample is the statisticians' Achilles heel. It stands for the battle he lost.

Some countries also resist research by outsiders. They identify it with espionage. They are, we sometimes say, "xenophobic." Their culture breeds secretiveness.[9] In such an at-

[6] For an interesting discussion of this topic, see Sidney M. Jourard, *The Transparent Self* (New York: Van Nostrand, 1964).

[7] Europeans have long been accustomed to filling in administrative as distinguished from research forms. The all-important "papers" that are so salient, the forms that have to be filled out when registering at hotels, custom forms, and the like, are very old. As is, also, of course, the fearful interrogation.

[8] Perhaps even by national custom. See footnote 5.

[9] Russia, for example, has been traditionally secretive. Not only in recent years but, apparently, for centuries. Even a hundred years ago

mosphere one would not expect much receptivity to science-building research and certainly not to fact-finding research. Even news reporting is limited.

It is well to remember, therefore, that research is not an impersonal, automatic process that, quite independently of personalities involved, grinds out valid, reliable, and testable findings. It is an utterly human and personal process. And not at all immune to conflict. Still, the situation is not hopeless, despite the Camelot incident. A considerable amount of cross-cultural research has been and continues to be done.

SOME LESSONS LEARNED

All cross-cultural research has its peculiar hazards, the "access problems" just discussed not the least among them. Among the first of the social scientists to face them were the anthropologists. On the basis of their experience, a fairly simple set of rules could be devised to help overcome the more serious hazards and a brilliant tradition evolved for research among at least preliterate peoples.

In addition to alerting and preparing us for the more obvious problems of communication, they taught us the importance of proper timing in one's approach to a people. They taught us the importance of the intermediary who introduced us to the people. They taught us the necessity of informal as well as of formal channels of approach to them. They taught us the importance of sensitivity in the scholar or scientist making the approach.

Not all they taught was relevant. Actually the work of

---

travelers reported they were not permitted free access to the country. And the closeness with which outsiders are even today observed and watched testifies to the survival of this emphasis on secrecy. The resistance of the U.S.S.R. to on-site inspection is only one example of the general close-mouthedness characteristic of its culture. Conversely, however, David and Vera Mace reported that they were given great freedom when researching the family in the U.S.S.R. It is currently reported that in Portugal it is forbidden to talk to foreigners.

the anthropologists was not a threat to their subjects. Much of the work was descriptive; they asked questions about the structure of the system for analytic purposes, but their data were primarily descriptive. (Often, in fact, the subjects were delighted, as when, for example, they learned from the anthropologists for the first time that their language had a grammar). Until recently, because of their discipline bias, the anthropologists' emphasis was on the integrity of the system, on its wholeness rather than on its conflicts, the presence of solidarity rather than on its absence. Only in the last generation has attention been devoted to the "schismogenetic" factors in preliterate social systems. But even when attention turned to the conflict aspects of preliterate cultures, it was only a matter of changing emphasis; the old methods and techniques could still be used. The researcher was in no sense involved in the conflicts; he was not a participant; he was not viewed as one. Research was not conflict prone. Still the lessons learned and taught by the anthropologists were useful and practical.

Cross-national research among more advanced, or literature nations also has an ancient and honorable tradition. Historians, economists, sociologists, and political scientists of the United States have studied scores of foreign countries and they, in turn, have studied us. Indeed, so-called area studies, have become standard disciplines. The fraternity of scholars from anywhere finds access to research resources anywhere. With only the traditional restrictions that guard documents for a certain number of years, it would be unthinkable if a bona fide scholar from any country were denied access to libraries and archives and museums. The more remote the subject studied, of course, the more accessible the data are. There is the rub. No one minds how minutely the revolution of a century ago is studied, down to the favorite drink of the major participants. It is the study of last year's revolution — or next year's — that is taboo.

Within the last generation, even survey research has gained widespread acceptance. Almost all advanced nations, as noted earlier, now have regular polling agencies available for such survey study. We have learned a great deal about how to conduct them. Still, even here there are sensitive areas and though conflict may be minimized, except in trivial research, it must still be reckoned with.

CONFLICT AS RESEARCH

If research is often a conflict process, so too is conflict itself often a research operation. It is not merely a cute *bon mot* to say that in a certain sense conflict may resolve itself into a set of research problems. Not traditional espionage for securing military intelligence, which has always been part of war, but civilian information-gathering or fact-finding research which is increasingly important in modern kinds of conflict.

The specific kinds of data, information, or facts sought in any research and hence the methods and techniques employed in seeking them depend, of course, on the theory or conceptualization with which one approaches the problem. In the area of conflict, if one approaches it with, let us say, a game-theory or decision-theory orientation, he looks in his research for data about the way decision makers or players in a game operate. If one approaches it with a social-forces orientation, he looks for data about long-time trends in variables he views as relevant for the conflict he is interested in — demographic, economic, attitudinal, and so on. In any event, whatever the conceptualization, research may constitute as important an element of conflict as hardware.[10]

[10] The hazards of lack of knowledge based on sound research were highlighted by columnist Joseph Kraft. He pointed out that American policy in Vietnam was based largely on "hunches, guesses, prejudices and assumptions — on propositions that are unknown and unknowable, untested and untestable. . . . The United State Government knows next to nothing about the politics of the Viet Cong. Systematic investigation was not even begun until late last summer . . . ." ("Insight and Outlook: The Agnostic Voice," *The Washington Post*, January 29, 1966). He lists a number of areas of ignorance and concludes that policy in Wash-

Before proceeding with this theme, mention must be made of a major trend in the nature of conflict itself.

CONFLICT OLD AND NEW

Industrial engineers tell us that every human being in a factory represents an engineering defect. When or if engineering solutions are correct, machines and instruments take over the performance of all tasks. In an analogous way, every example of violence[11] in a conflict may be said to represent

---

ington rests on "a foundation of guesswork" rather than on valid and reliable research. He points to a RAND study, based on an analysis of Lin Piao's article, "People's War," which, in the RAND researchers' opinion, reflected a situation diametrically different from that assumed by policymakers in Washington. Lin Piao, according to RAND, was advising the Viet Cong to abandon terrorism and militancy and revert to protracted guerrilla warfare and building greater popular support; according to Washington, Peking was goading the Viet Cong toward maintaining maximum belligerency (Murrey Marder, "China Urges New Viet Cong Strategy, Experts Say," *ibid.*, January 27, 1966). Joseph Alsop, very much the "hawk," "reads" the opponents' mind in a quotation from Sun Tzu's *Art of War* (about 350 B.C.) as follows: "When without a previous understanding the enemy asks for a truce, he is plotting" ("LBJ Meet Sun Tzu," *ibid.*, January 19, 1966). And from a commentator on this book more than a millennium later, Ch'en Hao, he quotes: "If without reason one begs for a truce it is assuredly because affairs in his country are in a dangerous state and he is worried and wishes to make a plan to gain a respite. Or otherwise he knows that our situation is susceptible to his plots and wants to forestall our suspicions by asking for a truce. Then he will take advantage. . . ." [*ibid.*]. Neither side has a monopoly on ignorance. [A definitive study of the Viet Cong has just been completed by Douglas Pike, who for the past six years has been with the U.S. Embassy in Saigon. See *Viet Cong* Cambridge, Mass.: The M.I.T. Press, 1966.]

[11] We are not here speaking of violence in the sense of an emotional explosion. The editor of a respected American periodical, *Harper's Monthly Magazine*, suggested in the January 1966 issue that a great deal of the violence that characterizes the modern world may be an explosive reaction against the loss of challenge and adventure which modern life suffers from. John Fischer argues for William James' moral equivalent for war. The implication is that conflict is the expression of a basic

a failure in strategy. For when or if strategic solutions are available, strategy may supplant violence.[12]

In a strictly technical sense, to be sure, violence may itself be a strategy;[13] certainly the threat of violence is. But the term is here used in the sense defined by Thomas C. Schelling:

> . . . strategy . . . is not concerned with the efficient application of force but with the exploitation of potential force. . . . It is concerned . . . with the possibility that particular outcomes are worse (better) for both claimants than certain other outcomes.[14]

The critical words for our purpose are "worse (better) for both claimants." For it is this specification that transforms the situation from a zero-sum to a mixed-motive game. There are alternatives that both parties may prefer.

William Kornhauser is of the opinion that although violence is not necessarily characteristic of revolution, extreme polarization (which renders it a zero-sum game) is.[15] But if this has been true in the past, the thesis of the present paper is that it is less and less so in the present; that in most modern conflicts, violence is a worse solution than some other

---

human need which, if not satisfied by life challenges, will find expression in violence. Psychologists have also been researching the biology and psychology of aggression and appear to find aggression intimately related to the human gene composition. We may be back in the nineteenth-century controversy about the inevitability of conflict. Hopefully, however, there will be no glorification of war, as there was at that time.

[12] Rudolf Rummel has studied violence as an index of both domestic and international conflict.

[13] Thomas C. Schelling, *The Strategy of Conflict* (Cambridge, Mass.: Harvard University Press, 1960).

[14] *Ibid.*, p. 5.

[15] "If violence and illegitimacy are not definitive of revolution, the search for the generic qualities of this kind of conflict must begin anew. One prominent feature of revolutionary conflict would appear to be extreme polarization, such that there is one and only one satisfactory outcome for the parties to the conflict, namely eventual *total victory*. Thus, revolution implies the large extent to which no compromise or exchange is possible among the parties to the conflict" (William Kornhauser, "Notes on Revolution," Mimeographed, 1965).

for both parties; and that if it was ever true that war constituted a zero-sum game, in an international system, it is no longer so.

We have become accustomed to the short life of much of our knowledge. It has become a cliché that ten years after one acquires his degree, half of what he learned is already outmoded. It has been estimated that more than half of what now constitutes basic science in certain fast-moving sciences is only ten years old, and so on. Still, the world to which much of past science pertained has not changed that rapidly; it is still possible to apply Newtonian physics, for example, to most earthly problems. Euclidean geometry may be old-fashioned, but it is still useful for many mundane tasks.

In the field of the social sciences, however, not only does new science replace old but the very world on which the old was based also changes. It is difficult to formulate any scientific generalizations that are relevant in sociological phenomena several hundred years ago and also today.[16] Those that are so formulated have to be so extremely general as to amount to little.

Conflict phenomena today, it is argued here, are different from conflict phenomena in the past, and much of our thinking about conflict in the past is outmoded with respect to conflict today. It is true that much of Schelling's thinking, let us say, is applicable to ancient history — as he has himself shown — but the reverse is not necessarily true, namely that the kinds of conflict that are characteristic (if not typical) of the present were also characteristic of the past.

For one thing, conflict in a social system characterized by mechanical solidarity, for example, is not the same as conflict in a social system characterized by organic solidarity. Conflict

[16] It is true that in many ways industrialization today has the same concomitants as those which characterized it in the nineteenth century. Urbanization results in the same kinds of social effects in an African or Asian city as it did in European and American cities. This similarity suggests that sociological processes have fairly wide and enduring validity. But in many ways, the processes are not the same and predictions based on western experience would be hazardous.

today is more likely to occur in a system characterized by organic than by mechanical solidarity. As the international world has become more integrated, it is more and more difficult to isolate conflict: it has wider ramifications. In biblical times, it was possible to raze villages without doing irreparable damage to one's own tribe. In a modern war, the victor often has to restore the vanquished.[17] It was once possible for nations to have their upheavals in decent privacy. Hardly at all today. The sociological setting for conflict in, let us say, the Congo a century ago was quite different from the setting today. Who, in fact, knew how many revolutions there were in the Congo in past centuries? Or cared? And when conflict could be quarantined, so to speak, it constituted a different kind of phenomenon than it does when it cannot be. The growing integration of the whole world into an interlocking set of systems makes it all but impossible to quarantine conflict. Precisely because they are increasingly parts of larger and larger systems, nations and states can no longer have their domestic conflicts in quiet. Big Brother, Little Brother, even Great White Fathers and Mothers all over the world are watching. And all may feel they have a stake. Zero-sum conflicts, which Kornhauser believes characteristic of revolutions, are transformed into mixed-motive conflicts, and the two are different.[18]

Schelling has highlighted the contrast between (old) zero-sum and (new) mixed-motive forms of conflict.[19] As contrasted with old types, new kinds demand not secrecy, feints, and miscommunication but precisely the reverse. Adversaries have to make themselves perfectly clear. Misinterpretation or misunderstanding may be fatal. Traditional concepts of

[17] The story is told of a small nation having fiscal difficulties. One minister advises a declaration of war on the United States. When it had won, it would, as a matter of course, rebuild the country and thus solve the problem. The suggestion was readily acceptable until one minister raised the question, but what if *we* win?

[18] It may be that a revolution is zero-sum at the local level but not at the international level.

[19] Thomas C. Schelling, *op. cit.*, pp. 160 – 61.

strategy and the research called for by them are thus less and less applicable to modern conflicts.[20]

RESEARCH, THEORY, AND DATA REQUIREMENTS IN THE FIELD OF CONFLICT

The data requirements of conflict-as-research vary. The structure of some kinds of conflict may render increased information irrelevant. A saddle point, so-called, is present. Neither side can do better with increased information. In other zero-sum games, however, this is not true. It is to the interest of both sides to know as much as possible and to be as secretive as possible. Here the research nature of conflict is clear.[21]

But the structure of the situation is not always self-evident. Research may be required to determine what kind of game situation is actually involved. Is it a zero-sum game? Is there a saddle point present? Is it a mixed-motive game? A pure strategy game? A mixed-strategy game? A tacit game? A bargaining situation? Does one party have first move? Or is this viewed as not a game situation but rather as a "parametric behavior equilibrium"? If one conceives the situation as a game, the kinds of data his research is designed to deliver will produce "understanding"; if as a parametric behavior equilibrium, knowledge.

KNOWLEDGE VERSUS UNDERSTANDING: PARAMETRIC VERSUS STRATEGIC BEHAVIOR

A generation ago, there was a lively controversy with respect to the several research approaches to sociological phe-

[20] The title of our session — "Research in Conflict Resolution" — is indicative. Why not "Research in Victory?" The concept of victory is extremely equivocal in modern conflict. In a mixed-motive game, both sides may win — or lose.

[21] Secrecy is so important for an optimum result that even the players themselves do not know in advance what they are going to do; it depends on certain odds determined by a mathematical solution.

nomena. One's position in this controversy greatly influenced one's data requirements in research. The positivists and the neopositivists argued for objectivity; they wanted knowledge. The advocates of "verstehen" wanted more; they argued for understanding, for insights, for intuitive, even empathic, experience. The neopositivists argued that one did not have to be a criminal to learn about crime; the "verstehen" advocates argued that it helped if one could get inside of the criminal and see the world from his angle. We hear little of this controversy today. "Verstehen" seems to be a method of finding questions to ask; objective research seems to be a method of finding answers to them. If an interviewer really shows "verstehen," he may elicit even more information than he asks for. But the issue is still relevant in conflict-as-research in the contrast between parametric behavior and game or bargaining behavior.

If the parties in a conflict situation observe one another's behavior and on the basis of these observations assign probabilities to the several alternatives open to one another, the result is not a strategic game, technically speaking, at least in the Schelling sense; it is what he calls a parametric behavior equilibrium.[22] That is, the parties are not interacting with one another either to communicate or to deceive but are, in effect, treating one another as things, as objects.[23] They are not attempting to read one another's mind or to influence one another by their own behavior. The conflict-as-research might take any form — scientific, investigative, fact-finding, espionage, or what-have-you.

But if they are in a strategic game situation, they want more. The data requirements or the information needed in conflict-as-research in a game-type situation has to do with (1) the subjective probabilities of both players for all the possible alternatives available to them and (2) the value assigned to the outcome of every pair of alternatives. Since

[22] Thomas C. Schelling, *op. cit.*, p. 225.
[23] In a certain sense, a "minimax" strategy in a game situation is a way of protecting oneself against interaction with an opponent.

the usual technical research procedures do not always apply, "mind-reading" techniques have to be evolved. "Kremlin watchers" and their opposite numbers, "White House watchers," learn to infer meanings from all sorts of behavior as well as from pictures, jokes, and protocol. Although they are behaviorists of the most orthodox kind, the objective of their research is more like understanding than hard data or information. They put induction to use for strategic ends.[24]

SOME IDEOLOGICAL LESSONS

Those who approach international conflict with an ideological bias are not likely to view it as a researchable phenomenon. They already have the answers. "Wars of national liberation" are to them simply the expression of historical principles: They do not require explanations. The research required is operational; it seeks data on how to prosecute such wars, not on how to interpret or explain them.

In a sense, a party that enters a conflict situation with an ideological commitment has the "first move" in Schelling's sense. If he believes that history is on his side, that he represents the wave of the future, his behavior is predetermined; he has no choice; he has to go along with history. Even if the idea should occur to him that he might make concessions to an adversary, he cannot; "history" would punish him. We call such adversaries fanatics; they cannot be bar-

[24] Game theory, it might be added parenthetically, is on the whole less insulting to subjects than is inductive research. In game theory, the researcher envisages situations of interaction, of "mind reading," or verstehen, of role taking, of recognition of opponents as manipulating and manipulatable human beings. In inductive research, the opponents are merely observed; they could just as well be objects or things. They are not interacted with but to; they are acted upon simply as data. It is true, to be sure, that in zero-sum games the effect of successful strategy is protection against having to react to one's opponent; one works out a policy that is independent of what the opponent does or, rather, that optimizes one's payoff no matter what he does. Even so, the game-theory approach cannot ignore the human nature of opponents, and the inductive approach sometimes can.

gained with; that is, they refuse to negotiate. Their behavior may look quite nonrational to others but it is the logical result of the game matrix as they see it. They do not view a world of probabilities, of uncertainties, or even of risks. The probabilities in their matrix are 1.0 and 0.0. They believe they are bound to win; if not today, then decades hence. Sure of themselves, they are willing to wait it out. Adversaries must challenge their subjective probabilities. It is not easy.

Project Camelot called forth a scrutiny not only of the ideological biases of others but of our own as well. Two examples are noteworthy, one having to do with a political and one with a theoretical bias.

Charles Wolf, Jr., for example, commented on the so-called "popular support" theory of insurrection, a theory which states that the "activating force behind insurgency movements lies in popular attitudes and animus, the erosion of mass support for established institutions, and the gaining of popular support and commitment by the insurgency. In the same manner, current doctrine contends that successful counterinsurgency programs require that support be won from the insurgents by the established government.[25] He called our attention to the fact that the American populist bias made us sympathetic with insurrectionists and as a result we had a "disposition to accept and to advocate the 'popular-support' view."[26] The result was a bias in favor of insurgents.

But this proinsurrectionist bias had its counterpart in an allegedly proincumbent bias intrinsic, it has been charged, in the social-systems approach characteristic of American sociology in the last generation. Project Camelot was asking: How do social systems operate and how do they fall apart? What causes systems to break down? Why do they disintegrate? What are the preconditions of internal war, revolutions, or insurgencies? Can these preconditions be rectified

[25] Charles Wolf, Jr., "Insurgency and Counterinsurgency: New Myths and Old Realities," RAND Mimeo P–3132 – 1, July 1965.
[26] *Ibid.*

or forestalled? Are there definite stages and sequences that can be clearly delineated? Are there general patterns applicable universally or is each instance *sui generis*?[27] This emphasis on social systems had ideological implications which are understandable only in the perspective of American sociology during the last quarter century.

WHAT DO YOU MEAN "SOCIAL-SYSTEMS APPROACH"?

For a whole generation, American sociology had shown great preoccupation with social systems and the emphasis had been overwhelmingly on factors and forces making for their stability. Some critics had argued that this emphasis had the effect of justifying the status quo. By implication, therefore, a systems approach to revolution or insurgency would be biased in favor of incumbents.

Actually, as W. J. Goode so cogently notes, an emphasis on stability implies, even if indirectly, instability or the threat of it.

. . . the social sciences . . . in effect *assumed* instability in the social system, and tried to explain why stability is so common. Contrary to much contemporary criticism, the dominant group in sociology has not defended the *status quo;* rather its members have explained why it *is* the current state of affairs, i.e., why things are as they are. At times, this seems to the dissidents an espousal of a Panglossian view of social action: everything works out to the greatest good, all contributes to the continued existence of current social arrangements. Constantly searching for the main factors in stability suggests, in fact, that there must be powerful sets of disrupting forces: otherwise, stability would not be problematic.[28]

Only in the last decade was attention turned to tensions and strains in social systems — to the question: "What are these forces against which the stabilizing factors operate?"[29] Understandably, therefore, in the minds of some social scientists

[27] See the Camelot papers edited by Samuel Z. Klausner, in *The Study of Total Societies,* for the total-system papers.

[28] W. J. Goode, "Mobility and Revolution," Paper given at Camelot conference at Airlie House, Warrenton, Virginia, June 1965, pp. 1 – 2.

[29] *Ibid.*, p. 1.

a systems approach implied, rightly or wrongly, a bias in favor of the status quo and hence of incumbents.

Actually, the systems approach, it soon appeared, had to be radically modified to fit the problems today. As soon as the social scientists turned their gaze from the vacuum of strictly theoretical models to the messy world around them, they noticed that the areas of the world characterized by revolutionary potential today were not, in the textbook sense at any rate, social systems at all. W. J. Goode, for example, on the basis of his own work in the Caribbean, stated as the most important problem for exploration the following:

> Contrary to most contemporary social, sociological and anthropological theory, I am asserting that major societies can operate with a substantial degree of anomie. Textbook discussions assert that this is impossible. Under the assumption that anomie is not by definition excluded from any society, we can begin to ask at what levels of anomie a society can continue to operate.[30]

And Charles Wolf, Jr., speaking of transitional societies, came to a similar conclusion:

> Transitional societies are inherently vulnerable to insurgency. Cleavages and antagonisms are endemic and pervasive: between landlords and tenants; between urban and rural areas; among ethnic, racial, religious, and linguistic groups. Inequities in the distribution of wealth, income, education, and opportunity are chronic, painful, and widespread. Resentment against the current or historic privilege and status patterns of bitterness and resentment are as much a part of the fabric of transitional societies as low-income levels. To change the patterns requires far reaching changes in social, political and economic structure.[31]

Quite aside from the fact that social systems in real life did not conform to the textbook models which had been so thoroughly analyzed and explained, there was the difficulty that it was not always clear which system needed examining. In a nonintegrated world, the system might well be a tribe or a community. But as the world becomes increasingly integrated, as noted earlier, the system itself expands. Increas-

[30] *Ibid.*, p. 36.
[31] Charles Wolf, Jr., *op. cit.*, p. 8.

ingly, revolutions occur in systems that extend beyond national or tribal borders.[32]

SOME TECHNICAL LESSONS

Not all the lessons learned from Project Camelot were incidental or serendipitous. Since the desire was to pick the best brains available, a wide gamut of freedom was built into the planning. Any lead that promised to have productive "fallout" was followed, whether or not it was finally incorporated into the design. Some contributors emphasized the preconditions of revolution, some structural aspects, some processual aspects, some decision making, some recruitment, and so on.[33] The result was a rich array of technical suggestions.[34] A few of the many approaches appear in this volume.

The Operations Approach.[35]

The school of thought which undergirds operations research has essentially an engineering orientation. Operations research

[32] The systems approach was too valuable to jettison. Insurgencies themselves may be viewed as systems *(ibid.)* and any game model may also be used, in the sense that any interacting situation constitutes a system. If anything that Ego does affects what Alter does, a system may be said to exist.

[33] It was interesting to note the difficulties resulting from Project Camelot's attempt to canvass all promising approaches. During the planning phase, seminars were held at which a wide variety of approaches was presented. Specialists in specific approaches often became restless during the presentation of different approaches; there was a feeling of looseness. It was interesting also to note how independent research agencies, accustomed to dealing with industry or with routine government operations, floundered in presenting their wares. The idea that Project Camelot wanted at all to shop the research stalls in the market was disconcerting.

[34] Unfortunately, there was not time for all these heady contributions to jell; it is not, therefore, possible to state unequivocally what would have been the final design or the final data requirements if the project had continued.

[35] It was noted earlier that some people object to being researched. Some object especially to being researched by industrial management.

studies how to do things, whatever they may happen to be, the best and most feasible way. As applied to industrial management and to public administration, it has developed a fairly extensive tool kit. Using these tools, it can show a client the true nature of his problems, what decisions have to be made, the alternatives available to him, the pros and cons of each one, and the best "trade-offs."

Among the operational questions raised were these: What criteria should be used in selecting variables for study? What techniques which have been found useful in civilian decision or policy making can also be useful to decision or policy makers in research dealing with conflict?

With respect to the criteria to be applied in selecting variables for study, Abt Associates suggested three, namely: "(1) the data accuracy requirements of the model, (2) the rate of change of the data required, and (3) the cost of data collection."

The designer can use these relationships to assist him in the selection of variables in the following way:

1. Balance the data accuracy requirements of the proposed design with the expected rate of change of the actual required data, to produce an expected error that is smaller than the maximum allowed, assuming accurate detection of the actual rate of change.

2. The difference in this expected error and the maximum allowed would then be taken up by the error incurred by less than accurate detection due to practical cost limits of collection efforts.[36]

William Whyte's book, *The Organization Man* (New York: Simon and Schuster, 1956) was, in effect, their list of particulars. In an analogous way, some critics of Project Camelot objected to what seemed to them to be its "managerial" orientation. It is quite true that some of those who contributed ideas to the thinking-through phase of the design had an operational approach. But if it had been as sinister as charged, this approach would certainly have been classified, certainly not published. Some of it is included in this volume. This is not naïveté but candor.

[36] Abt Associates, *The Application of Operations Research, Interdisciplinary Systems Analysis and Simulation to Internal Revolution Conflict and Its Pre-Conditions*, p. 24. The problem of variables was also discussed in connection with the problem of indicators of revolution. In-

Research on conflict, in brief, was viewed like any other kind of operation in which quality control (that is, data accuracy) and production costs (that is, of data collection) had to be balanced.

Kathleen Archibald, who has done extensive research on the processes by which scientific research becomes incorporated in government policy, stated that in selecting dependent variables, the criteria must include the possibility of judging them as good or bad, or, preferably, as measurably good or bad according to a set of preferences.[37] And the criteria for the selection of the independent variable must include feasibility of control.[38] This, in turn, involves specifications under which different requirements hold. Is the dependent variable continuous or a discrete future event? Is it valued positively, negatively, or mixed positively and negatively? She pointed out that critical variables may not be the same for all parties in all conflicts since they depend on both capabilities and value judgments. Nor are they the same from the point of view of practical application and of basic research.

The importance of operational criteria for the selection of variables was highlighted by a preliminary survey of the literature on revolution made by members of the project staff under the direction of Ralph Swisher, which revealed literally scores of variables that at least some researchers had found relevant.[39] It was a very sobering experience to have emphasized the fact that in responsible research in the work-a-day world the selection of variables has to be subject to operational limits. Not the theoretically most important and relevant variables but the operationally most feasible — bearing in mind, to be sure, importance and relevance — are the

---

dicators must be accessible, frequently redefined, and capable of check by historical research (p. 20).

[37] Kathleen Archibald, "Possible Criteria for a Theoretical Approach Useful to Policy," p. 2.

[38] *Ibid.*, p. 3.

[39] "Hypotheses Related to Conflict," Working Paper for Project Camelot.

ones that have to be selected. The freewheeling theorist may know exactly and precisely the most important and the most relevant variables; but if they are unobtainable, then the best "trade-off" has to be settled for. The operations approach is salutary but not exciting.

Applicable Models.

In addition to their discussion of criteria for the selection of variables, Abt Associates also canvassed current research procedures and techniques to see which if any could be applied to conflict research, especially internal war research. Some interesting analogies were suggested. Research on the social psychology of persuasion and influence, especially in small groups, has developed a considerable literature that, Abt Associates believed, could be relevant for studying the political recruitment aspect of internal war potential. In addition, they suggested that techniques developed for reliability and quality control could, by analogy, be applied to social systems, rebellious groups being viewed — rather whimsically — as failures in a particular component of the system.[40] Queuing theory, they also suggested, could be applied to the service activities required to make the defective part operable.[41]

Inventory control techniques, it was suggested, constitute another prototype with possible applicability to tactical aspects of conflict, such as reenforcement and garrison size, routing of arms, and disposition of weapons. Linear program models were proposed as possible ways for optimizing resource allocation, since they can "be used for almost any problem . . . in which scarce personnel or equipment have to travel from place to place."[42] Viewing popular disaffection and subversion as infectious diseases makes epidemiological models relevant.[43] Optimized sectoring theory for regional structuring was also suggested.

[40] Abt Associates, *op. cit.*, p. 31.
[41] *Ibid.*, p. 32.
[42] *Ibid.*, p. 33.
[43] *Ibid.*, pp. 33 – 34.

Since so many of these intriguing and imaginative analogies were more likely to be applicable for the actual prosecution of conflict rather than for researching its preconditions, they were viewed as highly stimulating, if not as intrinsically applicable to Project Camelot's assignment.

The Inductive Approach.

This research method, which has been peculiarly characteristic of American social-science research, relies heavily on empirical data. The aim usually is to gather enough data to generalize. A great deal of emphasis is placed on sampling, on clarity of definition of variables, on precise coding, on validity, on reliability, on tests of significance, on appropriate statistical analysis. Project Camelot was to rely heavily on this approach. As noted earlier, the extensive literature, historical and contemporary, on revolution was canvassed by Ralph Swisher and his associates, resulting in literally scores of hypotheses for testing by means of empirical research. The most sophisticated representative of this empirical point of view was the work of Rudolf Rummel, who applied factor analysis to instances of reported violence, arriving at three basic dimensions: turmoil, revolution, and subversion. On the theoretical side, Rummel's work on social space was in the tradition of Kurt Lewin's field theory.[44]

Robert Hefner and Sheldon Levy were also among the technical empiricists. Their concern was with methods of measuring attitudes. Inasmuch as customary methods of surveying attitudes are not always available in conflict research, they were interested in devising methods and techniques that circumvented this roadblock by alternative techniques, especially content analysis and expert judgment.

If Project Camelot had materialized, empirical findings in the inductive tradition would undoubtedly have constituted a major part of its contribution. But they would have been

[44] p. 25 ff. in Rudolf J. Rummel, "A Field Theory of Social Action with Application to Conflict within Nations," in *General Systems*, Vol. 10 (1965).

of the science-building rather than of the information type.

The Deductive Approach.

At present, the deductive approach tends to take the form of mathematical models that specify a set of conditions and then deduce the consequences. Manuel Avila's model — for the study of preconditions of revolution — illustrated this approach. It required data on no less than sixteen independent variables; but the data for most of them were of a kind that did not call for field surveys.

Simulation, both computer and manual (games), was also included in the hospitable design of Project Camelot. Manual simulation, or an appropriate game, is basically processual in nature; it seeks to determine how decision makers operate under given restraints. James Coleman, Robert Boguslaw, and Thomas Ireland contributed to this approach, all from slightly different theories and hence game specifications.

All in all, the lessons learned from Project Camelot — latent as well as manifest — constitute a real contribution to conflict research and research in conflict resolution.

SUMMARY COMMENTS: NO HARM IN DREAMING

The conception, design, and implementation of research — science building, administrative, or what-have-you — will continue to be creative arts, not routine chores. Especially in the social sciences where, as in the physical sciences, not only scientific knowledge and techniques change but the phenomena to be studied themselves also change.

These observations appear to be peculiarly applicable in the area of conflict, particularly of war, both inter- and intranational. For the nature of these conflicts has changed as the world has become increasingly integrated into a set or system or interlocking systems. They are, as a result, less and less likely to be zero-sum in nature, in which victory is possible. They are more and more likely to be mixed-motive games in which both sides may lose or win.

In the past, war was, in a way, a kind of trial-and-error research to determine subjective probabilities, values, and outcomes. It was a test of will, of resources, of skill, leadership, and the like; it demonstrated "the rules of the game." Do we still have to use such an expensive procedure? Is it conceivable that research can take the place of this costly form of experimentation and testing?

R. B. Braithwaite has suggested that in 300 years "economic and political and other branches of moral philosophy will bask in radiation from a source — theory of games of strategy — whose prototype was kindled round the poker tables of Princeton."[45] Is the idea so fanciful after all? Will it one day be possible that trusted researchers will be able to offer advice to decision makers which will convincingly optimize everyone's values? Perhaps one of the most useful things that, let us say, UNESCO could do would be to hold frequent seminars on the theory of conflict for social scientists from all over the world. Instead of a Project Camelot, let us have, say, a Project Braithwaite to research ways of substituting scientific research for the trial-and-error of war, research that would result in optimizing everyone's values in a world where victory is less and less possible.

[45] R. B. Braithwaite, *Theory of Games as a Tool for the Moral Philosopher* (Cambridge, Eng.: Cambridge University Press, 1955).

Herbert Blumer

University of California at Berkeley

Threats from Agency-Determined Research: The Case of Camelot

My intention is to invite social scientists to look anew at the Camelot affair in order to recognize and consider the implicit dangers to the integrity of social science that are embodied in the occurrence. My concerns differ from those which social scientists have seemingly had in viewing and interpreting the affair. In my judgment, social scientists have treated the occurrence far too lightly; and, where aroused by it they have been chiefly disturbed by the wrong things. The affair, in terms of what it represents, has very grave import for social science along directions quite different from those in which social scientists have mainly expressed their concern.

The response of social scientists to Camelot has been, in the main, surprisingly mild and nonchalant. I infer from a large number of conversations which I have had that many social scientists never even heard of the affair. Of those who did, seemingly most regarded it with passing interest — merely as an odd and momentarily exciting event such as might appear anywhere in the news columns. Apparently, they saw nothing to awaken any serious concern as to how the project might endanger the integrity of scientific study. Their criticisms of it — when they had any — were confined to condemning certain decisions and actions in the administration of the project, as showing poor judgment or mismanagement. For them, the lesson to be learned from the Camelot affair was that of being careful not to get into trouble – to do such things as employing tactful and discrete workers, establishing good lines of communication within the project, maintaining good relations with embassy officials, avoiding involvement in "cloak-and-dagger" activities, and being diplomatic in interagency fights. Such precautions reflect concern with the safety of projects; they show little awareness of, or concern with, any questions of scientific integrity raised by the Camelot incident.

A similar obtuseness to questions of scientific integrity is to be noted in the case of social scientists operating in some capacity as representatives of their disciplines. Scarcely any references to the Camelot affair are to be found in the professional journals in social science,* and where made, the discussion did not perceive the occurrence as threatening fundamental precepts of scientific study. More disquieting is the absence of items in the official proceedings of the various social science societies to suggest that such bodies saw anything in the Camelot incident that was ominous to fundamental ideals of scientific study. One must conclude, I think, that social scientists by and large were only mildly aroused by the Camelot affair and that they showed very little official concern with the implications of the episode for the integrity of scientific study.

In contrast, there seems to have been a considerable amount of concern with the *consequences* of the affair as affecting the status of social science, particularly sociology, in circles of the federal government. At least a number of influential social scientists who would be regarded as belonging to the "elite" in present-day social sciences were impelled to meet together for the purpose of planning action with regard to this line of consequences of the Camelot

* A notable exception has been the treatment of the Camelot affair by Irving Louis Horowitz in *Trans-action*, Vol. 3, No. 1 (November–December 1965).

affair. It is of great importance for our purpose to see what these social scientists were concerned with. Their concerns provide the best indication of how the Camelot affair was viewed and assessed by persons who came closest to being the representatives and spokesmen of social science.

There is no difficulty in pinpointing the concerns. They were: (1) an apprehension that social science might suffer a loss in its share of federal support of research; (2) a corresponding fear that the influence of sociology in federal circles might be lessened; (3) a fear that access to important areas of research might be severely restricted, if not closed to social scientists; (4) a fear that the interests of sociology might be caught up in and injured by departmental rivalries in the federal government; and (5) some apprehension of federal censorship of research.

How are we to evaluate these directions of concern? It seems clear that with the possible exception of the fifth one, they signified predominantly an interest in protecting the position or standing of sociology with regard to the *opportunities* for research and influence available in or through the federal government. The motivation was clearly that of seeing that sociology was not hampered or cut off from the largess of federal research funds, that its range and lines of influence in governmental circles were not restricted, that its opportunities for engaging in foreign-area research were not impaired, and that it be freed from the expense and disadvantage of becoming a "cat's paw" in interdepartmental rivalries.

That these were legitimate and worthy concerns is not to be questioned. But, I think one must ask if this is the central meaning of the Camelot project — the lesson that it is to convey. Is its central significance merely that of repairing the loss of influence of sociology in federal circles and that of ensuring the accessibility of sociology to large-scale federal research funds? Should the reaction in our discipline be merely or mainly a matter of establishing an apparatus — such as a suggested National Social Science Foundation — that will enhance the prospects of getting a larger share of federal largess and of extending the range of sociological influence in federal circles?

It seems to me that the primary significance of the Camelot affair for sociology lies along an entirely different line. The vital question it poses is not that of the status of sociology in the eyes of the federal government but of the commitment of sociology to the precepts of science. The major issue is not that of entrenching and extending the role of sociology in the federal government but of protecting the integrity of sociology as a scientific discipline. As one probes reflectively into the Camelot occurrence and ponders over its implications, one must recognize, I think, a number of conditions that pose threats to the premises on which sociology necessarily rests as a scientific undertaking. These threats, while highlighted by the Camelot episode, should not be viewed as confined to it. One must, I think, look upon Camelot in the context of the increasing dependency of sociological research on federal subsidization. Already, the extent of federal support of social science research is very formidable. There is nothing on the horizon to suggest that it is not going to increase. There is reason to believe that federal agencies will be led more and more to enlist the aid of social scientists to conduct research studies that will enable the agencies to execute more effectively their respective missions. One should see the Camelot affair not as an isolated episode but as spotlighting a number of questions that are indigenous in varying degrees in the general matter of using social science research for the purpose of achieving the aims of governmental agencies. The overarching question refers to the dangers that such participation in agency-determined research may set for the integrity of sociology as a discipline. It is to this matter that I wish to direct my remarks.

In order to clear the ground for my line of treatment, I wish to say that I am not concerned in this paper with the highly important question as to whether a given agency-determined project is ethically proper and defensible. This question is in order and should be faced by the scholar. In these days of intensified preparation for strife, of extension of national power, and of efforts to maintain established political stability in the face of a changing world, one may justifiably be led to question the ethics and wisdom of certain federally supported research enterprises. Thus, scientists may have proper compunctions about participating in research designed to perfect instruments of slaughter such as the atomic bomb or forms of chemical warfare, or to lend their aid in devising techniques of demoralization as in the case of psychological warfare, or to contribute to "cloak-and-dagger" activities. I suspect that most of the moral indignation aroused by the Camelot episode stemmed from the belief that the project represented an unwarranted and ethically suspect intrusion into the life of other peoples. However proper in their own right may be questions and criticisms of the moral character of given research undertakings, they are not the object of concern in my discussion. Such questions and criticisms center on the *use* to which the research may be put; they focus on the reprehensible character of the purpose for which the scientific act is undertaken. They leave untouched the question of the eroding effect that agency-determined projects may have on the integrity of the scientific undertaking itself. My analysis is concerned with this latter matter.

The threats of agency-directed research to the integrity of science that I wish to consider arise from matters other than that of secrecy. The threats that appear to me to be of crucial significance are (1) the restraints imposed on the scientific pursuit of truth, (2) a disrespect of the rights of the human beings being studied, and (3) an unwitting corruption of scholars engaging in agency-directed research. My discussion of these forms of threat will be confined to the social sciences. For reasons that will be made clear in the course of the discussion, the given threats are not likely to be serious in the case of agency-directed research in the physical and biological sciences; in contrast, they may become grave in the case of social science.

RESTRAINTS ON THE SCIENTIFIC PURSUIT OF TRUTH

The free pursuit of truth, *wherever it may lead*, is the basis of science and scholarship, indeed the reason for their existence as forms of collective endeavor. To pursue truth, science necessarily requires freedom of inquiry. This becomes its indispensable right. But also, in this pursuit of truth, science has the unavoidable obligation of submitting its assertions to tests of validity. I wish to examine agency-determined research in the light of these twin components of the scientific pursuit of truth.

Freedom of scientific inquiry means simply being free from restrictions imposed on what the scientist may investigate. This freedom means much more than the privilege of selecting and studying different topics in the field of study. It means, indeed requires, that the scientist be free to view critically and to question any and all parts of the scientific study and procedure in which he is to engage. The pursuit of truth in science does not allow for anything less. The scientist must be in a position to assess critically the choice of problems for study, to question the premises or assumptions underlying the study, to judge the empirical relevance of the dominant ideas which are to lead or guide the study, and to assess the methods of inquiry to be employed in the study. To the extent to which he has closed to him the right to scrutinize critically and challenge any or all of these parts of the scientific undertaking, he is forced to forfeit in corresponding measure the pursuit of truth. Within those areas of the scientific undertaking that are closed to his critical assessment he becomes a technician — an executor carrying out a predesigned task in place of being a seeker of knowledge. It should be added that this indispensable right of critical assessment is not limited to the intial period in which the study is being formulated but must extend to the study during the full course of its execution so that false starts and wrong directions may be corrected.

Agency-determined research is open to serious misgiving

when assessed in terms of this picture of what constitutes freedom of inquiry. Typically, such research excludes several vital parts of the research enterprise from scrutiny, challenge, and correction by the participating scientists. I refer to the selection of the problem that the project is to study, the premises that underlie the formulation of the problem, and the dominant ideas that give the study its character and its direction. These are obviously matters that are determined by the agency in response to its practical interests and ends — they are not devised to satisfy the interests of science.

Many social scientists would argue that within the framework of the project, the participating social scientist may carve out a legitimate scientific problem and study it with a high order of exacting method. Thus, participants in the Camelot project seemingly had no doubt that they could resolve the research task into a series of legitimate scientific problems whose study could be made without sacrifice of the freedom of inquiry. Their view would be that the pursuit of knowledge to serve the purpose of the agency need not imperil the scientific validity of the knowledge thus gained. This argument has a germ of truth. But it overlooks the easy possibility that the project may force the component research undertakings to fit its mold at the expense of an accurate analysis of the empirical area with which the project is concerned. One must bear in mind that in responding to the practical interest and policy orientation of the agency the project is given an "ideological" slant or perspective. This ideological perspective can be detected, in the first instance, in what the project presupposes to be desirable, good, and worthy of being fostered, or conversely, in what is regarded as reprehensible and to be curtailed. In addition, the ideological perspective is fashioned out of a variety of underlying images that are usually beyond detection by those who hold them and certainly beyond their critical scrutiny. This underlying imagery represents a scheme of how the world is organized. Thus, it will have implicit classifications of peoples, their relationship, their motives and stances, the deleterious or beneficial character of their position and intentions, the dangers and threats present in the operating milieu, and the general direction along which it is felt that social development should advance. An understanding of what I am saying is clear if one thinks of any social doctrine, such as communism, fascism, racism, antiracism, "the white man's burden," or "preserving the world for democracy."

I am not concerned here with the question — however appropriate it may be — of whether the given ideological perspective is good or bad. Instead, my concern is to point out that the ideological perspective underlying and shaping the agency project may impose a perceptual structure on the empirical area under study in such a way as to unwittingly misrepresent the empirical area. The questions asked, the data sought, and lines of analysis used in response to one perspective may lead to a set of findings and an interpretation quite different from those yielded by an alternate set of questions reflecting a different ideological perspective. Let me explain this important and much overlooked matter by dealing with one aspect of it and using the Camelot project as an illustration.

The area of human group life with which an agency-determined research project is concerned is marked, almost by definition, by the play of competing social tendencies, each striving to shape the state of things to be in the given area of life. The agency is interested in getting the knowledge that will enable the tendency that the agency favors to triumph over other tendencies that are striving in a contrary or different direction. Thus, study is focused on the desired tendency, seeking to ascertain the conditions that will enable it to thrive, or to withstand the pressure of contrary tendencies, or to become dominant. This mobilization of research interest on the preferred tendency can easily lead to the neglect, or inadequate study, of other or contrary tendencies that are in play in the empirical world — tendencies that may themselves be open to cultivation and progressive development. If one fails to study with comparable thoroughness such other tendencies, one is in danger both of misrepresenting the empirical area and of developing inadequate knowledge. This can be seen, it seems to me, in the case of Camelot, which was concerned with the question of how insurgency in developing countries could be prevented and contained. Yet it is equally legitimate in the case of this topic to ask how insurgency could be encouraged and promoted — to ask, for instance, how agitation could be organized and facilitated, how passions could be aroused and dissidence mobilized for action, how weak and vulnerable points in the social structure could be detected and exploited, and how control by a dominant elite could be undermined. As these questions suggest, the given area or order of life with which the Camelot project was concerned must be recognized as containing diverse tendencies or differing incipient lines of formation which were genuine parts of its empirical make-up. To pick out one of these potentials for study without giving the other potentials comparable study is to risk misrepresentation and faulty analysis. The potential line of formation selected for study has to contend in the empirical world with the other potential lines of formation and has to face the possibility that they, similarly, may be cultivated and developed. Consequently, they have to be brought within the field of study in order to have adequate analysis. Put succinctly, one cannot grasp scientifically the nature of counterinsurgency without understanding adequately the nature of insurgency. In a corresponding way, one cannot understand the mechanisms of agitation without understanding the nature of counteragitation; one cannot understand how a given type of political control can be maintained without understanding how it may be undermined; one cannot understand how a given condition of crime or disorganization may be remedied without understanding how that condition may be abetted and entrenched.

Enough has been said, I trust, to suggest how an underlying ideological perspective may prefigure the matters to be studied and thus impose unwittingly a restricted and slanted framework on the research, molding the research to fit the framework. It is easy for specific research projects that are fashioned inside of the framework, however carefully performed, to contribute to an erroneous depiction of the empirical world and to inaccurate scientific knowledge. It is against this danger, to which agency-determined research is so susceptible, that participating social scientists have to be on guard. The necessary corrective or antidote for the danger is obviously the freedom to question the premises underlying the project, to challenge its leading ideas, to scrutinize critically the problem that is set up as the objective of the research, and to move in new directions in the research quest. Yet, it is precisely these forms of freedom of inquiry that are likely to be closed to the scientist participating in agency-determined social research.

Not all forms or instances of agency-determined research are alike in terms of these largely unwitting restraints placed on the freedom of scientific inquiry. Generally, such restraints are likely to be strongest and most serious in the case of projects that reflect strong ideological bents. It is this latter type of project that is especially prone to endanger the integrity of social science — all too frequently without awareness by the participating scientist.

If agency-determined research is likely to restrain freedom of scientific inquiry, it is no less likely to restrict the other component of the scientific pursuit of truth — the demonstration of the validity of assertions. An empirical science has to square its propositions with the empirical field to which they apply. The empirical field in the case of social science research projects initiated by agencies is almost always constituted by a body of actual social life of given people — their activities, their organization, their interrelationships, their orientations, their career lines, their concerns and strivings, their tensions and conflicts, and their social controls. Such a body of actual group life is the empirical stuff against which the propositions have to be tested at any stage in their formulation as well as in their final form. There is no substitute for this ultimate type of test. The implication of this simple point is clear. It is that those engaged in the research must have or must develop an intimate familiarity with the given field of social life under study and that they have the opportunity to explore the area freely in their studies. This intimate familiarity is not yielded merely by working with a set of narrowly abstracted data that do not provide an understanding of their empirical context; nor is it given by working with sets of "indicators" when one lacks a concrete understanding of the nature and context of the things that they are supposed to indicate. The familiarity should exist in breadth and depth so that the social scientist has a grasp of the sensitivities and orientations of the people under study, their world as they see it, and the content of their experience from their point of view.

Rarely does the participant in agency-determined research begin his study with such familiarity. To expect all participants to have it is to ask too much. But the conditions of the research study should be such as to promote the cultivation and development of such familiarity. It is in this respect that agency-determined social research is likely to be very wanting. A number of conditions usually combine to compress such research inside a preestablished design that markedly restricts research workers from developing intimate familiarity with the people and area of life under study. Let me comment briefly on the conditions. First, as previously noted, the organization of the research around the value-objective of the agency supplies an ideological perspective that in itself seems to make unnecessary the development of intimate familiarity. Second, the project is typically designed in advance to yield the specific information that is sought. The faithful execution of the study requires close adherence to the design. This limits both the need and the occasion for developing free-ranging familiarity with the life of the people. Third, when the objective or target of the study is set up, reliance is placed on the application of established techniques, skills, and expertise in place of cultivating familiarity with the area. Whether specialists possessing such expertise and skills have an intimate familiarity with the area of life under study becomes secondary in importance. Fourth, the setting of time limits for the completion of the study, with the expectation of "results," is a powerful deterrent to engaging in the process of familiarization and exploratory inquiry because of the delays and uncertainties that this involves. Fifth, a project once organized and launched represents a heavy investment and commitment; those directing the project can ill afford to jeopardize its course and completion by allowing it to get outside of the confines of its predetermined scheme. These five conditions, singly and in combination, operate to keep participating scientists away from the flexible and exploratory widening of contact that is essential for the development of intimate familiarity with the given empirical area. The empirical test of assertions becomes confined to the data yielded by the circumscribed inquiry and is thus likely to escape assessment in the light of the broader area of natural experience. Propositions about people in their natural world need to be tested ultimately by faithful information of such people in that natural world. Agency-determined research, with its emphasis on specialized, prestructured, and circumscribed inquiry, does not lend itself readily to the acquisition of such naturalistic information.

The Camelot project was dissolved before it reached the point of actual research study. However, a perusal of the documents and accounts of its preparation suggests rather decisively that like comparable studies it was not oriented to develop intimate familiarity with the field of insurgency in the case of the peoples to be studied. The area and line of inquiry were restricted and slanted, information was to be sought for predetermined and circumscribed problems, reliance was to be placed on expertise in the use of specific techniques, participants were chosen without particular regard to their possessing intimate familiarity with the given area of life among the peoples to be studied, and the outline of the project did not apparently provide for the development of such familiarity during the course of the study. These observations are not advanced to criticize the Camelot project per se but to call attention to the ease with which agency-determined research may separate itself from intimate familiarity with the natural world against which its propositions have to be tested.

DISREGARD OF THE INTERESTS OF THE PEOPLE UNDER STUDY

The Camelot project epitomizes the ease with which agency-determined social research may ignore the interests, rights, and claims of the people who are the objects of inquiry. In my judgment, such disregard is a distinct threat to the integrity of social science. This matter should be put in perspective and be understood by social scientists.

Agency-determined research is prone to treat lightly the interests and claims of people who are the objects of study or whose lives are to be changed by applying the results of the study. The interests and needs of the agency on whose behalf the research is to be undertaken have priority in governing the research enterprise. If the interests and needs are felt to be urgent and acute, little consideration is likely to be given to the interests and rights of the subjects. The judgment of what is desirable or good for the people may readily be an expression of ethnocentric bias — whether the bias be that of a nation, of a social class, of a militaristic circle of a doctrinally minded group in power, or of some professionally minded group. This combination of agency interest and of ethnocentric bias may permeate the research project at the expense of a sensitivity to, and respect for, the wishes, interests, and rights of the people who are to be studied and whose lives are to be changed as the result of the study. This is especially likely to be the case if the people are a foreign group with a remote and alien culture; there is less likelihood of being sensitive to their collective rights, their institutions, their culture, and their future. But this may also be the case if the people are underprivileged and politically impotent as, for example, in the instance of urban renewal research in our American cities. In making these observations, I am not charging that agency-determined research is deliberately callous in disregarding the rights and interests of the subjects under study. Nor am I implying that all agency-determined research is suspect in such disregard. Instead, I merely wish to note the ease with which agency-determined research, as in the case of the Camelot project, can be unwittingly obtuse in considering and respecting such rights and interests.

Indifference to the interests and rights of people under study and the possible harmful effects to them that may come from applying the results of the study to their lives are both legitimate matters of ethical concern and, in given instances, of moral protest. Such an ethical stance seems to have been true of a number of social scientists with regard to the Camelot project. And it was this ethical stance which seems to have been the chief source of the indignation of laymen in the case of the Camelot project. However warranted such ethical doubt and moral protest may have been, my concern is along a different line. I am concerned here with the question of how obtuseness to the rights and interests of subjects affects the integrity of social science — rather than with the ethical consequences of such obtuseness.

In a way that I suspect is not sufficiently realized and appreciated, the integrity of social science requires that its research enterprise enjoy trust and respect generally among people. People are its data — their lives, their activities, and their institutions. The study of the social life of people depends to a large extent on their cooperation, whether in the form of subjects responding to questions or in the form of representatives making records accessible to use, or in the form of a collective body opening given lines of inquiry. While there are features of their life — usually the more superficial aspects — that are open to study without the permission or cooperation of people, social inquiry cannot go very far without their tacit or actual cooperation. This is not the case with the physical and biological sciences — where atoms, inanimate objects, cells or nonhuman organisms cannot "talk back," but it is clearly the case with the social sciences. Not only does social science require the cooperation of people in case of most specific research enterprises, but in the long run its prospects and fate as an ongoing collective endeavor depend on its favorable acceptance by people in general. In this important sense, general trust and respect for social science is integral to its makeup. Without such trust and respect social science cannot achieve its mission — either in specific projects where frank cooperation is called for or in its general over-all and long-run status as a scientific endeavor. There is enjoined on individual social scientists, in a way that few of them realize, the need of developing and preserving such public trust and respect as an indispensable condition for the growth and maturation of their science.

UNWITTING CORRUPTION OF PARTICIPATING SCIENTISTS

In my judgment, the most serious threat of agency-determined research to the integrity of social science lies in the corrupting influence that it may have in blunting or undercutting fidelity to the precepts and ideals of science. In voicing this judgment, I am well aware that the corrupting influence is mainly unintentional, that it is a result in large measure of special conditions currently surrounding agency-determined research, and that the individual scholar or research worker is all too frequently a willing, sometimes eager, accomplice to the corruption. Despite these features — perhaps because of them — it is important to note and consider how agency-determined research permits and in a measure encourages participating social scientists to sacrifice adherence to the fundamental principles of science.

The primary source of the corrupting influence is the lure

that agency-determined research casts in the form of sizable allotments of funds for research and in the form of the prestige that is seemingly yielded by connection with high-level governmental work. Many of today's social scientists are highly susceptible to this lure. There is great pressure among social scientists not merely to do research but to have funds for research; the social scientist today who does not have research funds is likely to be regarded as a lowly figure. Under the pressure to have funds, many are ready to bend their research interests and efforts in the directions laid down by available funds. Further, many attach a significant premium to commanding large-sized funds. To be engaged in a research undertaking of large magnitude, to have a large amount of money for its execution, and to command the assistance of a sizable corps of research workers on the project have become, I think unfortunately, a ponderable standard of successful achievement in social science research today. All too frequently, research scholars are assessed by colleagues, university authorities, and prospective donors in terms of the amount of money for research that they have raised or may raise. Aside from the eminence seemingly yielded by being in command of large funds and in charge of large-scale research undertakings, there are likely to be appreciable subsidiary benefits — secretarial assistance, travel funds, and the prospects of a series of publications as senior author with the collaboration of research workers on the project. All of these advantages and kudos bulk large today in the imagery and aspirations of many social scientists engaged in social research. Agency-determined research is one of the more munificent forms of research support, sometimes the only available source of sizable research support. This is certainly one of the reasons why numbers of social scientists are attracted to agency-determined projects. Of somewhat comparable influence is the prestige that seems to be yielded by connection with high-level governmental work. I suppose that this prestige reflects the importance of government as an institution in contemporary life and that like the latter the importance increases as one moves from the municipal level to the federal level, and on the federal level from lower placed agencies to higher placed agencies. I observe among many of my colleagues in social science a sense of eminence in being connected with high-level federal agencies in either a consultant capacity or a contract research relationship. Many social scientists construe such a connection as a form of professional recognition or as a sign that one is exerting influence in governmental circles. I make these rather trite observations merely to indicate that the sense of prestige of a high-level governmental connection is a further explanation of why agency-determined research is an attraction to many social scientists. The combination of the availability of sizable research support and the conferring of professional prestige lays the basis for a weighty reward system to which many social scientists are responsive.

One may appropriately ask why this attractiveness of agency-determined research should be regarded as a source of corruption to social scientists. The answer, put simple and baldly, is that the participating social scientist who responds to the attraction is likely to subordinate his commitment to the genuine ideals and precepts of scientific endeavor. To enter into agency-determined research requires an acceptance of the terms and conditions of that research. In a general sense, this means fitting into a web of premises, perspectives, expectations, demands, and controls. To accommodate to this web, the participant may be easily led at differing points to sacrifice full observance of the precepts of science. One may get an initial understanding of this matter by thinking of the position of the social scientist who is engaged in his own independent research. Such a person is not beholden to an agency. He does not have to tailor his research to meet the interests and perspectives of the agency. He is free to carve out his own problem and to set his own objective. He is free to question the premises of his own inquiry. He is free to modify his problem and to redirect his research as he proceeds. He is not under pressure to produce "results" within a specified time period. He does not have to put on a front, pretending a knowledge or expertise that he does not possess in order to maintain status in the eyes of project directors or colleagues on the project. He does not have to contend with opportunities to make a showing on the basis of qualities other than the merit of his scientific work. He is free from the entanglements of the reward-system that are likely to attend agency-determined projects.

These observations suggest, by contrast, the conditions which are brought into play in the case of agency-determined research. There are a variety of conditions in the latter that foster deviations from the precepts of scientific endeavor, short-cuts, equivocations, concessions, and pretense. The way and the degree to which such conditions affect participating social scientists vary greatly. But that they are brought into play is a matter that I think is not open to question. Instances such as the following are not uncommon: seeking to learn in advance the interests and preferential schemes of the agency officials in order to ensure favorable reception of one's research project; willingness to make concessions solely to secure desired funds; suppressing one's doubts as to the wisdom of the perspective and aims guiding the project; readiness to undertake a line of research, inside of the agency's scheme, that lies beyond current methodological means; refraining from voicing doubts to agency officials as to whether the desired results are achievable; readiness to embark on research in areas in which one is relatively naïve and uninformed; contentment with merely applying techniques in which one has expertise, without seeking to develop a concrete understanding of the area to which the techniques are applied; pressure to make some sort of showing of "results" in line with the objective of the project in place of admitting negative or inconsequential results; and the pressure, in meeting deadline targets, to dress up one's presentation with a façade of completeness which it does not genuinely possess. Such instances bespeak the corrupting influence that agency-determined research may exercise on the participating social scientist. The participating social scientist is particularly likely to remain mute with regard to the restraints on the freedom of scientific inquiry and on the naturalistic verification of propositions that we have previously noted.

Certainly, the matters which I am discussing were already evident, in part, in the Camelot project even though that project did not get much beyond its initial stage and even though we have nothing approaching a full report on the positions and views of the participants in the project. The scholarly account of the project given by Irving Horowitz suggests the lure of the project to some participants in terms of the sizable amount of research money that it was to make available and the professional distinction that connection with the project was to yield. The account suggests also a muting of doubts among some participants with regard to the aims and premises of the project; a reliance on rationalizations to justify participation despite such doubts; a readiness to participate by some who had little, if any, scholarly knowledge of "insurgency"; a corresponding readiness to participate by others who had scarcely any knowledge, much less intimate knowledge, of the peoples to be studied; and, of course, a general readiness in advance to tailor research projects to fit the over-all design of the project irrespective of the premises undergirding the design. I have no doubt that had the project been allowed to develop and run its course there would have been a series of concessions of scholarly and scientific desires, a cutting of corners here and there to meet the project design and get "results," a showing of expertise in applying techniques in place of free inquiry into the natural world under study, essentially no remonstrations against the restraints on the scientific pursuit of truth that I have discussed earlier, and little protest against ignoring the rights and claims of the peoples under study.

My observations and conjectures in the case of the Camelot project are not intended to impugn the social scientists in that project. I mention them merely to illuminate the more important topic, namely, the corrupting tendencies that are likely to be brought into play in the case of agency-determined research. Such corrupting tendencies would not be particularly grave if they were confined to just an occasional project, as in the case of the Camelot project; nor if they were merely an expression of the occasional ambitious and unscrupulous entrepreneur in our ranks. But this does not seem to be the case. Instead, the ominous character of the corrupting tendencies is that they may become implanted as a normal and acceptable practice in the structure of social science research. We should bear in mind two things. First, that the corrupting tendencies operate largely unseen, mainly in the restricted area of private experience; they escape the corrective restraints that would more readily come into play if they were easily detectable by public scrutiny. Second, that the individual social scientist, like other human beings, is likely to accept and follow what has the guise of legitimized practice among his colleagues. If he suspects that they are cutting corners to "produce results," to gain distinction, and to advance in their careers, and if there is no clear and decisive professional condemnation of such procedures, he is understandably likely to succumb to what he judges to be a common practice. What is needed is a strong professional ethic that will fortify the individual in adherence to scientific ideals and precepts.

CONCLUDING OBSERVATIONS

The foregoing discussion indicates what seems to me to be the real lessons of the Camelot episode for sociology and the social sciences. The calamitous feature of that episode is not the threat of a reduction in the share of federal largess alloted to sociology nor in a setback in sociology's place of influence in governmental circles. Nor should the episode be checked off as merely an unfortunate instance of mismanagement, to be avoided in the future; this short-sighted view with its unwarranted scape-goating of the project's director is singularly obtuse in seeing the real significance of the episode. Still further, the condemnation of the project on ethical grounds, however warranted, reflects the posture of the citizen — a posture that the scientist is privileged to assume — but does not deal with the special import of the episode for social science itself. This import, in my judgment, lies in the threats that are posed to the integrity of scientific endeavor. As I have tried to explain, these threats occur in the limitations that are imposed on the pursuit of scientific truth, in the disregard for the rights and claims of the people under study, and in the corrupting tendencies which may lead social scientists to sacrifice full adherence to the ideals and precepts of the scientific enterprise.

These threats exist in varying degree in the case of what I have designated as agency-determined research. It would be absurd to contend that they arise in all instances of such research or that they bulk-up large in most instances. I make no such contention. But I do think that it is necessary to be always alert to the likelihood of their play, particularly in projects of crucial importance. Social scientists need scarcely to be reminded of the prospect of a continuing expansion in agency-determined research and of the likelihood that much of such research will reflect the cast of mounting nationalistic concerns. Before such prospects, social scientists should be on guard to protect the integrity of scientific endeavor.

The development of the proper safeguards and of the necessary spirit of vigilance is, in my judgment, the function of the professional organizations of social scientists. From where else is the development to come? Such bodies should accept the responsibility of clarifying for their members the nature of the scientific ethic that is called for in these disciplines. Such clarification should certainly emphasize the need of understanding and respecting the character of the scientific enterprise in its totality — and not merely in some partial aspect such as observing the criteria covering the application of a special technique. The responsible professional bodies should also identify the typical conditions in present-day social research that are conducive to the sacrifice of the scientific ethic. And, finally, the professional bodies should dedicate themselves to a continual cultivation of the scientific ethic among their members. In these ways, we may hope for a bending of agency-determined research to meet the requirements of the scientific ethic rather than the reverse relationship.

PART IV

THE POLITICAL RESPONSE

Dante B. Fascell

U.S. House of Representatives

Behavioral Sciences and the National Security

More than three years ago, in the course of a stimulating session with the late Edward R. Murrow, the House Foreign Affairs Subcommittee on International Organizations and Movements launched an inquiry into the operations that comprise the fourth dimension of our foreign policy — the dimension that is concerned with the U.S. image abroad and with influencing the attitudes of the peoples and of the governments of foreign countries.

In the months, then years, that followed, we held numerous hearings, probing into the organization, the management, and the direction of a multitude of governmental programs designed to lend support to the diplomatic, economic, and military components of our foreign policy.

We also consulted extensively with individuals and organizations in the private sector — with communications-media specialists, with behavioral and other social scientists, and with the representatives of American voluntary organizations and of U.S. firms conducting business abroad.

Our findings and conclusions, as well as our recommendations for actions that we deemed to be in our national interest, were outlined in a series of reports and studies published by the Subcommittee. I shall refer to some of those publications in the course of my remarks.

One area that was of particular interest to our subcommittee in this investigation deals with the role of the behavioral sciences — with what they tell us about human attitudes and motivations and how this knowledge is being — or can be — applied to governmental undertakings designed to carry out our foreign policy objectives.

SERIOUS SHORTCOMINGS

Much to our surprise and regret, we found that the situation prevailing in this area — insofar as governmental operations and our government's relations with the academic community are concerned — is in a state of considerable disrepair.

We found, for example, that a disproportionately small part of our government's annual 16-billion dollar outlay on research and development is being devoted to research in the fields of the social and behavioral sciences — and that funds spent on foreign-policy-related research account for only a fraction of the latter amount.

We also found that the bulk of research relevant to the achievement of our national objectives on the international scene is being conducted by agencies that do not have direct responsibility for the formulation and execution of our foreign policy.

We found, further, that coordination between governmental research programs in these fields was inadequate — that duplication and research gaps mar the results of our national effort in this area — and that the allocation of scarce resources, both manpower and financial, is not related to any orderly, long-term projection of our national needs and resulting priorities.

We found, in brief, that our effort in the field of the social and behavioral sciences is fragmented and uncoordinated — and that this is creating increasing problems for the government as well as for the academic and professional communities that have endeavored to assist in meeting our national requirements.

Most of our findings on this subject were detailed in two reports — in House Report 1352, of the 88th Congress, entitled "Ideological Operations and Foreign Policy," and in House Report 1224, of the 89th Congress, entitled "Behavioral Sciences and the National Security."

REMEDIES PROPOSED

In submitting our findings to the Congress, our subcommittee made a number of specific recommendations for correcting the disorder that exists in this area.

Some of those recommendations appear to have produced encouraging — although very modest — results.

In 1964, for example, an interagency Foreign Area Research Coordination Group (FAR) was established under the chairmanship of a Department of State representative to serve as a forum for the interchange of information between government agencies sponsoring research relating to foreign affairs.

Again — last year — following the widespread publicity arising out of Project Camelot and the initiation of hearings on this subject by our subcommittee, two steps were taken — one within the Department of Defense and the other on an interagency basis — to reduce the risk of government sponsorship of foreign affairs research that could adversely affect our foreign relations:

The Department of Defense moved to designate a central point for the coordination and clearance of all research relating to foreign affairs, performed by or for the military establishment.

And the Foreign Research Council, created within the

Department of State, was given the task of reviewing all government-sponsored research relating to foreign affairs.

These and other steps, while helpful in some respects, fall considerably short of curing the basic problems to which I just alluded.

BILLS BEING INTRODUCED

For this reason, I am today introducing three separate bills in the House of Representatives, with the hope of stimulating discussion — and constructive action — to further remedy the flaws that continue to plague our government's approach to the social and behavioral sciences.

These bills result from our subcommitte's continuing investigation of the formulation and implementation of our foreign policy. Two of them are based directly on the recommendations embodied in our subcommittee's last report on "Behavioral Sciences and the National Security." Nevertheless, all three of them have implications which transcend the field of foreign policy. They should be of interest to social and behavioral scientists and governmental agencies specializing in other fields.

I shall describe the three bills briefly and then include their full texts in the Record at the conclusion of my remarks.

WHITE HOUSE CONFERENCE ON THE SOCIAL AND BEHAVIORAL SCIENCES

My first bill proposes the establishment of a Presidential Commission to prepare the groundwork for a White House Conference on the Social and Behavioral Sciences.

Pursuant to the bill, the commission would be appointed by the President and confirmed by the Senate.

It would be composed of twelve members selected from private life among recognized leaders in the social and behavioral sciences.

The purpose of the commission would be to conduct such studies and investigations as it may deem necessary to make recommendations to the President with respect to the time for convening a White House Conference on the Social and Behavioral Sciences, the subject matters to be included in the agenda of such a conference, the individuals and organizations to be invited to participate, and related issues.

The commission is directed to submit its report within one year after the enactment of the authorizing legislation.

To aid it in its work, the Office of Science and Technology in the Executive Office of the President is authorized to provide the commission with the necessary staff assistance.

This is the first step. It is directed to the examination of our national effort in the social and behavioral sciences. It is also intended to bring to bear upon government policy, the knowledge, the experience, and the insights of the leading social and behavioral scientists in our country.

OFFICE OF BEHAVIORAL SCIENCES

My second proposal calls for the establishment, in the Executive Office of the President, of the Office of Social Sciences.

This proposed office is modeled on the already existing Office of Science and Technology, which advises the President with respect to scientific policy and matters having a bearing on the national security and welfare.

The director of the new office, created under my bill, would have a triple assignment:

First, it would be his responsibility to develop and encourage the pursuit of a national policy for the promotion of basic research and education in the social and behavioral sciences;

second, he would be charged with the task of evaluating research programs in the social and behavioral sciences undertaken by agencies of the federal government;

and, third, he would assist the President as he may request with respect to the coordination of federal activities in the social and behavioral sciences.

NATIONAL BEHAVIORAL SCIENCES FOUNDATION

My third bill deals with a proposal that has been discussed for a number of years but has never been implemented: a proposal to establish a National Social Science Foundation.

The bill would create such a foundation as an independent federal agency.

The foundation's affairs would be managed by a board composed of twelve members appointed by the President for six-year terms, an executive committee elected by the board, and a director. All of these presidential appointments would be subject to Senate confirmation.

The functions of the foundation can be summarized as follows:

first, to initiate and support basic research and programs to strengthen research potential in the social and behavioral sciences;

second, to award scholarships and graduate fellowships in these fields;

third, to foster the interchange of information among social and behavioral scientists in the United States and foreign countries;

fourth, to evaluate the status and the needs of the various social and behavioral sciences, and to correlate its own programs with those undertaken by agencies of the federal government, by individuals, and by public and private research groups;

fifth, to maintain a current register of social and behavioral scientists and technical personnel, and in other ways to provide a central clearinghouse for the collection, interpretation and analysis of data on the availability of, and the current and projected need for, information in the social and behavioral sciences;

and, sixth, to ascertain, and report to the President and the Congress, the flow of federal funds for research in the social and behavioral sciences.

There are many other provisions in this legislation that

deal with the general authority of the foundation, international activities, security matters, personnel, coordination with foreign policy, and other subjects.

TO BEGIN A DIALOGUE

I wish to make clear that the three bills I have authored are not intended to abolish any existing institutions or programs — to disrupt any projects that are underway — or to supplant any other efforts that may be undertaken to correct the shortcomings that have been of concern to our subcommittee.

I want to repeat that my sole purpose in introducing this legislation is to begin a dialogue between the United States Government and the academic and professional communities on how best to resolve the problems that confront us in the area of the social and behavioral sciences.

I am not wedded to the specific provisions outlined in my bills. Some of them may prove to be unnecessary and should then be discarded. Others may need to be modified. Still other proposals, not mentioned in my bills, may warrant inclusion in this legislation before it is enacted.

We must, however, begin some place. And the bills which I am introducing are intended as such a beginning.

I hope that this effort will be accepted in the spirit in which it was conceived and carried out.

I hope that interested individuals — in the Congress, in the executive branch of our government, and in the private sector — will take up these bills, study them, and offer us their views and comments.

Together, we should be able to resolve this very complex situation to the mutual advantage of our government and of the academic and professional communities, thereby strengthening our nation's ability to cope with the multitude of problems that confront us at this troubled juncture of history

FINDINGS

I. Project Camelot

During recent years, Communist support of "wars of national liberation" and U.S. commitments to aid the developing nations of the free world to meet this threat propelled our Military Establishment into an expanding involvement in research relating to foreign areas and foreign populations. Noting the extent of this involvement, the Director of Defense Research and Engineering of the Department of Defense on April 24, 1964, requested the Defense Science Board to conduct a study of Defense research and development programs "relating to ethnic and other motivational factors involved in the causation and conduct of small wars . . . ." The report produced by that study disclosed various deficiencies in the behavioral sciences research program of the Department of Defense. Among others, the report cited the need to improve "the knowledge and understanding in depth of the internal cultural, economic and political conditions that generate conflicts between national groups," urged increased emphasis on the collection of initial primary data in overseas locations, and criticized the Military Establishment for "failure to organize appropriate multidisciplinary programs and to use the techniques of such related fields as operations research."

Prompted by these findings, the Department of the Army, having the responsibility for the administration of the military assistance program as well as for research, planning, and organization for counterinsurgency and limited wars, embarked upon what became known as Project Camelot. Working through a contractor, the Special Operations Research Office (SORO) at American University, the Army began to prepare a project which sought to integrate many disparate research problems in pursuit of a single operational objective by attempting to develop a generalized model of a developing society. The purpose of this project was to produce a better understanding of how the processes of social change operate in the developing countries. On the one hand, Project Camelot was intended to assist in identifying the forerunners of social breakdown and the resultant opportunity for Communist penetration and possible takeover; on the other hand, it was also expected to produce basic information which would furnish some guidelines with respect to actions that might be taken by or with the indigenous governments to foster constructive change within a framework of relative order and stability.

The first phase of Project Camelot — the phase which was to be completed this past summer — was devoted to developing the research design, together with recommendations as to where the overseas fieldwork should be done. The preliminary proposals were then to be submitted for review by the Army Research Staff, by the Department of Defense, and by other government agencies, including the Department of State. Subject to their recommendations and final approval, the actual research work was to commence either late this year or in 1966. However, Project Camelot never passed phase 1. While the preparatory work was going on, a representative of the contractor, traveling to Chile on personal business, attempted to ascertain the interest and resources available in that country in order to determine whether Chile should be included in the tentative program of research, or the research design. A distorted version of his activities and of the project appeared in a local newspaper, reported to be pro-Communist, and led to considerable adverse publicity in Chile, elsewhere abroad, and in the United States. The American Ambassador to Chile, having no previous knowledge of Project Camelot, protested to Washington and the resulting furor prompted the Army to cancel the project on August 2, 1965.

II. MILITARY SPONSORSHIP OF RESEARCH RELATING TO FOREIGN POLICY

The issue which was brought to the fore by the experience of Project Camelot and which is indeed central to the entire government-sponsored behavioral sciences research program in the field of foreign affairs, is whether it is necessary and proper for the Military Establishment — or, for that matter, for any other government agency — to engage in activities of this type except at the direction of the authorities entrusted with the responsibility for the conduct of U.S. foreign policy. This issue was raised by our subcommittee almost 2 years ago and we continue to be of the opinion that institutional arrangements must be worked out which will insure that the scope and the direction of our governmental effort in this field receive full and continuous attention from the appropriate high-level foreign policy officials.

This does not mean that the Military Establishment should be denied the informational and research tools which are necessary for the proper fulfillment of its assigned role in the conduct of our foreign relations. On the contrary, events of recent years have clearly demonstrated the pertinency of behavioral sciences research to the effective implementation of the military assistance program, the Army's civic action undertakings abroad, and the provision of assistance to countries requesting help to combat Communist-inspired insurgency and guerilla warfare.

In this regard, we must remember that since World War II, the foreign relations of the United States have increasingly involved the developing nations of Asia, Africa, and Latin America. In all of those areas, independent nations have been struggling against great odds to establish stable governments and to advance the task of economic development. In the meantime, the major Communist powers have sought to exploit the instability and economic problems in these nations to expand their control over large parts of the world. Khrushchev's statement of January 6, 1961, pledging the Soviet

Union's support for the so-called wars of national liberation, elevated these subversive activities to the level of official policy, consciously and intensively pursued by the Communist powers.

The State Department, the Defense Department, and other key agencies of our government increasingly have had to turn their attention to helping the developing countries meet this threat. Because of its involvement in military assistance activities — and because the Communist threat encompasses the political, economic, social as well as military spheres — our Military Establishment's missions in this area have become much broader than the traditional mission of providing U.S. Armed Forces for the national defense.

To carry out these missions, our Military Establishment has concerned itself not only with the development of weapons and other military hardware but also with the human element involved in an effective defense against Communist subversive warfare. This requirement was explained by Mr. Seymour J. Deitchman, Special Assistant for Counterinsurgency in the Department of Defense, in the course of his testimony before our subcommittee, in these words:

. . . whether the military is involved in direct conflict or in preinsurgency military assistance, U.S. military people all over the world must work with and help local military personnel at all levels plan and implement the counterinsurgency programs. The war itself revolves around the allegiance and support of the local population. The Defense Department has therefore recognized that part of its research and development efforts to support counterinsurgency operations must be oriented toward the people, United States and foreign, involved in this type of war; and the DOD has called on the types of scientists — anthropologists, psychologists, sociologists, political scientists, economists — whose professional orientation to human behavior would enable them to make useful contributions in this area.

To sum up, the U.S. Military Establishment, in carrying out its assigned missions, continually comes into contact with individuals and institutions in foreign countries. Our own military personnel abroad — some 1 million today —

must draw upon knowledge obtained through behavioral sciences research to avoid situations and activities which can cause friction, antagonize local foreign populations, and create other difficulties. At the same time, "wars of national liberation" with which the free world is confronted, are unlike conventional wars, and new instruments are needed to fight them. There are no fixed frontlines in those conflicts. The problem here involves the behavioral patterns of the insurgents as well as of the people of the nation where the war is being fought. To do their job in assisting the nations defending themselves against Communist subversion, U.S. military personnel — and the people who are being aided — must understand the motivations of the enemy, its weak points and its strengths. Behavioral sciences research helps to provide this basic information. It constitutes one of the vital tools in the arsenal of the free societies.

III. SOME BASIC PROBLEMS

Nevertheless, as the recent experience with Project Camelot has demonstrated, some U.S. research efforts can provoke extremely unfavorable reactions abroad not only from the Communists and their sympathizers but also from academic and political groups that are generally friendly to the United States. There exists in every country a sensitivity to foreigners probing into delicate social and political matters. Also, the level of sensitivity varies according to who does the research and its subject matter. Careful attention to these factors is certainly indicated in the allocation of responsibilities for research on subjects related to our foreign policy, in the preparation of research designs, and in the selection of foreign areas for on-the-spot field investigations.

Further problems arise when the military become involved in foreign affairs research and when the scope of such undertakings appears to exceed the bounds of the legitimate interests of a particular research project's sponsors. In both instances, the motives of the sponsors often are suspect. In some countries there is a strong aversion on the part of the local population to any involvement by the military in social and political matters. These considerations appear to have played a part in the disposition of Project Camelot. That project, as mentioned previously, addressed itself to the basic dynamics of change in the developing countries. This subject, as pointed out by Secretary of State Dean Rusk in the course of his testimony before our subcommittee, "was and is important not only, and not even primarily, to the military services or to the other United States government departments and agencies but to all who are concerned with the peaceful economic, social, and political progress of the less developed countries." It is not entirely surprising, therefore, that the U.S. Army's sponsorship of Project Camelot aroused some concern. What is more to the point, however, is that others who have more central responsibility for the conduct of our foreign affairs and who are directly involved in the task of promoting economic and social progress in the developing countries had not initiated this type of research themselves.

The problems attendant upon government sponsorship of research in foreign affairs are not limited to the adverse reactions which such undertakings may produce abroad. Here again, the identity of the agencies sponsoring the research is important. At present, the bulk of research on subjects relating to U.S. foreign policy continues to be conducted or sponsored by our Military Establishment. Secretary Rusk testified that approximately $30 million is spent each year by the U.S. government on research in the behavioral and social sciences and that the Department of State accounts for less than 1 percent of this annual outlay, even though this type of research can have far-reaching impact on foreign affairs. We should like to reiterate that such obvious imbalance in the allocation of resources raises some serious questions regarding its potential impact on the formulation and execution of U.S. foreign policy.

Further, whenever the federal government becomes a powerful sponsor of policy research in our universities, the situation is not without some risks to our academic community and, ultimately, to the entire nation. At a minimum, careful planning is indicated if the increasing size of the federal effort is not to distort the direction of research, lower its quality, or erode the independence of our private scholars and academic institutions.

IV. COORDINATION OF GOVERNMENT-SPONSORED RESEARCH

In view of the above-outlined considerations, effective coordination of the government's research in the behavioral sciences under direct supervision of the authorities responsible for the conduct of our foreign policy is certainly imperative. Some progress in this direction is finally being accomplished.

On the military side, coordination within the Department of Defense has been attempted through information exchange, joint planning, discussion, and recommendations to and adjudication by the Director of Defense Research and Engineering. More recently, the Army was assigned the responsibility for coordinating the Military Establishment's research effort in the behavioral and social sciences applied to counterinsurgency. No single military department, however, may order another department to perform, or desist from, any project. A significant development in this regard occurred on July 12, 1965, when the Secretary of Defense directed that "all studies done in or for the Department of Defense, the conduct of which may affect the relations of the United States with foreign governments, are to be cleared with the office of the Assistant Secretary of Defense (International Security Affairs) before they are initiated." The latter office thus became the major contact point in this field of research between the Defense Department and the State Department.

On an interagency basis, the Foreign Area Research Coordination Group (FAR), chaired by a representative of the Department of State, has served during the past year as an instrument for the exchange of information between government agencies sponsoring research relating to foreign affairs. The Foreign Area Research Coordination Group has no budget of its own to support research and has no authority to request agencies to conduct particular tasks or studies. According to the testimony of Secretary Rusk, "its present terms of reference specifically forbid it from seeking to veto or to direct the research of any agency. Its major accomplishment to date has been in the area of improved communication, both among contract research administrators and substantive research specialists in the Government." In a move applauded by our subcommittee, the Department of State is currently upgrading the level of Foreign Area Research Coordination Group and initiating efforts within it to work out, on a voluntary basis, some agreement on the priority of research tasks in certain areas.

Within the Department of State, the External Research Staff systematically collects and disseminates information on private and government-sponsored research related to foreign affairs. In addition, a direct outgrowth of the Project Camelot episode, the recommendations of this subcommittee, and President Johnson's letter to the Secretary of State dated August 2, 1965,[1] has been the establishment, in September 1965, of the Foreign Research Council. Chaired by the Director of the Bureau of Intelligence and Research, the Council will include a member of the Policy Planning Council, a member of the Deputy Under Secretary's office (Politico-Military Affairs), and, as necessary and appropriate, representatives of the State Department's geographic bureaus. The functions of the newly established Council will include a review of all government-sponsored research relating to foreign affairs, the exercise of a veto power over individual

[1] The President's letter directed the Secretary of State to establish procedures to insure that the United States government may not undertake to sponsor foreign area research which, in the judgment of the Secretary of State, would adversely affect U.S. foreign relations. The text of the letter appears on p. 107 of the hearings on "Behavioral Sciences and the National Security."

projects, and the formulation of Department of State policy with respect to the criteria, the priorities, and the implementation of this type of research.

V RECOMMENDATIONS

The above-described arrangements, particularly the establishment of a focal point for the clearance of all foreign policy-related research in the behavioral sciences, represent a substantial advancement over the situation which prevailed in this field when this subcommittee's report of April 1964 was issued. Nevertheless, they appear to us deficient in two important respects:

First, while the coordination of foreign-policy-oriented research is being greatly improved, this effort still lacks an effective direction-giving system. There is no provision in the existing arrangements for the determination of needs and the setting of priorities relevant to an effective implementation of U.S. foreign policy. Under the current system, each department is still free to go in its own direction, to establish priorities and parcel out tasks on the basis of its own particular needs and inclinations. Neither the voluntary and limited charter of Foreign Area Research Coordination Group nor the veto power of the new Foreign Research Council resolves this difficulty.

Second, there is no single focal point within this growing Government-wide effort for a sustained and fruitful collaboration with private scholars and the academic community. The Department of Defense, it is true, receives counsel from the Defense Science Board which, at least on occasion, includes representation of the behavioral sciences. The relationship here, however, is limited by the Military Establishment's primary concern with military matters. The Arms Control and Disarmament Agency has its own Social Sciences Advisory Board which focuses upon subjects of interest to that Agency. The Department of State, through the External Research Staff and other offices in the Bureau of

Intelligence and Research, compiles information about private research pertaining to foreign affairs and, as necessary, seeks the advice of individual specialists on particular problems that the Department may encounter in the field of behavioral sciences research. These and related arrangements are in themselves specialized and fragmentary.

To help correct these deficiencies, the Subcommittee recommends that there be established an Office of the Behavioral Sciences Adviser to the President. Such office would provide the direction essential to an effective government-wide effort in the field of behavioral sciences, develop mutually beneficial long-term relationships between the government and the academic community, strengthen both the formulation and the implementation of foreign policy, and assure orderly development of the government's programs in this field. (*Representative H. R. Gross does not concur in the above recommendation.*)

In addition, it is our view that a very useful purpose would be served by the convocation of a White House Conference on Behavioral Sciences to examine our national effort in these fields and to bring to bear upon government policy the knowledge, the experience, and the insights of the leading social scientists of our country. We recommend that urgent consideration be given to this proposal.

Finally, we wish to reiterate our earlier recommendations made by this subcommittee in 1964 that the civilian agencies' — primarily the State Department's and AID's — input into behavioral sciences research be substantially augmented and that effective methods be devised — such as the use of automatic data processing equipment — to modernize the flow and handling of information derived through such research in order to bring it within reach of the officials responsible for making foreign policy decisions. Without such improvements, research activities themselves, no matter how productive, will be unable to exert maximum impact both on policy formulation and on our operational programs in the field of foreign policy.

VI. CONCLUDING REMARKS

The structural reforms which we recommend may not, of themselves, cure the disorder of our foreign policy research program. The latter, as we pointed out, is symptomatic of the deeply rooted problem of maldistribution of responsibilities for certain key foreign policy operations. To remedy this maldistribution, further thought needs to be given to the assignment of operational responsibilities to executive departments and agencies on the basis of their ability most effectively to achieve our international objectives. Research activities should always be related to each department's or agency's specific operational responsibilities. The structural reforms which we have proposed will facilitate the achievement of these tasks — but will not supplant them.

With respect to the objectives of our foreign policy undertakings, it seems to us that too little attention has been paid in the past to the long-range requirements of economic and social development in the developing countries. In the long run, the attainment of these objectives will depend in large part on the development of the social structures of these countries — on the proliferation and maturation of the many forms of group and social organization which can assure popular participation in the development of these countries and provide the means for bringing to bear on their respective national undertakings the talents, the aspirations, and the political convictions of their people. Too frequently, there has been a tendency for U.S. economic, military, and related assistance to be programed without regard to the degree of progress achieved in developing effective democratic institutions in the aided countries. Unless progress toward true self-government by the people accompanies economic development, a large part of our aid effort may not produce the desired results.

We wish to reiterate, therefore, that the agencies primarily responsible for our economic aid and development programs should take more active interest — both through social science research and through positive support of the incipient social and economic organizations in the developing countries — in assisting the development of the social fabric of those countries.

There is one more point we wish to make which relates to Project Camelot. In addition to the basic issues discussed in this report, the course of events which led to the termination of this project has been of some concern to us. We cannot condone the type of interdepartmental rivalry which was evidenced in the steady stream of "leaks" originating in the State Department, undoubtedly intended to preclude any other disposition of this proposed undertaking. This type of contention between agencies of our government can hardly serve to advance the interests of our foreign policy or of our national security.

Senator J. W. Fulbright

U.S. Senate

*America in an Age of Revolution**

There are moments in world affairs when a new atmosphere and a new direction can be perceived for the first time. I am apprehensive that we are now at such a turning point in international relations. I fear that we may be moving from a time of adjustment and accommodation to a time of tension and conflict, from a time of international community building to one of chauvinism and militant nationalism, from a time of peaceful civilian programs for the advancement of human welfare to a time of armed might for the suppression of aggression, subversion, or revolutions.

Change is in the air. A year or two ago, people concerned with foreign policy were talking of Atlantic community and bridges to the East, of India's five-year plan and of land reform in Latin America. None of these ideas have been abandoned; they are still being pursued with varying degrees of enthusiasm and energy. But they are no longer the principal focus of public and official interest; instead we are preoccupied with matters of military escalation and counterinsurgency in southeast Asia, with the unforeseen consequences of a military intervention in Latin America, with warnings and threats among the great powers.

---

* Reprinted with the permission of the author and the *St. Louis Post-Dispatch*.

Nowhere is the new atmosphere more in evidence than in the nation's universities. On the one hand, students and professors conduct marches and teach-ins to protest the war in Vietnam. On the other hand, the campuses are inhabited by proliferating institutes and centers with awe-inspiring names that use vast government contract funds to produce ponderous studies of "insurgency" and "counterinsurgency" — studies which, behind their opaque language, look very much like efforts to develop "scientific" techniques for the anticipation and prevention of revolutions, without regard for the possibility that some revolutions may be justified or even desirable.

The spirit of crusading anticommunism, which poisoned our politics in the early fifties, is once again on the rise, threatening to undermine the hard-won gains of the past decade toward better East-West relations. Our policies have been distorted again and again since the end of World War II by a tendency to confuse Communist ideology with Communist imperialism. It is the latter which threatens us, just as German and Japanese imperialism threatened us twenty-five years ago. Because Russia was expansionist under Stalin and China is expansionist under Mao, we have inferred that all Communist regimes by their very nature are expansionist and that, therefore, they must be regarded as threats to our security regardless of how they actually behave.

Experience of the last twenty years shows that some Communist regimes are aggressive and others are not and that all, including the Soviet Union, are subject to change. This is not a theory but an inference from experience. Unless we act on this inference and make the clearest possible distinction between the ideology and the actual behavior of Communist states, war is virtually certain to result. We must recognize, as many Americans are not now recognizing, that Communist totalitarianism as practiced within Communist countries, though profoundly distasteful to us, is no more a threat to our security than the right-wing authoritarianism of Spain or South Africa. Our prospects for avoiding a third world war depend largely on our willingness to distinguish between ideology and policy and to act toward Communist countries according to how they act toward us.

The critical question for the months ahead is whether it will be possible to limit the effects of the war in Vietnam or whether it is going to undermine past achievements in East-West relations and draw the great powers into a new round of conflict. Unless both sides are able to resist mounting pressures for expanding the Vietnamese war, the Soviet Union and the United States may be drawn into the direct confrontation that both want most fervently to avoid.

We are threatened with a situation somewhat like that of 1914, when the great powers of Europe, largely to prove their loyalty to weak and irresponsible dependent states, allowed themselves to be drawn into a conflict that none of them really desired. In the coming months it will take a high order of statesmanship in Moscow and in Washington to save the two great powers from being drawn toward catastrophe.

Our policy makers face the task of resisting pressures that are certain to mount while the war insists upon an undiscriminating "tough" policy toward all Communist countries. Difficult as it will be, we must apply the test of policy rather than ideology, and bear in mind that the Communist countries of Eastern Europe have had little to do with the war in Vietnam and that the Soviet Union itself has been restrained in support of its North Vietnamese ally.

We must bear these facts in mind and we must act on them. We can alleviate the strains on East-West relations by negotiating at Geneva for an underground nuclear test ban and a nuclear nonproliferation agreement and by expanding our commercial and cultural relations with those Communist countries such as Rumania that demonstrate a desire to pursue independent foreign policies.

At the same time, in addition to repeating our willingness to negotiate an end to the Vietnamese war, we might also begin to indicate what we would consider honorable terms for ending the war. Looking beyond the war in southeast Asia, it would seem to be time for us to reevaluate the policy toward

China that has proved so unsatisfactory over the past decade.

A new emphasis in American foreign policy is apparent in our relations with Latin America as well as in our relations with the Communist countries. Since President Kennedy took office in 1961, the United States has been concerned both with economic development and social reform in Latin America and with the need for security against Communist subversion.

Our government remains concerned with both social reform and security, but in recent months, partly because of the influence on our thinking of the war in Vietnam, there has been a marked shift in emphasis. We are not hearing much about the Alliance for Progress these days, although it was reported prior to the Dominican crisis to be doing quite well. Instead United States officials seem to be preoccupied with the danger of Communist infiltration of reform movements in Latin America and accordingly are showing more interest in counterinsurgency techniques than in housing and road building and land and tax reform.

• • • • • • •

A recent expression of this altered emphasis was the so-called "Project Camelot," a study conducted by a research organization at the American University with funds provided by the Department of the Army. This ill-advised project was purportedly studying the likelihood of insurgent movements developing in Chile and means of combating them. As any sensible observer might have anticipated, the Chilean government — and the United States ambassador in Santiago — took offense at this project, with its implicit connotations of counterrevolution and possible intervention. Happily, Project Camelot was promptly canceled (and in fact never got under way in Chile), but there are indications that similar projects are planned for other countries.

It would be a signal service to the countries involved and to the national interests of the United States if the intellectual resources devoted to these dubious "studies" of insurgency and counterinsurgency were diverted to the more constructive projects of the Alliance for Progress — projects of social and economic reform that offer the only real hope of avoiding violent revolution.

In their concern with matters of security, some of our officials seem to have forgotten that virtually all reform movements attract some Communist support, that there is an important difference between Communist support and Communist control of a political movement, that it is quite possible to compete with the Communists for influence in a reform movement rather than abandon it to them, and, most important of all, that in the long run economic development and social justice are the only reliable security against Communist subversion.

There is a growing feeling in some parts of the world of a new direction in American foreign policy. It is felt that after a period of sympathy and support for political and social reform in the emerging nations the United States has set itself against these forces and has made itself the champion of the militarists, reactionaries, and privileged minorities. Somehow the term "counterinsurgency," of which we hear so much, sounds very much like "counterrevolution."

This view of American policy is substantially inaccurate, but people act not on objective truth but on what they believe to be true. In fact, what Americans fear is not social reform but Communist aggression. It is our misfortune that we have confused Communist imperialism with Communist ideology and Communist ideology with any reformist doctrine or movement that attracts Communist support. Thus, contrary to our own will and intentions, we sometimes find ourselves arrayed against the forces of political and social reform and on the side of reactionaries whose ideas and actions are an affront to our own democratic values.

The aspiration to national dignity and social justice is the most powerful force in the world today. It would be a tragedy of enormous proportions if the United States, in fear of communism, were to allow the Communists to make themselves the champions of nationalism and social reform throughout the world. Our interests and our ideals require us not to abandon the field in exaggerated fear of communism and its power but to compete with the Communists as vigorously as we can in the advancement of the world-wide aspiration to national dignity and social justice.

This is not and cannot be easy for us. We are not, as we proclaim in Fourth of July speeches, the "most truly revolutionary nation in the world." We are much closer to being the most truly unrevolutionary nation in the world. We are rich and satisfied in a world of desperate poverty and human degradation. We delude ourselves when we suppose that our own revolution has any real relevance to the profound social upheavals that are taking place today in Latin America and Asia and Africa. We delude ourselves further if we suppose that the forces of change in the emerging nations are likely to be consummated everywhere without violence and profound social dislocation.

Our own revolution was a conservative one in the sense that it represented a successful effort by relatively free and prosperous people to recover traditional rights that had recently been infringed. Thereafter the American people acquired wealth and power by the relatively peaceful habitation of an almost empty continent. The point that we must grasp about our own experience is its uniqueness.

The social revolutions of twentieth century Latin America and Asia and Africa are not sober efforts to recover traditional rights but angry movements by people who have always been poor to acquire the national dignity and social justice that they have never known. These are total revolutions, like the French Revolution of 1789 and the Russian Revolution of 1917 and not like the American Revolution of 1776.

There are no empty and fertile plains waiting for cultivation in India; there is no promised land in Pakistan or Egypt. There are only great numbers of people with limited resources and unlimited needs. They have come awake in the twentieth century, and they are making revolutions. The aims and ideals of these movements may be similar to those of the American Revolution, but their nature and intensity are profoundly different.

We are required by our interests and our ideals to understand things of which we have little experience and to accept and support profound social change, sometimes by means that are contrary to our traditions and our strong preferences. We, an unrevolutionary nation, are required to make ourselves the friends and supporters of fundamental change, with or without revolution. For a time, we were moving toward doing so, but in recent months we appear to be moving in a different direction.

It is not an easy thing for a nation like the United States to associate itself with revolutionary change, but neither is it impossible, and a great deal depends upon our doing so. Whether our own domestic values are to be conserved in the world or are to be swept away in a tide of violent upheaval is likely to be determined by America's own ability and willingness to support social revolution.

Theodore R. Vallance

Special Operations Research Office, Army

Project Camelot: An Interim Postlude

Project Camelot, the largest, most ambitious and probably the most widely heard of — I will not say most widely known — social science research project of the early 1960's came to a sudden halt on July 8, 1965, at the direction of the Secretary of Defense. The activities immediately preceding and following the termination of the Project, including the hearings in Congress, have been widely reported, vehemently discussed, frequently misunderstood.

It is interesting to note that practically all of what has been written or said publicly pro or con about Project Camelot has been said by social scientists or administrators only marginally connected with the project, by journalists working on close deadlines with limited information and frequently a predetermined point of view, and by an occasional professional science writer seriously concerned with both accuracy of fact and significance of issues. There has been as yet no extensive statement by anyone authoritatively associated with the project. I hope that as director of the organization in which Camelot was being developed I can add a few facts not yet recorded, correct a few misimpressions that have been recorded, and continue a helpful speculation about the essential lessons that may be gleaned from the experience. It should not be assumed that these subsequent comments reflect all the facts or information available to officials in the Department of the Army.

So far as concerns the general story, this has been on the whole fairly well told in the Horowitz (1965) article as it first appeared in *Trans-action*, including the general statement of what the project was all about, the chronicling of the comedy of errors in Chile that led to the ultimate demise of the project, and most of the élan of the project staff itself. Report No. 4, "Behavioral Science and the National Security," of the Fascell Committee, parts of which are reprinted in this [book], contains additional detail. Therefore, my own summary here of the objectives and general configuration of the project will be very brief, skimming over the 2,000 pages of design and conceptual papers that were prepared leading to the research plan whose implementation was to begin a scant two months beyond the cancellation date.

To summarize the design, then, Project Camelot was a large-scale multidisciplinary study of the early phase in the development of internal war potential and the effects of government actions vis-à-vis that development. The objective of the study was to analyze the feasibility of developing and testing a system for analyzing a country that would provide the means to (*a*) identify and measure indicators and causes of potential internal conflict; (*b*) determine the effect of various government actions to influence that potential; and (*c*) obtain, store, and retrieve the information required for the above system to be operational.

It was planned as an objective, nonnormative study concerned with *what is or might be* and *not* with what *ought to be*.

A balanced course between theoretical and empirical work was planned. Being multidisciplinary, the project was bringing to bear all the relevant disciplines and talents required, whether they be drawn from the fields of sociology, psychology, anthropology, mathematics, economics, political science, or military science.

Finally, Project Camelot was considering a country as a

system of interrelations which were to be examined from various perspectives, including external relations. In this sense, the project was a system analysis making use of the techniques of operations research as well as other methods.

Procedurally, the project planned to use a societal model, emphasizing processes of social change, as a heuristic device to guide data collection which would in turn feed back with refinements of the model, and so on through several iterations.

The data were to have consisted primarily of analytic case studies of about 23 prior revolutions or revolts, using parameters stated in the model. Additionally, empirical analyses of contemporary developing societies, again with parameters deriving from the model, would be conducted in a second effort to assess the predictive value of the model.

As a continuing effort, drawing from and providing guidance to the empirical and analytical case studies, there was planned an extensive simulation project to study closely the model and its functions at first hand.

Some additional points to emphasize, I believe, are these:

First, the project was from the start planned as a basic research effort, with no requirements to deliver a product that would have application to anything but further research and development activity. In fact, the entire project was openly presented by its Army Research Office proponents to higher Defense offices as well as to the public, represented in part by a special advisory committee established for the Army by the National Research Council, as a feasibility study only. Its basic, continuing, and final objective was to produce the proper qualifying statements to either a "yes" or "no" answer to the question of whether or not it is feasible to conduct intensive, extensive, and enduring research into the problems of identifying, forecasting, and perhaps influencing (ends uncommitted) the actions of the social forces potentially leading to internal war. The willingness of the Army to call what was by far the largest single integrated social science research project ever undertaken (total costs programmed at from three to five million dollars in a three- to four-year period) just a *feasibility study* was indeed impressive and foretold, given a generally affirmative conclusion, great things to come for and from social science.

Second, clearly deriving from the open nature of this project, it is evident that no "espionage," not even the development of a technology for espionage, was envisioned during or even as an outcome of the project. Scientific techniques and models for information analysis and prediction purposes, yes; undercover activities, clearly no.

Third, any research to be conducted in foreign countries would have been conducted only with the full knowledge and consent of the local government and with the fullest possible cooperation of local scholars, universities, and other resources. Indeed, the activity that contained the triggering of the Chilean debacle, of which Horowitz writes, was just an activity — albeit clumsily conducted — of ascertaining the interest of local social scientists in participating in the project, when and if it were later jointly determined that parts of the project should be conducted in their country.

Fourth, the scope and openness of the project quickly attracted the affirmative interest of nearly everyone with whom we discussed it. The number and stature of social scientists who willingly lent their names and contributed their time to planning committees, seminars, and advisory boards was impressive and most gratifying. The Fascell Committee's report contains a partial listing.

It would probably not be profitable to attempt a detailed consideration of the minor errors and misunderstandings in the public record. Nor does space permit a thorough examination of some of the philosophical arguments that have been raised. It will be best, therefore, to delay for later treatment a detailing of such issues.

With reference to Irving Horowitz's generally fair article, I believe it correct to say that much of his interpretation and many of his observations about Camelot's design, philosophical assumptions, and ethics, as well as the extent and effects of the sponsor's intrusions into these matters are to a degree gratuitous and reflect Horowitz's late and fleeting acquaintance with the facts and purposes of the project.

A minor error of fact that should be corrected is the misstatement of the size of the Camelot effort in relation to its parent organization. The Project's funds for the year of its life came to something like one fifth of the total Special Operations Research Office (SORO) funding level, and at no time was Camelot likely to have become as much as one third of the total SORO budget.

Now I turn to a consideration of lessons learned or suspected. Again, shortage of space precludes developing these ideas very fully. Therefore, I shall list only a few items that appear as fairly strong conclusions or moderately strong suspicions.

1. Carrying out in a foreign country empirical, new-data, social science research, that has the possibility of producing applicable results, if that research is funded by the U. S. government, contains difficulties of relating the researcher to his local publics that are not shared by researchers working under nongovernment auspices.

a. These difficulties are especially acute if the branch of the U.S. government happens to be openly and traditionally concerned with extending or maintaining United States influence in the part of the world in which that country exists. This is not to say that foreign governments do not want research projects that are sponsored by the Departments of Defense or State — indeed they have collaborated willingly and effectively on many occasions — but rather that internal political climates may be conducive to projects sponsored by the U.S. government becoming internal political issues, leading to a condition of technical infeasibility or to a necessity for the host government to withdraw its hospitality for the project.

b. There is probably no general solution to this problem

beyond a willingness to invest a large amount of time in careful preparation and establishment of good faith and intentions with all parts and parties of the country likely to be concerned — officially or unofficially — with the project in any way. This suspicion does not stem uniquely from the Camelot experience — for there were no data collected outside the United States on that project at all — but from that, plus observation of several other social science projects. There can be no doubt that the use of any kind of "front" organization is fraught with the most extreme hazards to the good name of social science and to international relations and should never be attempted. Complete openness and assurance of the sharing of results, on the other hand, may go a long way toward disarming suspicions as well as encouraging the best form of cooperation from local people and institutions.

2. Basic social science research that is sponsored by an operation arm of the U.S. Government — as compared with an arm that has solely research responsibilities — may be faced with a unique set of internal bureaucratic problems.

Here I am thinking of the very practical fact that the executive branches of the government — the elements of the Defense establishment, the Departments of Labor, State, Agriculture, and other specialized agencies, such as the Agency for International Development or the National Security Agency — have as their very practical justification for existing *the getting of something done.* True, most of the executive branches and specialized agencies have their research elements, but these elements are uniformly justified mainly in terms of assisting the parent department to do *its own* job better. Research cannot normally be justified in the name of science *alone.* Basic research may be most easily conducted, I believe, for the executive departments in support of a better understanding of processes suspected of being an element of an applied problem.

On the other hand, the National Science Foundation, the National Research Council, the Smithsonian Institution, and a few others have as their primary charter the conducting or the stimulating of research for the sake of advancing the frontiers of science. This is a different orientation and one that allows the defense of basic research to be conducted in consistent terms and — this is important — without the need to justify it in practical terms to a skeptical internal bureaucracy whose elements are always competing for limited resources or to a Congress which has become accustomed to looking at the practical side of executive department operations.

Thus, Camelot was occasionally troubled by having two lines of supporting argument within the Defense establishment, lines that were not always consistently supporting one another. On one hand, the Army Research Office, which has in its charter the monitorship of most of the Army's basic research programs, took pride in defending the basic scientific nature of the Project. Simultaneously, however, this same office had to present the Project to people skeptical of social science or to representatives of the competing interests of "immediately useful" research as addressing some of the most pressing practical problems of the times — the wars of national liberation, insurgency, turmoil growing from the revolution of rising expectations, and the like. The use of both arguments allowed one to question — and many did — just what it really was that the Army wanted to accomplish.

Horowitz has observed, and I corroborate, that this dual support produced some confusion among our scientific colleagues as to whether the Project was really to do basic research, and even generated some skepticism about its underlying philosophical and, if any, political assumptions.

3. University association with social science projects that are potentially sensitive in the international field is different from the associations of other research institutions with such projects.

This is not yet wholly clear so far as the Camelot implications are concerned. Most prominent, however, is likely to be the tradition of free speech and free publication within the university context when associated with politically sensitive yet unclassified research subject matter and results. Thus, I believe that it is important for a university embarking in research areas in which there may be implications or sensitivities associated with government sponsorship to anticipate a policy or position with reference to its willingness to submit to the strictures of government information policy when a government agency can reasonably make a case for silence in the best interests of the nation on an unclassified project being conducted by a university.

A university should also weigh the risks of being exposed to the hazards of charges of espionage and toolery if its research happens to find disfavor within certain elements of foreign countries in which the work is being done, or in other countries wherein the work arouses some kind of interest.

Likewise, a university faced with the opportunity to undertake significant social science projects with foreign affairs implications must weigh the considerations just outlined against the obligations it feels to perform a public service for which it might be uniquely qualified, and the opportunity to reap the advantages to its own institutional development.

In conclusion, the experiences gained from the entire Camelot adventure, from its early and humble beginnings through its days of rapid growth and enthusiastic commitment, to its period of trauma and sudden death have been valuable in many ways and costly in others. Another day will doubtless come when a major social science project of similar scope and ambition will be attempted. If it succeeds where Camelot failed, perhaps Camelot will not have been a failure after all.

George C. Denney, Jr.

Department of State

State Department Procedures for Reviewing Government-Sponsored Foreign Area Research*

Last year a number of events drew attention both to the increasing role of the federal government as a sponsor (mainly by contracts with persons and institutions outside the government) of social science research related to foreign affairs and to some of the problems associated with this sponsorship. In June, an ambitious outline of a study of the social roots of political instability, financed by the Army and named Project Camelot, provoked such hostile reaction in Chile, where it was discussed by an indiscreet consultant to the study designers, and elsewhere, that the Defense Department felt compelled to cancel it. In early August, President Johnson, noting that some federally supported social science research could "raise problems affecting the conduct of our foreign policy," asked the Secretary of State to take steps to "assure the propriety of government-sponsored social science research in the area of foreign policy." On November 18, 1965, after weeks of internal discussions and consultations with other agencies, the State De-

* Based on remarks made May 6, 1966, at annual convention of the International Studies Association, Wayne State University, Detroit, Michigan.

partment issued a set of procedures for its review of "possible adverse effects upon foreign relations" of government-sponsored research.[1]

These developments have been accompanied by controversy, some of it resulting from misunderstandings of the facts of the matter and some of it stemming from legitimate differences of opinion on important issues of public policy affecting both the government and the academic community. In the year since Camelot, however, there has been a growing recognition that certain types of United States government support for social science research take on a political significance that neither the government nor the academic community can afford to ignore. The way in which such research is viewed abroad affects not only the foreign relations of the government but also, in many cases, the "image" of the private American scholar and his opportunities for carrying out valuable investigations. The procedures issued last November and the formal and informal practices that are growing up around them are part of the government's efforts to obtain the social and behavioral studies it needs in the area of foreign affairs without provoking counter-productive foreign reactions and without "contaminating" the atmosphere for private scholars whose work is not supported by the policy-making agencies of the federal government.

This paper discusses several questions. What was wrong with the government machinery before the new review procedures? What determined the timing of the new review process? What is the scope of the procedures? How is the review process working? What changes in the system may lie ahead?

What was wrong with the government machinery before the November 18, 1965, procedures went into effect?

Before November 1965, the responsibility for assessing foreign relations risks connected with external research contracts

[1] The text of the procedures was published in the *Federal Register*, Vol. 31, No. 7 (January 12, 1966).

was not clearly fixed. This does not mean, as some critics of the procedures have thought, that in the past federally supported research was never assessed in terms of its potential for creating difficulties for the government and embarrassments for the scholars involved. But each agency was responsible for its own contracts for research and each felt it was responsible as to all questions that might arise. The judgment of the State Department of the risks that might be run with research intended to help the foreign policy community in Washington was sometimes sought and sometimes not. The department had no recognized veto, indeed no recognized right even to be consulted, and it had inadequate information about the research proposals of other agencies and about ongoing research projects. If the State Department happened to hear of a proposal for a contract, or if an agency came to State for advice, that was fine. If not, there was not likely to be any consideration by the department of the risks that might be in the offing.

In recent years, however, some department officers began to realize that the gradual increase in the number and cost of contract research would create serious problems, though what these problems might be was only dimly perceived. For the same reason other agencies were increasingly feeling the need to consult and seek the advice of the State Department and of other agencies interested in the same research topic. In addition, the various research-supporting agencies wanted to avoid project duplication, and they also wanted to be able to prove that there was no duplication of their projects in order to justify them to their own budget chiefs and to the Congress when they explained their programs. In response to this felt need, a voluntary coordination of contract research was just beginning before the new review procedures were adopted. The Foreign Area Research Coordination Group was established in 1964[2] and there was agreement in principle

---

[2] The Foreign Area Research Coordination Group (FAR) is a voluntary cooperative arrangement bringing together the research administra-

that agencies sponsoring research should exchange information and discuss common problems and thus prevent duplication and maximize the usefulness of research findings. As of last year, that information exchange was still rudimentary and tended to be about projects that were already completed or were well under way and not about planned research.

TIMING OF THE PROCEDURES

A coincidence of events was heavily responsible for the development of the procedures that came into effect last November. The blow-up in the summer surrounding the Camelot project, and the scheduled hearings of the House Foreign Affairs Subcommittee on International Organizations and Movements (the Fascell subcommittee) in August drew the attention of the White House to an unsatisfactory situation. There resulted the letter of August 2, 1965, from the President to Secretary Rusk, telling the Secretary to review proposed research contracts.

The directive calling for the procedures was the beginning of negotiations. From August until November, there was consultation and debate among a few agencies, not the whole list of agencies now subject to the procedures. The Bureau of the Budget engaged itself heavily, did a lot of consultation, and presented the views of many agencies that were not directly approached by the State Department. The views of the Office of Science and Technology, also in the Executive Office of the President, were brought in too. Agreement was eventually reached and the procedures formally went into effect on November 18.

---

tors of some two dozen federal agencies that support foreign-area studies through grants and contracts. It is continuing to function, entirely separate from the risk review process, for the purpose of coordinating the planning of foreign area research.

SCOPE OF THE PROCEDURES

It is important to realize what these procedures do not cover. The following kinds of research projects are not reviewed by the State Department. First, privately financed research of any kind, anywhere, for any purpose is of course completely outside the department's purview. Second, in-house government research done by regular employees is also not subject to State review and clearance. Third, the procedures do not apply to studies other than those in the social and behavioral sciences on international matters or foreign areas and peoples. Even in the social and behavioral sciences, moreover, certain types of government-supported research are exempt from review; research projects that result from general-purpose grants that government agencies may make to a university for buildings or for strengthening faculty or for a general program, without reference to specific research topics, are also excluded from review. Finally, domestic grants by the National Science Foundation, the National Institutes of Health, the Fulbright scholars program, and the National Defense Education Act are all exempt from the review procedures.

How does the department deal with research projects not included in these broad exemptions? There are three main categories of research. The first category consists of projects which must be submitted to the State Department and cleared by it. These are projects involving foreign travel or contacts with foreign nationals which are sponsored by military and foreign affairs agencies — that is, the Department of Defense, USIA, AID, the Arms Control and Disarmament Agency, and CIA, and, of course, units of the State Department itself. Projects in this category will be considered cleared unless other action by the department is communicated to the sponsoring agency within fifteen days after the department receives the required information. In this category are projects most likely to pose problems of political sensitivity.

At the other end of the spectrum are projects that do not

require State Department clearance. The typical project in this category is one which is classified and is conducted entirely in the United States without contacts with foreign nationals. These projects do not need to be submitted for clearance, but brief information about them is to be furnished to the department, either just before the project is undertaken or in a quarterly report if the agency would rather do it that way. The department retains the option to ask for more information or to ask that the particular project be reviewed.

Everything else, all other kinds of projects, fall into category two — in between those just described. These are projects on which the "clearance point" within each agency — each agency has a central action office for these matters — decides whether or not such projects need to be submitted to the State Department for clearance. Two typical kinds of research are included in this category: first, projects, either classified or unclassified, sponsored by domestic agencies and involving foreign travel or contact with foreign nationals; and second, unclassified projects, not involving foreign travel or contact with foreign nationals. (Experience has shown that even projects involving no field work abroad can sometimes embarrass foreign relations.) The fifteen-day-clearance rule applies here also. If the sponsoring agency decides that the project does not require clearance, it nevertheless sends a brief summary of information to the department, and the department, again, has the right to ask for more information or to review a particular project.

At an early stage in discussions of the procedures, concern was expressed that if all classified research were exempt from review this would encourage overclassification as a device for avoiding department clearance. The obligation to keep the department informed of all projects, regardless of classification, removes one bureaucratic temptation to overclassify. There remains some danger that classification might be used as a means of obtaining department clearance for otherwise sensitive projects, but experience has been encouraging to date. Another antidote is that some scholars do not like to work on classified projects, and this provides an additional incentive to make a project unclassified if possible.

PRINCIPLES OF REVIEW

The Department of State wishes to avoid features of research projects that could stir up sensitivities overseas. It is not concerned with controlling the findings of government-supported research. It does not "censor" research reports or in any other way attempt to influence the conclusions of the scholars whose work enjoys government funding.

The sponsoring agency is the best judge of the need for a project related to its mission. The department has no intention of second-guessing the agency as to that. On the other hand, the fact that it clears a project for foreign relations risk is not necessarily an endorsement of the study by the department. Clearance means only that State has determined that, whatever other merits or deficiencies a project may or may not have, it is not likely to prove seriously embarrassing to the government. This judgment is now made deliberately and with due process, so to speak, by the department of government primarily concerned with the conduct of foreign relations.

The responsibility for the wise expenditure of research funds remains in each agency. The State Department has not become and does not wish to be a fiscal controller. It does not ask whether the agency is paying too much for its results or whether the agency has hired the wrong man to do the work. If the department were to encounter a clear case of duplication, that is, if the files were to show that somebody else had done or were about to do the same thing, the fact would be pointed out to an agency. No such clear case of that has occurred as yet.

Experience dictates that the Department of State must take an especially careful look at military-sponsored research. The history of many countries is such and the political realities in many places in the world is such that Pentagon-financed research is more likely than that sponsored by other agencies to be resented or to cause trouble of some kind.

THE REVIEW PROCESS

The Department of State has tried to create such review organs and to assign action in ways that would give proper consideration to the political implications of sensitive projects and to the potential value of research. The key State units involved in the review process are a Foreign Affairs Research Council (RC) established by the Secretary and a review staff located in the Bureau of Intelligence and Research.

The Research Council is a fifteen-member body chaired by the Director of the Bureau of Intelligence and Research and including senior officers of the Policy Planning Council, the Politico-Military Affairs office, each of the geographic and functional bureaus, and the Foreign Service Institute. The typical representative from a geographic policy bureau is the officer in charge of "regional affairs," an officer who has a view of his whole area and is not responsible for just one country. The council sets general policy, but it does not often deal collegially with a particular project. It does, however, meet periodically to discuss staff reports on the whole review process, listings of actions taken, and general problems that emerge from time to time.

The review staff is located in the Office of External Research (XR) of the Bureau of Intelligence and Research. This is an important point, because it means that in the review and clearance process a key role is played by a bureau that contains a large number of social science research specialists engaged in political, economic, and sociological analyses; that traditionally maintains liaison with the academic world; that systematically collects and disseminates a vast amount of information on private and government-sponsored research related to foreign affairs; that makes extensive use of consultants; and that has a modest contract research program of its own.

Before a project comes to the department, it has had some review in the sending agency. In the case of the Department of Defense, this has become a substantial step. There the Office of the Assistant Secretary of Defense for International Security Affairs (ISA) has established a staff that looks at the proposals of Army, Navy, Air Force, the Advanced Research Projects Agency, and ISA itself and passes a foreign relations risk judgment on them.

The first thing the department must concern itself with is whether there is adequate information about a project sent to it for review. The required information is spelled out in the procedures. There is something of a dilemma here. It is preferable to be informed of a project at an early stage, other things being equal, but the trouble is that at an early stage there are not always available the substantive and methodological details about a project that are helpful and sometimes crucial in determining whether or not it is likely to cause any problems.

Once a project is sent to the department, it is handled by the review staff in the Office of External Research. Each project is assigned to a reviewing officer who carries the thing through from beginning to end. Ideally, this man would be a Foreign Service officer with experience abroad and sensitivity to the kinds of things that irritate foreign governments or people, but at the same time he would be an experienced researcher alive to the potentials for research, the nuances of design, the problems of data collection, and so on. The Department does the best it can to get some of each quality and a mix of people for this work.

The reviewing officer first studies a proposal and discusses problems with other staff members. Then he consults other officers in the Department, beginning in most cases with the Research Council member of every geographic bureau affected by the project. Usually he then consults with the "country desk" man of every country involved in the project. He may talk also with other parts of the Department or with some other agency. Sometimes before the project is received there has been some consultation with State's overseas missions by field representatives of the sponsoring agency. It may come in already cleared, with the ambassador indicating that he thinks it is a good project and poses no problems. If that does not happen or if the department has some reason to think there has been an inadequate discussion in the field, or if there are additional questions, including problems of timing, that the field may not have thought of, the department will consult with the embassy further by aerogram or cable.

When this consultation process is finished, the staff officer prepares a memorandum discussing the project and any problems that are seen in it and makes a recommendation to clear the project without question, to clear it with certain conditions to be met by the sponsoring agency or the researcher, or to deny clearance altogether. This memorandum, which is approved by those in the department who participated in the process, goes to the Chairman of the Research Council. A letter or memorandum is then sent to the sponsoring agency, giving the department's decision and the reasons for it and sometimes suggesting changes in the proposed research that would reduce its sensitivity. Usually the letter or memorandum is preceded by a telephone call, informing the agency of the department's views, and frequently there are telephone conversations or meetings with officers of the sponsoring agency during the consultation process. Finally, when the agency gets its letter, it can appeal an adverse decision to the Foreign Affairs Research Council, but that has not happened as yet.

CHECKLIST FOR THE REVIEWER

What does the State Department reviewer think about as he looks at a project? First, he asks about the adequacy of the information that is submitted. At what stage is the project planning or implementation? Is there enough information on subject matter, methodology, field research needed, and so on, to enable the State Department to make a really sound judgment? He takes note of the statements made by the sponsoring agency about the importance of the project. What priority is given to it by the sponsoring agency? Is there any special matter of timeliness or urgency? Does it appear to duplicate any other past or planned project?

With this basic information in hand, the reviewing officer then considers the possible risks in terms of foreign relations. Attitudes in the country where the work is to be done are very important. Does the country have some policy or other that would affect the work? Has there been some incident or history that might be pertinent to what is proposed? Is an election imminent, or something else affecting the timing that should be taken into account? Is the host government already cooperating in the project? Is there some kind of problem with the political opposition in the country? Of course the sensitivity of the research subject itself has to be considered — is it a subject likely to offend people, to be resented by significant groups, to be exploited for propaganda aimed at the United States or at friendly governments, to appear linked with U.S. policies opposed by the host government? Then there are sponsorship problems. Does the agency sponsorship itself create problems for what may otherwise be a good piece of research? Are there serious objections to the particular contractor or the individual researcher? Are there some disclosure questions? What is the classification of the project? What is the proposed extent of disclosure of details about the contractor and the project? What are the publication expectations?

Research techniques also have to be looked at. What is the extent, and what is the nature, of contacts in the host country? Is there a questionnaire involved? How widespread is the distribution? What sort of controls are envisaged? Is it to be purely documentary research or some other kind of research? Are local scholars going to participate? Are the data to be shared in the country? Is the final product to be shared with local social scientists?

When all these questions are looked at, and there appears to be some risk, various modifications that might reduce the risk are considered through consultation within the government in Washington and with U.S. diplomatic missions in the areas concerned. Sometimes the subject or the research techniques can be modified somewhat, the sponsorship may be changed or shared, or disclosure policies changed. Consultations with the host government or other elements in the host country may prove useful. Foreign scholars or institutions may be associated with the project to make it a joint undertaking. Occasionally, review of final reports before publication by the embassy and by the department may be prescribed. Sometimes the country of the study can be changed without affecting the value of the study.

A checklist something like the foregoing can be made of questions which ought to be asked in determining whether or not a proposed study is likely to run into difficulties or is likely to provoke criticisms and attacks on the U.S. government. It has, however, become clear with experience in these matters that the criteria of sensitivity cannot be defined precisely and applied mechanically. The political circumstances affecting the atmosphere for social research differ tremendously from place to place and from time to time.

Some "sensitivities" are pertinent only to the U.S. government but some are equally problems for researchers doing field work abroad done under completely private auspices. There may be differing intellectual traditions that hamper communications between American social scientists and foreign intellectuals. Some popular cultures are hostile to empirical social research. Some foreign scholars may feel that they are patronized or not involved as thoroughly as they should be in projects of joint interest. There is occasionally a problem of the "saturation" of a geographic area, an elite group, or an individual by a succession of American scholars working on the same or similar subjects. These are obviously matters of considerable importance to the American academic community as a whole as well as to the government.

Although the State Department's assigned responsibility is to avoid political or diplomatic embarrassment, it is equally interested in facilitating private research from which the American people and government benefit. If sponsoring agencies or government contract researchers are indifferent or careless about the attitudes of foreigners they will often find it difficult to carry out their field work and they may even, as Secretary Rusk noted before the Fascell Subcommittee, "create or increase hostility . . . toward American scholars who are completely unconnected with government agencies." "We must take care," the Secretary added, "that official sponsorship of research does not increase the difficulties of independent American scholars who are doing or plan to do private research abroad."

TABLE I
Statistics on Review Actions

	Projects Reviewed	Other Actions*	Total	Number of Professional Staff
July (1965)	1	2	3	1
August	5	12	17	2 permanent 4 temporary
September	3	5	8	2 permanent 2½ temporary
October	2	10	12	2 permanent 3 temporary
November	7	12	19	3 permanent 2 temporary
December	8	17	25	4 permanent
January (1966)	12	11	23	5 permanent
February	8	19	27	6 permanent
March	7	17	24	6 permanent ½ temporary
April	22	19	41	6 permanent ½ temporary
May	24	17	41	6 permanent
TOTALS	99	141	240	

*Scrutiny of reports for unclassified publication, amendments or extension of ongoing projects, and travel plans are not included in "Projects Reviewed."

	Average	Range
Time needed for action (number of working days)		
August–January	7½	½–43
February–April	7½	½–27

Table I provides a few statistics on the review process so far. These cover the period from last July through May of this year. In the aftermath of the Camelot affair, some offices of the Defense Department informally began to clear projects with State even before formal review requirements were issued. The statistics say nothing about many research projects started before the procedures were adopted which, because they seemed to pose no serious problems of sensitivity, have not been formally reviewed by the department. It is likely that an occasional new project still escapes review for a variety of reasons. With these qualifications, the table shows that the Department of State and other agencies have substantial accomplishments, in the past six months especially.

A total of 99 new projects have been reviewed and cleared and 141 other actions have been taken (review and clearance of final study reports, decisions on extensions of ongoing projects to new countries, review of travel and field work plans of researchers working on particularly sensitive projects, and so on), with a grand total of 240 clearances of some kind. In about 60 percent of these cases, clearances have been unconditional; in the remaining 40 percent mild or severe conditions for clearance have been imposed, but in only a handful of cases have the conditions imposed by the department led to a complete stoppage of the project.

After starting with one professional staff member in the Office of External Research handling these clearances, there is now a review staff consisting of six professionals working full time and helped on occasion by other members of the office. In addition, study and advice have been contributed by Research Council members, research and policy specialists in the department and senior officers in the Bureau of Intelligence and Research and elsewhere. The projects reviewed by the department add up to more than $10,000,000 worth of contract research sponsored by 15 federal departments and agencies.

BENEFICIAL BY-PRODUCTS

There have been some incidental benefits from the review process apart from whatever has been accomplished in reducing risks. Suggestions on the goals or the conduct of a project from officers in the department have been useful to the designers from time to time. The department has sometimes been able to make source materials available to researchers. Some of these materials the researchers did not know were available or did not know they could get from the Department.

The strengthening of the education of Foreign Service officers in the useful possibilities of social science research has been good. The review process has begun to stimulate some additional research requests from officers in the department's geographic bureaus. A similar development seems to be taking place in U.S. missions abroad. For the first time, embassies are kept fully aware of government-sponsored social and behavioral research on their areas of responsibility, and the frequent involvement of mission officers in the clearance process encourages these officers to look at research proposals closely and to maintain an active interest in field work going on in their countries.

There is one paradoxical benefit: On at least one occasion, the review process has resulted in the relaxation of excessive restrictions on data gathering imposed on the researcher by the sponsoring agency. The agency tried to make it less "sensitive" by confining data to official sources of the government of the country involved. Such a biased study, it was felt, would be potentially more embarrassing than one drawing also on unofficial data, including that provided by political opponents of the government in question. So clearance was made conditional upon the project being broadened.

The review process is also resulting in a broadening and deepening of relationships between the Department of State and the academic community. It would be cumbersome to involve academic consultants in every clearance action; nevertheless, in about one quarter of our actions the project has been discussed with the researchers, and, with the consent of the sponsoring agencies, this practice will be continued. Moreover, it is now planned to call an ad hoc meeting of some outside consultants representing the major disciplines to discuss the entire review experience thus far, to examine the typical "problem cases" and to seek improvements in the operation.

The reactions of other agencies have been mixed. Some have welcomed the review while others have been more cautious or critical but none has raised any serious objections to the clearance process on principle. Some agencies have found it difficult to organize themselves internally to centralize information on their multifarious contract research activities, and, occasionally, the department has been blamed for delaying decisions on projects that in fact were being held up elsewhere in the sponsoring agencies. These problems are being worked out. On April 19th, the department held a half-day meeting with Defense Department representatives to describe our review mechanism and to discuss some outstanding problems. While it is clear that there are some things one or both agencies may want to change in the future, no one questioned the need for the review process in some form or other. At the April 21st meeting of the Foreign Area Research Coordination Group, no agency representative was moved to raise the question of research review. The process seems to be working fairly well.

The irony, of course, is that no amount of risk review can guarantee that there will not be another Camelot; it cannot prevent an individual researcher from doing something silly that will reflect adversely on him, his academic colleagues and his government patron. But the review mechanism can minimize the risks of another such development and other similar, though less dramatic and less publicized, incidents.

POSSIBLE CHANGES AHEAD

What changes may there be ahead? Recently, a letter went out to all agencies reminding them that the six-month re-examination of the procedures called for by the November 18, 1965, document was due and that changes should now be considered. One open question is the treatment of the research programs of RAND, IDA, and similar institutions which are largely the financial creatures of one Defense agency or another but which also carry out some research with nonappropriated funds. The Department has not done much in this area as yet, having been too busy with the more primary contracts.

It may be possible to simplify paper work somewhat. There is a subcommittee of the Foreign Area Research Coordination Group which is seeing whether the papers that are used for submitting projects for review could be also used for exchanging information among all agencies about research plans. There are obvious difficulties with this because the timing of research planning and research review are not the same, but maybe something can be worked out to benefit all agencies.

Another change may be an indirect but important one. At the last meeting of the Foreign Area Research Coordination Group, there was agreement on the text of an interagency research planning procedure. The gist of it is that the agencies initiate action at an appropriate stage to let other interested agencies know of their plans before they get down to the contract-making stage and get comments back from the interested agencies. Hopefully, this can be done expeditiously with benefit all around. Now as such coordination gets more detailed and as it gets broken down in the various geographic and functional subcommittees of FAR, it may be that there will be a fair amount of risk screening in the interagency planning process; and certainly in many cases the sponsoring agency will have the benefit of the Department of State's comment on a research plan (including sensitivity aspects) before it gets to the contract stage. So the formal review process may ultimately be a lot simpler and a lot faster.

Finally, there is interest in producing for the use of government research administrators and for scholars working on government contracts some guidelines for the conduct of field research — not "directives" by any means but checklists of problems that are likely to confront the American reseacher abroad. Guidelines of this sort might help to reduce the risk of adverse foreign reactions to research done under certain kinds of government auspices. This business of formulating "guidelines" is going on elsewhere. A number of professional scholarly groups in the past year have dealt with the problem of "access." The National Academy of Sciences has a committee on government-sponsored behavioral science research that will deal with this problem also, and the interagency Foreign Area Research Coordination Group (FAR) has agreed to cooperate with this committee. The Department of State, together with FAR, is sponsoring a government-academic symposium in June to discuss intensively this question of working principles for American researchers abroad. The objective we share with the academic community is to improve the acceptability of foreign area research and, of course, to improve the research results and their wider sharing with all nations.

Aniceto Rodríguez

Chilean Senate

A Socialist Commentary on Camelot

As a proof that Project Camelot is being implemented in Chile, I must point out that an agent of the Government of the United States, an ex-Chilean and now a naturalized North American, Mr. Hugo Nuttini, took the first steps in our university environment with the purpose of engaging some sectors of the faculty of our major training school, and even students in their first year, to make a survey. He was first denounced, if I recall, at the School of Sociology of the University of Chile. There Professor Eduardo Hamuy decisively rejected Project Camelot. He described it as a plan of Yankee espionage. He further was unwilling to offer either his own person or the prestige of the university to the success of such an aim.

According to information of the press, not satisfied with that, the agent Hugo Nuttini brought the problem to Dean Bunster, the General Secretary of the University of Chile. There, after having stated his aims and his ideas, this agent of the Department of State, this degraded Chilean who disowned his country to become a Yankee spy for the purpose of piercing the security of our country, was also categorically rejected.

Since tomorrow there shall be a debate on international affairs, I request that the Minister of Foreign Affairs be notified of this situation now with the purpose of informing him of these facts before the session begins. We should receive official notice, since there are contradicting items on this point, if the Chancellery intends to raise objections to Project Camelot through some form of diplomatic channels. I have privately consulted the Secretary of State when he arrived in Congress this afternoon, and he told me that there has as yet been no official intervention on the part of the government on this matter.

The problem is serious, because should we carelessly allow everything concerning Project Camelot to pass unchecked, we will be flooded by North American agents, aside from those which are already here. It is being said, for instance, that in the past months twelve Yankee consuls have been authorized to operate in Santiago. Twelve consuls. For what purpose? We know that the CIA, as well as the Pentagon and the FBI, disguise their agents behind diplomatic masks in order that the latter may be free to enjoy immunity and penetrate the national scene.

We (the Socialists) are having a General Congress of our Party in which we shall extensively analyze international problems in a responsible manner. Naturally, in this meeting we shall affirm once more our incorruptible anti-imperialist position. Undoubtedly there will be a political reply to the great new international challenge of Mr. Johnson and his set of North American political hacks who still see in Latin America the backyard of the great colossus of the North. In advance of this Congress, we can say that we pick up Mr. Johnson's challenge. It shall prevent neither the Socialists nor the popular forces from fighting on, with greater daring, courage, and fortitude, for the abused great political postulates of the authentic Chilean Revolution.

The list of North American intervention in Latin America is long. When Sandino, that giant of free men, shook the world with his example of courage and abnegation in Nicaragua, fighting for the independence of his country, we thought at the time that he might succeed. Unfortunately, the murderous bullet, well paid for by mercenary troops, by the Yankee troops, ended Sandino's life.

Later, they wanted to bring down the Cuban Revolution. They have not succeeded. This nation is conscious of the new Socialist society that has been built at the cost of sacrifice and devotion coming from the Cuban people. Yet Cuba has to hold its arms ready to hand; it knows that it is insecure because of the aggressive presence of North American imperialism. It also knows that it can count on the wide and generous solidarity offered by the popular sectors of Latin America.

We are surprised that Frei's government, which has healthily and honorably normalized the field of international relations, should have disregarded Cuba. Frei has established relationships with the countries of the Socialist orbit, with the Soviet Union and the Balkan countries. Yet Cuba remains solitary, rebellious, revolutionary, and unrecognized. Chile made a mistake during Alessandri's right-wing government when, toward the end of his term in office, he unjustly broke relations with the Government of Cuba, following weak instructions of the Organization of American States. This mistake, in the judgment of Socialists and of the popular movement, and even of a vast sector of Christian Democracy, should have been corrected. Let us hope that soon the Christian Democratic Government will understand the necessity of repairing this mistake, committed, I repeat, at the end of Alessandri's term.

Jorge Montes

Chilean Chamber of Deputies

A Communist Commentary on Camelot

A number of newspapers, and particularly *El Siglo*, have been referring to a so called "Project Camelot." What is this project? In order to define it, we shall textually quote from an official document. [See Document No. 1, pp. 47–49, from which excerpts were cited. I.L.H.].

These quotes from the project reveal the determination on the part of U.S. foreign policy to intervene in any country of the world where popular movements might threaten its interests. To this end, they use a covert form of espionage, which they try to present in terms of scientific research, thus violating the most elementary norms of sovereignty.

Indeed, our own country, Uruguay, Colombia, and Venezuela in Latin America, Senegal and Nigeria in Africa, and India, Vietnam, and Laos in Asia are the countries in which organized espionage, under the appearance of sociological investigation and under the rubric of "Project Camelot," is being carried out.

It has already been pointed out that both the Director of the Project, Rex Hopper, and Hugo C. Nuttini, its agent, have been in Chile. The latter, born in Chile and naturalized a North American, and an ex-student at the Naval School, tried to bring about the engagement of 20 to 25 Chilean scholars in order to carry out the studies implied in the project. He offered salaries of two thousand dollars a month plus all the necessary equipment to different university agencies. We are in a position to affirm that, at the General Secretaryship of the University of Chile, where Nuttini went, the true character of the project was unmasked. Nuttini had presented it with an especially prepared wording in order to make it appear to be an innocent scientific research undertaking. But his hope to recruit Chilean scholars for this work of espionage against Chile was rejected. Such response was due in part to the fact that the official document for the project, such as it is, had been previously known. This document had reached Chileans owing to a European sociologist. He had been offered a position in the direction of the project which he refused with dignity, making its contents known to his colleagues throughout the world.

This official document, worded for the highest level, is now in the hands of His Excellency the President of the Republic, who received it through the Minister of the Exchequer, Sergio Molina. The latter received it in his role as Dean of the Faculty of Economics of the University of Chile. Thus, the Government of Chile has full knowledge of the antinational content as well as the serious attack against our sovereignty implied in this North American project.

The gravity of this situation is made even more manifest if we consider the fact that different kinds of espionage researches fulfilling diverse partial objectives have been carried out for years. We are in a position to point out that the North American Walter Guzardi carried out in Chile a study of the middle classes that was oriented toward influencing them politically to the advantage of the United States. Further, Andrew G. Frank made a study of the Communist Party and the FRAP. And right now, others are carried out, among which there is one aimed at analyzing the structure of the Christian Democratic Party, and which is also sponsored by North Americans.

Bearing a direct relationship to this unmasked espionage being carried forth by the United States, with the tolerance of its authorities, is the proposed goal of creating an Inter-American Defense Force. This issue will be debated in the next Conference of Chancellors, to be held in Rio de Janeiro on August 24th of the present year [1965 I.L.H.].

The extreme pressure exerted by the United States upon Latin American Chancelleries in order to achieve this Inter-American Defense Force is a well-known fact. Imperialism tries to conceal its interventionist policy by means of this shadow-army, which, as project Camelot proves, is carried forth in every way. It is not impeded by any considerations whatsoever. Indeed, the confidential document 520.1 (22) of the Ministry of Foreign Affairs of Brazil shows the concomitance of the Castelo Branco Government with that of the United States. It also shows the brutality with which North Americans are trying to bring about the creation of this armed force.

In compliance with the latest suggestions of the Government of the United States, Brazilian authorities will prepare a broad documentation of subversive activities in Brazil which occurred before April 1964. There are also proofs of extremist infiltration in high government echelons in various countries of the Hemisphere. The Brazilian Government hopes that the presentation of these facts might have a positive influence upon the representatives of the Latin American countries in the Rio de Janeiro Conference.*

For another part, Itamarati is preparing the probing of Latin American countries and hopes that the idea of the Alliance shall be accepted with sympathy by the majority of the countries within the Organization of American States. In the specific cases of Chile and Mexico, the Brazilian Government shall follow the agreed line which, as the results show, corresponds with reality. In the case of Uruguay, Brazil has no possibilities of achieving the agreed upon objectives. It would view with pleasure the assistance of the United States Government in setting forth Brazil's aims before the Government of Uruguay. Brazil believes that through the exploitation of economic factors, it might obtain from Uruguay a favourable position with respect to said alliance.†

* Article 7.
† Article 8.

This text constitutes one more piece of evidence of the cynical and insolent intervention of the United States and its servants in the internal affairs of Latin American countries. Within this framework, in Chile and in other countries, the application of Project Camelot is being carried out. Let us recall President Johnson's statement at Baylor University where he contended that there are no longer internal wars but only international wars. In this way, he underlined his decision to perform military intervention in any nation of the world.

We Communists have appreciated the Chilean government's worthy attitude before the aggression to Santo Domingo, and its refusal to accept the creation of an Inter-American Defense Force. That is why we are surprised by the fact that this government (of Chile) should not have taken a stand concerning the serious threat to Chile's sovereignty that Project Camelot and other such studies imply. In order to avoid saying it in our own words, we shall quote Eduardo Hamuy, Director of the Center of Social and Economic Studies of the Faculty of Economics of the University of Chile. To him this is simply a plan of "systematized espionage" and a method for providing information of state secrets to an eventual enemy.

Because of the situation described, we request that these observations be transcribed in the name of the Honorable Chamber and should there be no quorum, in the name of our committee, to the Minister of Foreign Affairs, and that he be invited to the session of the corresponding committee next Friday in order that he should report concerning this situation.

At the same time, we believe that the Committee on Foreign Affairs, in addition to considering the situation, and within the possibilities allowed by regulations, should inquire into all facts related to these claims in order that the Chilean Parliament and Chilean public opinion be widely informed on an issue that compromises our national sovereignty. Further, we believe that the majority of the Honorable Chamber will have no objections to convene a special session during the first days of the coming week for the purpose of bringing wider information on this serious claim and that the different sectors of Parliament should state their opinion concerning this problem. It is necessary that we adopt a well-defined attitude in defense of our national sovereignty.

PART V

THE GENERAL IMPLICATIONS

William R. Polk

University of Chicago

*Problems of Government Utilization of Scholarly Research in International Affairs**

Tension between the academic community and the government is a corollary of the American concept of politics. That this tension should exist is probably essential to the wellbeing of both, and that a large number of the concerns of each are common is in the nature of a democracy. Our way of life is not conducive to a sterile scholasticism in which the scholar is forced to eschew worldly affairs; rather, the scholar who seeks to retire from the world is punished with the "disincentives" of smaller research and travel funds, fewer students and lesser acclaim. Nor does our form of government permit its executive either a free hand with knuckles unrapped by academic criticism or a pragmatic mind with concepts unchallenged by academic theory. In all aspects of public affairs this is the norm of our open society. But, because Americans are now acutely aware of their newly assumed world-wide responsibilities and are dissatisfied with existing

* A paper given at the 1965 Annual Meeting of the American Political Science Association, Washington, D.C., September 8–11, 1965. Copyright 1965 by William R. Polk. By permission.

This paper appeared in *Background*, Vol. 9, No. 3.

answers to dangerous international problems, it is in the area of foreign affairs that the academic community and the government attract and repel one another with the most vigor.

This troubled, stimulating, and obscure relationship is the subject of the following paper. By the very nature of the subject, it will be highly subjective and somewhat speculative. Small profit would accrue from a formalistic account or catalogue of contacts and contracts;* here we are concerned with the problems in this relationship.

A large government, like a great university, is a congeries of institutions. Generalization is almost as difficult about the one as about the other. At base, however, it is possible to say that the government is concerned with action and the university with thought. Having said this, one is immediately conscious of parts of each in which this is either untrue or so near to being untrue as to mislead. The government has its research and analysis offices and the university has operating branches. In general, though, the concentrations of activity and interest do contrast: where the government is concerned with analytical concepts, these are often at the level of what might be termed operating maxims and where the university is concerned with action it is often for training purposes or to test a theory.

Questions arise from this basic dissimilarity: what are the needs of the government; what are the requirements of academic research; is this likely to come to be a fruitful area without careful stimulation; is this stimulation likely to hobble academic research; if it is given, what are the dangers and what can be done to alleviate them; if a useful product results, is it communicated; and if so to whom and how; what are the problems of compartmentalization and classification;

* The External Research Staff of the Bureau of Intelligence and Research in the Department of State and the Foreign Area Research Coordination Group have published inventories and very useful analyses of gaps in research in which the government is interested.

how open are administrators to new ideas which challenge existing policy; how much can be absorbed; what are the advantages and disadvantages of the layers between the scholar and the administrator; who really are the consumers of academic research; what do they need from the academic community; what are they now getting; and where can scholars contribute the most in the period ahead?

THE NEEDS OF GOVERNMENT

It has been said that if a scheme similar to the Marshall Plan were proposed today, it could not be undertaken because expertise is so diffused in the government that such a plan would be studied to death.

Whether or not this is true, it is a fact that a very large number of people who work for the government have experience and knowledge covering most parts of the world. Very few are the areas or issues on which the government cannot assemble an imposing interagency committee of experts.

The growth of governmental expertise has been truly astonishing in the period since 1945. In conducting a wide variety of programs throughout most of the world since the Second World War, the American government has been a vast school. Its graduates now number in the hundreds of thousands. This diffusion of knowledge and experience is, of course, a great asset in the administration of programs. If a decision is made to assist in the building of a road in Nepal, there will be men throughout the government who know Nepal or who know about road building in similar areas.

In contrast, the diffusion of knowledge on this level can be a hindrance to the growth of new knowledge. In government, in academic life, and in industry, we have all encountered the expert "who has been there" and for whom all learning ended when he left. Additionally, knowledge of a single task often must be generalized into expertise on a large area: the man who knows about the roads of Nepal is forced by the nature of his job to serve as an expert on the politics of Nepal.

More commonly, a responsible administrator is pressed by urgent problems for which answers must be found quickly. It is this urgent but limited concern which commands his attention. He wants to know whether or not the granting of a loan to build a grain storage unit makes sense within the development plan of a country or, even more narrowly, out of three options which are currently possible, is the grain storage unit the most feasible. He is not professionally, or probably even intellectually, concerned with the complex relationships within the culture which will be disrupted by grain storage or with the changes in economic patterns which a regularization of the grain market will bring about or, even more remotely, with the theories of economic development. In his every action and every inaction, the administrator of the large and powerful programs now conducted by the American government changes the face of the world. If he is to do his job, he cannot be hobbled by considerations of the far-flung implications of his action or inaction. There are those who would claim that his efforts would be nullified should he even try. But, others, and I among them, would maintain that his actions would be much more economical and beneficial if he had a broader and fuller grasp of the materials with which he was working.

Perhaps not for these reasons but simply for the imperatives of time and limits of intellectual energy, it is often true that the government administrator does not read works in the social sciences beyond descriptions of countries in which he is concerned or particular processes with which he must deal. Left to themselves, most government officials would seek operating maxims which would enable them to do their jobs better. Consequently, they are often frustrated by the intellectual fare they are offered by the universities. When they ask for information, they often receive information in reply which compares poorly with that available to them through their own resources.

THE REQUIREMENTS OF ACADEMIC LIFE

Just as the best people in government service strive to improve their operating capabilities, the foremost scholars work at refining their knowledge and building conceptual schemes which will enable them to account more adequately for the complexities of life. Aquisition of information per se is, of course, important but this cannot be an end in itself for many scholars today. Rather, it is the ability to deduce from description of reality conceptions which will elucidate and simplify perceptions of reality which is important. The leaders in most academic fields are, therefore, often those who are the most theoretical and the least concerned with an ability to answer the sorts of questions posed by the administrator.

Whereas the administrator is concerned with a specific problem in a specific country, the scholar is often thinking in terms of comparative politics; where the intelligence analyst is concerned with those groups which matter politically, the anthropologist is often dealing with remote tribesmen or villagers; whereas the AID official is concerned with the effects of a program on the change in gross national product, the academic economist, if he is concerned about the world outside Western Europe and North America at all, may be interested in a part of an economy in which the American government will never have a program; and whereas the information officer is concerned with current public opinion, the historian or orientalist may devote himself entirely to a tradition whose impact on current affairs is at best tenuous and complex.

Even in those cases in which the political scientist or sociologist is concerned with the gathering of highly specific information, his own questions, dictated by the requirements of his own particular brand of research, may have led him to consider groups of people and kinds of problems which are not relevant to the tasks before the government official. One of the larger projects in the social sciences now underway, for example, deals with the attitudes of people remote from the centers of power. It was not, of course, hostility to the government which caused the scholars to pick these subjects; it was that they were interested in the problem of transmission of ideas and of opinions from the centers of power in the several societies rather than the influence of the citizens in the society upon political power.

In the social sciences today, particularly in political science, a great deal of attention is being given to methodology. From the perspective of the administrator, this is an "in-house" problem, as unuseful to him as is his thought on governmental organization to the scholar. Each subject has, indeed, developed its own particular esoteric language with "governmentalese" matched by the jargon of each scholarly field. Thus, quite apart from the problems of relevance of subject matter and methodology, a problem of mutual incomprehensibility has arisen. Few are the administrators who find in this strange new literature a message for themselves.

IS THERE A MEETING GROUND?

If the most advanced scholarly research of the academic is not of obvious utility to the government official, is his activity of use to the scholar?

Dealing as the American government does with virtually the whole range of human endeavor in most parts of the world, it is difficult to conceive of a political, economic, or cultural problem with which the government cannot offer experience. However, that experience may be seriously compromised by the involvement of the government: If one were concerned with the study of malaria, he might not be wise to study in an area being sprayed with DDT by U.S. public health workers. Nor would Vietnam today be the best place to study village administration.

Yet, unquestionably, the entry of the American government into these sorts of problems has furnished both the occasion and the impetus for a wide variety of specific academic and quasi-academic studies. Even in those areas in which the American government has no current concern, it has often been prepared to sponsor studies by members of the academic community as individuals or by large-scale research organizations.

A review of public and private research programs would reveal, I believe, that no one presumed to stake out a "meeting ground" between the government and the academic community. Nor does there appear to have been an attempt to mark out a middle layer between the operating maxims of the government and the theory of the scholar. In both of these cases, something "just growed" like Topsy. How this came about is not of immediate concern. But no one can deny that the almost accidental nature of its growth affects the relations between the academic community and the government and the quality of the product that passes between them.

Is there really a meeting ground on which the administrator and the scholar can contribute, one to the other?

Within the government there has long been a recognition that some few officials should be held apart from daily concerns to think about the larger if less concrete problems. It was General George Marshall who, as Secretary of State in 1947, created for this purpose the Policy Planning Staff in the Department of State. His one instruction to his new staff was to "avoid small stuff." Similar planning staffs exist now in most major government departments dealing with foreign affairs. Additionally, several of the larger government agencies concerned with foreign policy have special staffs which deal with research and analysis.

Relations between these "staff" officials and those with "line" responsibilities are always difficult. They are a miniature version of the relations between the government as a whole and the academic community. The planning officer, to do his job, must withdraw from operating responsibility. But, in doing so, he removes himself both from the power to command activity and from the current information on which it is predicated. If he is to take the "larger view," to some degree his vision will become blurred to the immediate. Accomplishment of his task depends primarily upon two factors: On the one hand, he must provide a service to his action-oriented colleagues which is sufficiently close to their day-to-day concerns as to be of obvious utility. On the other hand, he must be supported by those in authority or, in the normal course of events, he will simply be ignored. If the government's approach to world affairs is characterized by a high degree of pragmatic flexibility, there is obviously little scope for the planner or the intelligence analyst. If, on the other hand, there is a recognition of the utility of efficient planning toward longer term objectives and the mobilization of resources to accomplish policy within recognized political limitations, the roles of the planner and the intelligence analyst can be extraordinarily productive ones.

Within the academic community, likewise, there are many whose primary — or at least sole — interests do not lie in the further reaches of theoretical research. Two general categories of these people have been of great importance to the government in foreign policy matters. The one, with whom we are not primarily concerned here, is the thousands of teachers who have made possible the enormous expansion of expertise among government personnel particularly in foreign language skills. The second group comprises those who are concerned with information or analytical concepts that make them particularly valuable as consultants or writers on foreign affairs problems. It is perhaps not accurate to think of these as the less theoretically oriented scholars. Some of them, indeed, are among the pioneers in the social sciences. But, in general, it is rare that the theoretically oriented scholar is attuned to the problems of governmental action sufficiently to have been drawn into participation as advisor, consultant, or contractor in governmental affairs. Periodically, however, there is a normal emigration from the academic community to the government, in which many of the foremost social scientists have come into key governmental planning and intelligence functions. But many remain totally independent of the government and are able, therefore, to play a highly useful, independent role.

Several things must be said about this meeting ground and those who tread upon it:

First, the foreign policy issues which have been justified in it are often the less speculative and the more specific. It has been suggested that the question the "operator" wants answered is on the order of "will they rumble at four o'clock on 97th Street?" The social scientist's theoretical response might be: "What forces in society cause young men and women in urban society to rumble?" The middle range of policy-oriented question might run on the order of "what are the factors in the neighborhood of 97th Street which cause rumbles and what properly can we do to alleviate these and to blunt the intensity of the violence?" In practice, this has proven a difficult question to formulate, study, and usefully answer.

Second, the number of people in government concerned with the development of sharper analytical tools as opposed to better information or clearer operating maxims is limited just as the number of scholars who are concerned with more than the gathering of information but somewhat less than — or different from — "pure" theory are few.

Third, the position these people must maintain is precarious since they are pulled away from their fellows. Those in the government find that they get left out of the main stream of action and are often not in a position to exercise a major influence when policies are formulated as they usually are by the accretion of day-to-day decisions. They become "academic" in the worst sense of the word, forever looking at the big picture when those responsible for this afternoon's decision want to know whether to give or to withhold aid or whether a particular coup d'état will harm or help U.S. interests. Their counterparts in the academic community, likewise, become somewhat suspect among their fellows. They are thought to have compromised themselves. At best, they acquire information whose validity cannot be confirmed openly in the approved academic manner and at worst they are assumed to slant their research to the whim of the leviathan to whom they have prostituted themselves.

These views make for both waste and ruin. The government clearly needs far more precise analytical concepts and better formulation of its goals and means of achieving them than it now has. It is evident to most that the clever tactician is not necessarily a good strategist and that "muddling through," coping with each disparate problem as it arises, gradually learning from it, outliving it, and then forgetting its lessons when confronted with a similar problem a few years later is not the best approach to world affairs.

Within the academic community, the costs are less obvious but they are real. When the best men in a field eschew work that the government needs, others will do it in such ways as may harm the whole field or will, at best, not contribute what could have been contributed to our knowledge. The government certainly has reason to undertake some research related to national security affairs which many scholars will not wish to do. There are real reasons for this decision. But, in granting this, it must also be said that there are many other areas of scholarly concern in which we have been badly served.

WILL THE "MIDDLE GROUND" BE FERTILE WITHOUT CAREFUL CULTIVATION?

In most of their professional lives, the scholar and the administrator will not meet on the middle level. Neither, in his own terms, lives at his full capacity there. At best, each may regard this middle level as a reservoir of stimulation in which both should take an occasional dip: the academic by a tour of duty in the government and the government official by an occasional period of advanced study in an academic environment. The scholar believes that he can only keep his keenness and prepare for the challenges of tomorrow by working at a higher level of abstraction than this middle level calls for, while the administrator, in his empirical role, is judged by his ability to deal in rather crude approximations, under great pressure, and with the tools at hand.

Recognizing this factor, the government has undertaken in various ways to provide stimulation to scholars and officials who choose and have the talent to spend at least some of their time in this middle ground. Some of this stimulation has come quite accidentally as a by-product of other programs. In RAND, for example, study of problems of "hardware" netted a nonprofit organization profits it could not keep; such an opportunity among men of curiosity is the perfect condition for the spontaneous creation of life, even life in the social sciences! RAND's aggressiveness and government indifference allowed a venture into the social sciences where one had not been foreseen.

Much of the government's subsidy grows from a highly limited conception of research in the social sciences. As has been pointed out on our research in the China area, by Allen Whiting, studies completed through 1955 "fell largely under the category of know your enemy. They had a forced focus and might be considered apart from what basic research should be designed to achieve and to accomplish." Of the total amount of money spent on research and development in the foreign area, the Department of State, with general political responsibility, spent only 1 percent. In most areas, research projects were highly programmatic. For example, in Africa 94 percent of the money spent on government sponsored research came from the AID program and 5 percent from the Armed Forces and the Department of Defense.

The academic observer can easily get support from the government to do a study which is related in an obvious way to a major government program. The economist who will deal with the effect of an aid program on the monetary system of country X stands squarely in the midst of that rallying ground while his colleague who would deal with the monetary system in a country in which we have no aid program may be obscured from view. This is true even if the contribution to our understanding of economics is far greater from the latter or even if we ultimately undertake an aid program in that country. Put another way, the inclination of the government is to deal with problems at hand; within those problems, the inclination is to deal with issues on which we can contribute or on which we are somewhat informed. Thus, the economist who would understand a whole economy may not find the information gathered by an AID team to be a coherent view, and the AID team may not be concerned with a coherent view in which there will be many elements outside of the capabilities and concerns of an AID program.

In mounting most large programs, the government commissions studies on a variety of aspects of the countries: their economies, their trade, their cultures, and their politics. In 1964, for example, the government spent approximately $8.6 million in the social sciences.

One of the favorite items of research in which the government is investing a great deal of money is "counterinsurgency." Dozens of classified reports and shelves of books have been written to order on this subject.

To take the dark side of the mirror first, three things can now be said:

First, almost all the studies concentrate on the simpler and more obvious aspects and avoid the complex political problems which have made guerrilla warfare possible. This remains true despite the fashionableness of quoting Mao.

Second, probably the whole mass of literature on this field has been less read and has exercised a lesser influence than Jean Lartéguy's *The Centurions*.

Third, there is clearly no way in which the better writings in the field are regularly called to the attention of those who should know all there is to know on such a topic. For example, however much one may dislike or disagree with Roger Trinquier's *Modern Warfare*, it should be required reading for all of those engaged with the Vietnam problem. Yet, I doubt that more than a handful of those so engaged in Washington have read it. It is sobering also to reflect that, if it is important, it has been important for some time. It has been available in French almost four years longer than in English.

Perhaps the brightest aspect of the picture is simply the fact that a significant number of senior government officials realize that we need keener analytical tools than we have and that these cannot be supplied from inside the government itself. Consequently, the government is willing to spend a small proportion of available resources on the acquisition of more detailed information and better methods of analysis.

Serious government-academic problems are shown in a vivid light by the Vietnam issue. Among them are these: First, the political dimensions of the problem of insurgency have never been satisfactorily examined. In lieu of this insight, we have concentrated on the military aspects of the problem. Precious and painful experience indicates that this is a mistake.

Second, we lack historical sense. How much do we know about guerrilla warfare from experience in Greece, Malaya, the Philippines, Korea, Kenya, the Congo, or Yugoslavia? If one discounts the military tactics to focus on the political, economic, and cultural problems, the answer is shockingly little.

Third, we know little of politics as seen by local politicians and their constituents. After all of our aid efforts throughout the economically underdeveloped parts of the world, we know less about the politics of any than any of the bosses in America knew about his city 50 years ago. From our distant and lofty perspective, and aware as we are of the major tasks of the free world in the cold war, we cannot understand why the local people act on the basis of their view of their obviously petty politics. Perhaps we can blame Jonathan Swift for this. In each one of the world's crises, we are Gulliver in Lilliput. With his great force and ability to rise above the petty, Gulliver sought honestly and benevolently to put the Lilliputian's affairs aright. What was brilliant about Swift's usage of Lilliput, as satire of the world's Gullivers, also shows of much Gulliverian political analysis. The political reality is that on their scale, the issues of Lilliputians were as real, compelling, and vital as those of the Gullivers on their scale. We have not, I believe, come to terms with this in international affairs as we have so brilliantly in domestic affairs.

Take Vietnam as an example. First, we have not approached the information we have had available on Vietnam with a consistent set of questions to force that information to yield to us a pattern of human activity. Take the recent and widely read article by George A. Carver, Jr. in *Foreign Affairs* in April of this year. Although about the best article I know, it surprised me by hardly treating the period of the 1920's and 1930's when presumably the major structural changes usually resulting from modernization occurred. More crucially, to understand the present scene, what a priori would appear to be the heart of the political problem is totally neglected. This is the question of "legitimacy."

To survive, except in a military occupation, a government must be accepted. The French, I gather, were accepted as legitimate rulers of Indochina (at least to the extent that their rule was not effectively challenged) until the Japanese invasion and suppression of French rule in March 1945. During the war years, however, the Vichy-Japanese agreements tended to compromise the French in the eyes of those opposed to either; then with the defeat of the French by those who were clearly newcomers and had no trace of public acceptance, the Japanese made it possible for a native underground to lay claim to be the legitimate authority. The spell of legitimacy was broken and the return of the French with overwhelming military force could not turn back the clock. Then, when the French finally evacuated the country, they divided it along an arbitrary line and so created what we in the Middle East used to call an "artificial State," with a government led by an emperor in the south, while another "artificial state" was led by a vigorous, ruthless government which had aspired to legitimacy by warfare against the Japanese and French in the north. The contest was always unequal. But the key weakness of the southern regime has never been touched by all the aid and succor we have given. There are, indeed, those who believe that the more massive is our help, the more nonnationalist the southern government becomes.

I do not wish to belabor this point because, frankly, I know very little about Vietnam. However, our experience in Vietnam would suggest to me that neither in the government nor in the academic community have we as yet been able to make a very deep analysis of the major factors that shape politics in the country. If such an analysis were available, we could judge the government's receptivity to it, but since it is not available, we should not wonder that the government has had to use what it had while seeking better, if still crude, approximations to an analysis of guerrilla warfare.

Second, our lack of attention to the politics of this, our Lilliput, is, however, evident in our view of the Buddhists as totally irresponsible. From our point of view, the Buddhists have been playing Lilliputian politics while the big issue is on the scale of Gulliver. But the complex nature of the problem of Catholic-Buddhist relations appears to be little appreciated. Adam Roberts, in an article entitled "Buddhism and Politics in South Viet Nam" in *The World Today* of June 1965, makes the case that their actions and attitudes stem not from simple perversity but from real and present dangers.

Those who have grappled with the problems of the Middle East will remember the frustration of our elders who in the 1950's tried to get the Arabs to forget their "petty" quarrel with Israel in order to defend themselves against the massive Soviet peril which was so clear to us.

The important thing is not whether the issues are grand or petty from our perspective but rather whether or not one understands what issues move men. These are issues, I suggest, which we as authorities on foreign affairs may be less apt to appreciate than a working politician. Perhaps as we come to understand more deeply the affairs of many parts of the world, we will turn a larger part of our attention increasingly to petty issues which are the stuff of politics. It may be that Vietnam will force us to learn this approach to world affairs. If so, it may be a salutary lesson although in probably the most expensive school we have ever attended. Parenthetically, we should remember that the Lilliputians, in their fear of Gulliver's great power — and lack of discernment of their feelings and property — trapped and almost destroyed him.

A third factor is the lack of historical sense in the government. There is very little that we have been able to extrapolate from our previous experiences in other guerrilla situations which has helped us as we have become embroiled in Vietnam. The little that we have been able to derive has been in the nature of gimmickry — the "strategic hamlet" from the Malayan fortified village, the concept of closing the frontier from the Greek civil war, and various other techniques from the Philippines. But what all these situations should have taught us is not a tactic or a device but rather an awareness of the factors in politics which have made guerrilla warfare possible.

The government, obviously, cannot be expected to be an historian. Events which are a few years old are, from the government's point of view, "nonevents." Certainly the academic community must be the repository of historical information. But where is the first-rate history of any of the major political crises since the Second World War? Surely these histories are no less a part of general history than are those of other rebellions and wars. Yet we know remarkably little about them. It is, perhaps, a measure of the failure of the academic community that the only history of the Communist conquest of China, surely a major historical event of all time, is by a French general and was published in English 14 years after it appeared in France. When the best minds in the academic community turn aside, we get poorly conceived projects like Camelot, which is now in the public press, whose very clumsiness threatens research of social scientists in several parts of the world. If such projects are bad, perhaps we need to think more broadly of means to safeguard both the field and those who plow it. One answer might be large-scale, carefully controlled public research organizations or stimulators of research that are amenable to academic influence if not control.

Whether scholars like it or not, whether they join or stand aloof, there is a clear public need for more and better information and analysis, and the government must seek it. The better the government, the more it will seek. Therefore, the academic community will not protect itself from such fiascos as Camelot by closing its eyes or, like the lady of Shalott,

Like some bold seer or in a trance,
Seeing all his own mischance —
With a glassy countenance
Did she look to Camelot.

WILL GOVERNMENTAL STIMULATION HOBBLE ACADEMIC RESEARCH?

One of the most sensitive problems in governmental use of scholarly research is a simple and very human one: We all like to use ideas and concepts that bolster our own conceptions and prejudices and that protect our previous commitments.

The consultant or the concept, therefore, who or which opposes the main line, rather than suggesting refinements of it or ways to implement it more successfully, is apt to be rejected. Offices which deal with problems develop vested interests and invest prestige in them. It is very difficult, for example, to conceive of the various offices dealing with NATO affairs commissioning or being receptive to studies which imply that NATO should be disbanded. It was no doubt very largely for this reason that throughout the 1950's the foremost scholars in the major American universities dealing with Far Eastern affairs were not used as consultants by the government, nor did their thinking seriously influence American governmental planning for that area.

In short, not only does government-sponsored research tend to be concentrated in areas of reasonably immediate and practical application but also tends to deal ultimately with how to carry out something already assumed to be the right course of action. Studies that concentrate on nonpriority areas, or which suggest that current policy may be wrong, generally have to be financed privately. In the academic "market," the availability of research funds clearly shapes the growth of the field. Excessive government stimulation of scholarly activity, consequently, in its concentration on the immediate, the practical, and the orthodox, can prevent scholars from exercising two other major functions.

The first of these is "pathfinding": The scholar alone can mark out new areas beyond the immediate concern to the administrator. Of course, if scholars did not think ahead of their market, reality and our perception of it would be very different. It is a major task that the scholar alone undertakes when he moves ahead into new and yet uncharted areas. Like a horse going up-hill, he must be given his head or the rider is apt to pull him backward into the plain below.

The major reason why the government cannot be expected to finance basic work in the social sciences is the considerable lag between the time when an idea is first advanced, is amplified by research, published, gradually wins acceptance, and finally passes into the mainstream of thought. Between the birth of a concept and some practical result may be a decade. For a large part of this decade, the government has no operational interest in the idea. Indeed, activities in which the government has a direct interest may have only a remote relationship to the original concept. So it takes an unusual government official to see the importance of government assistance to "pure" research.

Nor can the government be expected to finance the work of the scholar as critic. Critique is not necessarily a major function of scholarly activities. But, in an open and democratic society, the scholar is to some extent the conscience, the educated conscience, of the public. It is the essence of the scholar's value that he be irresponsible, that is to say, not tagged with the responsibility for action. It is for this very reason that the government itself maintains cadres of officials who have no responsibility for previous decisions so that, theoretically at least, they can think each problem through *de novo*. In practice, of course, they can do so only within limits. It is the essence, moreover, of our system that a major part of the criticism of governmental activity be in the public domain. It is vital for the health of our two-party system that policy issues be brought out into the open by those who have the leisure and the equipment to elucidate them. Many of us in the government and out, I believe, felt that the recent debate on Vietnam was not very enlightening. Some of us were annoyed at the level to which parts of it descended. But, in a democracy, the importance of such public debates is clear. Only if the academic community is vigorous and well informed can such public confrontations prove useful.

Obviously, to some extent, the scholar loses his freedom when he becomes, even indirectly, an employee of the government. At the very least, he acquires access to confidential information. In the government work, as in private business, this gives him a privileged position and imposes restraints on his pen.

Much information is classified and restricted not because of its inherent sensitivity but because it was acquired by sensitive methods. Much which is sensitive today is not so after a short period of time, but it is extraordinarily difficult to declassify information because it is a terribly time-consuming operation and those who know the information and its state of sensitivity well enough to exercise this judgment are usually very busy people. Historically, "automatic" systems of declassification have not worked, since at each moment everyone is apt to believe that his project is likely to be sensitive (read "important") for a long time to come and that if he makes a mistake, it is far better to make a conservative mistake. Often, therefore, one cannot say what would prove or illustrate his point.

More important is the fact that access to this information has deprived the scholar of some of his valuable irresponsibility. To some degree, the scholar who is employed in a staff position in the government has more freedom than does his colleague outside the government who has access to restricted information as a consultant. At least his lines are clear. No small part of the fear many scholars have even of a tenuous involvement with the government is that this will somehow ensnare and deprive them of their ability to speak frankly and openly. This contributes to a failure of communication between the government and the academic community. I do not believe there is any simple prescription for this problem. The simple answer would seem to be that the scholar should not seek to acquire governmental information. But, obviously, this is not a sensible solution. It is the very nature of scholarship that the scholar seeks his information wherever he can find it. Some do not. Others even deny that the government has anything to offer, but no one who has had access to the treasure house of information within the government can deny that it is extremely difficult to write on contemporary international affairs without such access. This, I suspect, will remain an extraordinarily thorny problem of governmental-academic relationships. Perhaps the best that can be hoped for is that both the government and the academic community will recognize it as a problem and do their utmost to minimize its pernicious side effects.

IS SCHOLARLY RESEARCH ACTUALLY COMMUNICATED TO THE GOVERNMENT?

Who uses scholarly research? Are the seminal books in the social sciences or the major professional journals read by administrators?

Without undue exaggeration, one can say that very little of the product of academic research reaches administrators. If one were to question the foreign service officers engaged in political analysis as to what works on political theory or the social sciences in general they have read in the last five years, one would conclude that they read little more than the general public. Most of us who receive royalty checks know how little this is. About the best that can be hoped for is that those men and women charged with a particular problem will read reasonably widely in that particular field. But, alas, it must be admitted that this is often not the case.

A major problem is the sheer bulk of the works produced in the social sciences today. A vast amount of material is developed and even those who are temperamentally and intellectually receptive to it simply do not have the time — or one must admit, the energy — to read more than a fraction. I suppose that during the past four years I have read somewhat more than the average on my particular area of responsibility and on theories of social and political analysis; yet, as I look over the bibliography of works in progress on my area, I know in my heart — or in my eyes — that I shall not even skim a small part of the available literature.

Another, and very serious problem, is that often many layers are interposed between the "consumer" and the "producer." I have seen studies which dealt with subjects of major interest to me and others engaged in planning policy that were not so posed as to contribute on the most crucial aspects of our concern. Others, which were so designed to deal with priority affairs often, from my point of view, focused on the wrong priorities.

A large part of this is the fault of the consumer who fails to make his needs known. In my own experience in government, this has not been overwhelmingly difficult because many of the "brokers" of research are anxious for suggestions. And, in most of the major studies in which I was involved, a considerable amount of what outside the government would be regarded as basic research was used or specifically commissioned. However, some government departments are more research minded than others: historically, the Department of State has been far down the list. The 1 percent it now commissions in the field of international affairs is ten times what it financed in 1960. Consequently, major programs are undertaken without the sort of preparation which would be regarded as normal in most American industry.

The Department of Defense has been very active in stimulating research in international affairs. Clearly, it is true that with a huge Defense budget, a tiny percentage is a big amount of money, but I believe that inhospitality to research is more than a question of funds. A cause may be the feeling that the Department of State should be the expert on world affairs and that, for it to seek outside help is to suggest that it is not doing its job; the Department of Defense clearly need feel no qualms. In any event, without the layers of staff officers involved in planning and analysis, it is possible that little research would be commissioned. As it is, however, all too often the products of research, like Christ at Eboli, stop short of those whose needs are greatest.

Often a major influence comes from a general book which, for obscure reasons, catches an influential audience and then becomes almost required reading because everyone is talking about it. Such works, which may or may not be good scholarship, perform a pathfinder task to make others receptive to more specific studies. Such a book as Barbara Tuchman's *Guns of August* exercised a profound impact at a crucial moment in our government. Few who read it were concerned about its subject matter *per se* but it left one clear message: events tend to acquire a momentum of their own. Thus, while Step 12 is not inevitable, it is such a logical extension of Step 11 that an extra effort of will and intelligence is required to avoid it once one has taken Steps 1 through 11. So, as one reaches Step 11, he can look back and see that Steps 1 through 11 constitute a "policy" which now makes its own demands upon the policy maker. This was the central message of Miss Tuchman's book that came across in Washington and clearly influenced the attitude of those who made policy.

Another sort of impact is made by works which leave vivid phrases or conceptual notions which bring order or, at least, some light into the darkened lanes of our international affairs. Such a book was Walt Rostow's *Stages of Economic Growth*. Here again, it was a single point which has changed the thought of many about economic development: that was the concept of "take-off."

Both of these works illustrate, by contrast, a central problem of much of the social sciences today: Like some modern art and poetry, the literature of the social sciences does not communicate efficiently or gracefully. We have some of the snobbery of wine tasters — ours is a superior vintage which can be known only to us because it does not travel well. Let us admit that this is true, in a minority of cases, but we have come to make almost a fetish of noncommunication in the social sciences as so much more of our society has become geared to the mass media. I do not suggest for a moment that scholarship need be popularized but the clear, the sharp, and the vivid presentation of ideas need not damage those ideas and might help to cut down significantly the long gap, mentioned earlier, between conceptions and influence.

There is an interesting passage in Lartéguy's *The Praetorians*, in which the author describes the way in which thought on the political process is communicated through a military bureaucracy. He says: "*The Rape of the Masses*, 600 pages. What captain on active service could find time to read it from cover to cover? So one, who has dipped into it, mentions it to another, who discusses it with a third, and everyone has the impression he knows the book by heart. The same applies to Mao's instructions on guerrilla warfare." It may truly be in this way that the scholar and the official meet.

Occasionally we are not "open" to a direct approach from the social sciences. Then, it may be a novel or a historical analogy that leads us to a new perception. Lartéguy's books have certainly been a major influence in thought about guerrilla warfare although they deal with a particular period in a highly personalized form. One major danger of this sort of writing is that in the requirement of the genre the message may be distorted. Thus, Lartéguy certainly exaggerates the importance of those heroes who operated with determination and bravery and the contrary weakness of those villains who did not. Take as an example of this romanticism Lartéguy's description of the Subprefect Denis Pellegrin in *The Praetorians*. Clearly, this figure could only make a hash of any administration because, while delightful and colorful as a drinking or fighting companion, he is highly unpredictable. Yet, this dash of Elizabethan robustness is exactly the riposte to guerrilla warfare Lartéguy boils down to. Perhaps the best that can be said is that Lartéguy has made it possible for us to read Roger Trinquier. Is there something else? Clearly there is. But what it is has not yet been given to us by the social sciences.

In a similar category of indirection, though quite a different sort of work, is the use of history to make a contemporary point. The last issue of *Foreign Affairs* contains such an article by Henry Owens. All historians, consciously or not, are dealing with the relevant factors of today, as they perceive them in their views of the past.

MAJOR CONTRIBUTION OF THE ACADEMIC COMMUNITY

In the postwar years, in addition to supplying a tremendous amount of information, having trained legions of people with various skills needed by the government and sensitizing our society to some of the problems of world affairs, the academic community has made a major contribution in forcing us to think, for the first time, in terms of a "world view."

Two major approaches to the world have dominated American thought in the past 20 years. While they are intertwined, they can be usefully separated. The contrast is that of the tactician and the strategist or the pragmatist and the theoretician. In practice, the "operator" believes or acts as though he believes that human events, if not totally unconnected and unique, are so nearly so that the development of patterns and plans is an unprofitable "exercise." The task, however described, is really to cope with the problem at hand.

But most of us would agree that in virtually all human activities the disparate moves of the clever tactician often do not add up to a brilliant strategy. The classic example is, of course, in chess where it is occasionally the single tactically wrong move, the sacrifice, which wins the game. Knowing this, we seek a strategy, or are impressed by those who have one. It is largely for this reason that the major postwar development of a theory of international action, the mechanistic view associated with the RAND Corporation, became so influential. This approach had immediate practical application in military planning in the cold war and spread far beyond to a new field called "politicomilitary affairs."

In this "Game Theory" approach, foreign affairs problems were reduced to "Scenarios," were "gamed out" and thus revoked. The *Strategy of Conflict*, as Thomas Schelling called his book, pitted two antagonists against one another in a "confrontation," and logical responses to given moves were analyzed so that a sequence could be played, "escalated" to a showdown. In the course of this, the perception of international politics changed. Not only was a confrontation implicit in each scenario, if both "teams" carried through to the conclusion, but essentially there were just two teams, with some irritating interruptions by bit players. And, perhaps more important, the real stuff of international relations, the peculiarities of the several "players" were washed out so that a sort of "world-man," who logically and coolly could understand and rightly play the game, was posited. That this school of thought deeply affected our thinking on the Berlin and Cuba crises is evident.

However, when it comes to affect the attitudes and acts of the United States outside the framework of the cold war, this theory and its extensions into "counterinsurgency" so simplify politics as to mislead. Behind such problems as Vietnam are enormously complex political, psychological, and economic forces quite apart from Communist subversion, however much they may offer a fertile field for that subversion. To attempt to deal with these forces as though they were mere plays on a world gaming board is inappropriate and likely to be unsuccessful. No American politician faced with local forces and attitudes he can clearly perceive would attempt to bypass these with broad and, to the electorate, vague issues, or cope with local forces with devices comparable to "strategic hamlets," lightweight rifles, "choppers," defoliation, etc.

It seems to me that it probably will only be from the academic community that the government can receive now the kind of stimulation in coping with world affairs beyond the cold war, that the Game Theory and the mechanistic view of the cold war contributed in the 1950's.

WHERE CAN SCHOLARS CREATE MOST IN THE PERIOD AHEAD?

Anyone who has served in the government, particularly those of us who came from academic life and were privileged to have a wide vista of governmental activities, will have his favorite area, his chosen field wherein he can see current and potential contributions of other scholars to be most important and/or most needed. Those who deal, or have dealt, with specific areas will stress perceptions on a given area — obviously we need to know a great deal more about Brazil to get along with the Brazilians — or those who have grappled with functional problems will feel the same way about their functions — much more needs to be done about economic theory before we can deal adequately with the problems of development and economic growth.

Beyond the specific, however, I believe that there is a more important if a more vague category. This is the perception of the very complexity and rapid transformation of our world. Everyone knows that mankind is complex, although as we begin to perceive more, particularly through comparative politics, we can derive a greater understanding of the view of the Lilliputians and become less Gulliver-like in our myopia. Then, and perhaps only then, can we come to appreciate more of the dynamics of the politics of our world revolution. We have come far but we have a long way to go.

In my field, in Middle Eastern studies, the upward push since 1945 has been truly astonishing. Perhaps we are still too close to our own past work to distinguish all of the upward surges within that period. But I am fairly confident that we have been on a plateau for the past 5 or 6 years. It is not an uncomfortable or barren plateau. Many of us in the government found the view from it a bit breathtaking. I, for one, was really staggered by the amount of detailed information already accumulated and being gathered in the Middle East and by the battalions of men who could read the local languages and who knew a great deal about the local cultures.

But it is perhaps here where the scholar makes his most significant contribution, for he is restless. The comforts of this plateau are his boredom for he seeks a better view, even if it is of areas where the sun has not yet fallen.

In the next move upward, we cannot go alone or even so much alone as we have often been in the past. Rather, we will have to go hand in hand with those who would know their own countries. For in the social sciences as in the natural sciences from here on massive inputs of energy will be required for each new advance.

It is well that this should be the case for the scholars of other lands have developed some of the same sensitivities about their intellectual raw materials that their politicians have about their oil, rubber, and copper. Africans want to participate in developing African studies, for example, and feel somewhat exploited when we move ahead without them.

To the degree that the academic community joins in such an enterprise to develop a better world view with greater sensitivity to an understanding of the myriad of local forces and issues which make people act the way they do in the world's Lilliputs, our government, like Gulliver, can grow in discernment and skill to match its power and can, more effectively and safely move us and them toward the goals of life, liberty, and the pursuit of happiness.

Ithiel de Sola Pool

Massachusetts Institute of Technology

The Necessity for Social Scientists Doing Research for Governments

The social sciences can be described as the new humanities of the twentieth century. They have the same relationship to the training of mandarins of the twentieth century that the humanities have always had to the training of mandarins in the past. In the past, when one wanted to educate a prince, or policy maker, or civil servant to cope with his job, one taught him Latin, philosophy, history, literature — most of which had very little obvious relationship to what he was going to do. Yet in some way, these disciplines were supposed to enable him better to understand human affairs. This training worked to a considerable degree. Today, by means of the social sciences we are able to give him an even better tool for understanding the world around him. The day of philosophy, literature, etc., is not over. They have their value. But there are a great many things that we have learned to understand better through psychology, sociology, systems analysis, political science. Such knowledge is important to the mandarins of the future for it is by knowledge that men of power are humanized and civilized. They need a way of perceiving the consequences of what they do if their actions are not to be brutal, stupid, bureaucratic, but rather intelligent and humane. The only hope for humane government in the future is through the extensive use of the social sciences by government.

The social sciences are one way of finding answers to the questions which politicians and policy makers must always answer, namely, what are the human consequences of what they do? Max Weber in his classic essay on *Politics as a Vocation* pointed out that in a complex modern mass society political leadership is more important than ever before. Without political leadership of a certain kind, he said "the dark night will be upon us," a prediction that he wrote only a few years before Nazism did come over Germany. It was a very vivid prediction of what actually happened in Germany. Max Weber pointed out that if the kinds of government that we have in the modern world are going to function humanely, we must have political leaders who will be true to what he called an ethic of responsibility, that is an ethic that concerns itself with the human consequences of what the politician does. The alternative is what he called an absolute ethic, an ethic that derives from ideologies, dogmas of one sort or another. That is essentially the choice that we face, the choice between policy based on moralisms and policy based on social science.

We see this choice all around us in American government today. I would like to use as an example, the Department of Defense. The McNamara revolution is a star example of how the introduction of social science systems analysis and other relevant kinds of knowledge has had the effect of taming what would otherwise be a terrifying institution. What could be more terrifying than a gigantic military establishment possessing nuclear weapons. We are all aware of the expansionist, mission-justifying character of any bureaucracy. A 50-billion-dollar bureaucracy justifying its nuclear mission is frightening to contemplate. What has tamed it? I think it is fair to say that probably the most important contribution to arms control over the past decade has been the introduction of cost-effectiveness analysis. This rational process poses the question against every new proposal whether it really serves the purpose of maintaining order in the world. It compels a measurement of consequences rather than asking whether the better weapon fits the military cliché of always seeking a bigger bang. That is the ideological goal to which a military man is committed by his professional role.

The McNamara revolution is essentially the bringing of social science analysis into the operation of the Department of Defense. It has remade American defense policy in accordance with a series of ideas that germinated in the late 1950's in the RAND Corporation among people like Schelling, Wohlstetter, Kahn, and Kaufmann. These were academic people playing their role as social scientists (whatever their early training may have been). They were trying to decide with care and seriousness what would lead to deterrence and what would undermine it. While one might argue with their conclusions at any given point, it seems to me that it is the process that has been important. The result has been the humanization of the Department of Defense. That is a terribly important contribution to the quality of American life.

An organization like the Department of Defense has manifold needs for the tools of social science analysis as a way of understanding its world better. From the days in World War I when the intelligence test became an operational instrument in manpower management, the defense establishment has been a major user of psychology. As the world's largest training and educational institution, DOD has immense needs for scientific knowledge about selection, training, and human engineering. At least equally significant is DOD's need for foreign area knowledge. The Department of Defense is certainly the world's largest consumer of the skills of the geographer. It also needs linguistics. It also needs knowledge of the culture, values, and social and political structures of every country that is a potential enemy, or ally, or scene of turmoil — and that is virtually all the world.

One could go on and make the same sort of case for the use of social science by any department or agency of government. Some departments or agencies of government everybody likes, and the case for research for them would be noncontroversial. Everybody likes the Department of Agriculture. It helps farmers and that is a good thing. Nobody objects to social scientists making their contributions to agricultural extension programs. Everybody likes the Department of Labor and would agree that if we could introduce better human relations, better mediation, etc., it would be a good thing. Nobody objects to social scientists making contributions of that sort. Everybody among liberals likes AID and I am glad they do because I can think of no more important program in the world today. Nobody objects to social scientists making their contribution to trying to figure out how to raise living standards in the developing countries around the world. But I do not want to make such easy cases. I want to make the hard case. I want to make the case that agencies like the FBI, or prisons, or the CIA need social scientists just as much as do the agencies that everybody likes.

I do not think there is any advantage to the world to have prisons run by "dicks" whose only knowledge of what to do is the proverbial lore of their profession on how to keep men in line. It is a fine thing for social scientists to address themselves to trying to figure out how to achieve the results that society has asked of prisons in a more humane, more sensible, and more rational fashion. Perhaps social scientists can teach some of their insight and skills to prison wardens. I am not asking that every social scientist necessarily address himself to punitive problems. If you do not like hanging around prisons, you do not have to. This, however, is an important role for social scientists.

I would say exactly the same thing for the CIA. The U.S. government made a decision that it needs knowledge about the outside world. It needs to act with a certain amount of intelligence (small i or big I) instead of stupidity. Most of the knowledge of the outside world that the CIA collects it collects by social-science research methods, that is, through reading newspapers, listening to radio broadcasts, and asking people questions. Social research including area studies, history, anthropology, sociology, political science, and statistics provide both important inputs and important knowledge of methods of analysis to the Intelligence community. The CIA, as its name implies, should be the central social research organization to enable the federal government to understand the societies and cultures of the world. The fact that it uses as little social science as it does is deplorable. We should be demanding that they use us more. Do you feel that the U.S. government does not seem to understand Vietnamese villagers, or Dominican students, or Soviet writers? If you think that Washington could act better if it had a deeper comprehension of the social processes at work around the world, then you should be demanding that the CIA hire and write contracts with our best social scientists. The research now done by the CIA is sometimes well done and sometimes not very well done. I can think of no greater contribution a social scientist could make to the intelligence of the U.S. government than to help improve this effort at knowledge of the outside world. I would say the same thing for the FBI, which many academic people do not like because they do not like particular policies of it. But as long as we agree that it is a useful and necessary thing for the civil order of this country to have some kind of federal assistance in policing, then I would hope that it would operate with as much humanity and knowledge as the social sciences can bring to bear by working with it.

The organization with which I am affiliated, the Center for International Studies of M.I.T., has in the past had contracts with the CIA. A year ago, we decided regretfully not to take any new ones, not because some people do not like the CIA but for the simple reason that the classification placed on the existence of contracts, even though the work was unclassified and published, prevented disclosure of the party for whom the work was being done. This was a condition we were unwilling to accept. We were perfectly willing to do public, published scientific research for the U.S. government via any of its departments, but we had to be able to say who the sponsor was.

So far I have talked only about the United States. You remember my title was "The Necessity for Social Scientists Doing Research for Governments." I have been talking to a group of primarily American social scientists about the work that they might do in relation to their own government. But exactly the same thing applies to all governments around the world. Let me talk specifically about the developing countries, where it is perfectly clear that the social sciences have an enormous contribution to make. Without their contribution, the process of development, if it ever occurs, will be very much slower, more painful, more violent, more cruel, more arbitrary, and more unequal.

One of the key problems in the developing countries is the relationship of the intelligentsia to the masses of the people, to the peasantry in most cases. This has always been a key problem in the process of development. In Russia in the nineteenth century, there emerged the Norodniki movement of intellectuals who went back to the people. They went to villages and tried to work with them there. They were a kind of early Peace Corps if you wish. This motivation among the intelligentsia to create a nation, by bridging the gap that has made most developing nations two or more nations within one, is essential to the achievement of modernity. This drive to join "the people" has been one of the most important sources of political movements in all the developing countries. It has been the source of revolutionary drive from Norodnism, through social democracy and into the Bolshevik movement, which was just another approach to the problem. The same drive today is the key problem in Vietnam. The relation of the intelligentsia to the people is also a key problem in India. Indeed, it is a key problem in every developing country.

The social sciences provide a new and better way of linking the intelligentsia to their masses. The link will be made somehow with or without us. If it is made by ideological political movements, it will be made by revolutions and it will be made in turmoil and struggle by people killing each other. There is a better way now of making this link and that is through social science research. The social sciences provide a way in which the intelligentsia can begin to discover what their country is all about. They can begin to learn what their peasants really want and think, and learn how to bring them into a common society. Through social science they can begin to make one country out of two. So there is a tremendous impetus behind the social sciences in developing countries, as well as conservative and competitive revolutionary resistance to them. There is every reason to expect an enormous growth in the social sciences in the developing countries in the coming years. There will be a great desire on their part for the cooperation, assistance, and help of experienced social scientists from abroad who are willing to turn their interests and attention to the kind of problem that is meaningful to them.

The growth in the social sciences and in the demand for them in the developing countries is the big picture and the one which we should keep in mind. During the last year, since the Camelot episode, however, our attention has been excessively focused on a perturbation to the big picture. We have been preoccupied with the problems that arise in international cooperation in the social sciences (as they do in international cooperation in any field). We have taken the attacks upon social science by its natural foes on the Left and Right as representing the dominant trend rather than as representing counterattacks by ideologists who recognize that the power of pragmatic social analysis is a threat to them.

Nonetheless, I do not wish to minimize the problems created by rampant nationalism or emotional revolutionism. The dark night of reaction can take over a country. Progressive intelligent programs can be defeated. If the social scientist acts tactlessly and badly in sensitive conflict-ridden situations, he can make things worse, just as badly conducted exchange programs can make intercultural relations worse rather than better.

Considering the sensitivity of the situation in which the social scientist engaged in foreign area studies works, he certainly must give close attention to how he conducts himself. What can be said about the proper principles for the conduct of international research? In ethics, there is one principle that encompasses all the rest, the Golden Rule: Do unto others as you would have them do unto you. So also, in the field of conducting research abroad there is really one basic principle for university scholars. That one basic principle is that you, as a social scientist, have no right to ask foreign persons to contribute time, money, cooperation, or political support unless the purpose of the project is one which they see as their own, that is, one that they see as a service to their own country and people, and one to which they are themselves deeply and personally committed. It is not proper for us to go into the field to use fellow social scientists or interview subjects solely for an advantage of our own or even for the advantage of science per se. Note that I am not talking about the kind of research that does not make any demands upon the foreign country. The individual traveler who has a passport and a visa and goes some place and observes and talks to people and does not force them to submit to a questionnaire, but is solely observer, talking informally to them, is likely to be accepted in almost all countries of the world. He makes no demands upon the limited resources of time, personnel, and commitment of the host country. Even poor and dictatorial countries generally recognize the right of the individual traveler thus to serve his own curiosity. But the minute you start making demands on the scarce resources of a country, you have to consider that in most of the world the research resources that you are asking for are extremely scarce indeed. Note also that I am now talking about university social scientists. Intelligence personnel such as diplomats do not limit themselves to seeking information that serves the country in which they are seeking it. That is one reason that they are not always welcome. The academic social scientist on the other hand, if he is working on a research project abroad that demands the cooperation of foreign people, must find a common ground in terms of his interests and his needs. If he does that, most other probems of human relations take care of themselves.

Sponsorship is really a secondary question. It is not a nonexistent question but decidedly secondary. The primary question is whether the people with whom you are working abroad see the activity as one that is theirs, in their interests, and one that they want. The sensitivity of where the money comes from varies from country to country and from situation to situation. It is obvious that one would not propose cooperating in a contract under CIA auspices to a Soviet institute of sociology. There would be sensitivities. But that is an extreme example. It is certainly not true that Defense-sponsored research is, *ipso facto*, unpopular in all countries of the world. On the contrary, there are countries that see their problems in terms of security and are anxious for cooperation with and support of their own security research. They may welcome the cooperation of American and other agencies that are able to provide that kind of help.

The record of experience is perfectly clear. ONR, RAND, and a variety of Defense-connected organizations have had extensive research activities in friendly countries, welcomed by both scientists and statesmen in those countries.

The primary question is always the relationship of the American social scientist to the foreign social scientist.

With regard to that consideration I have laid down a condition that many social scientists would reject because they reject the obligation of political responsibility. Many social scientists would say that our job is to advance science. They would not concede that research cannot be conducted if it is not approved or liked in foreign countries. While conceding that is a high price to pay, I believe that in the present state of the world it has to be paid. We happen to come from the richest and most powerful country in the world. We go to countries that are very sensitive about this power relationship. This being the case, the academic social scientist going abroad cannot claim that power relationships are not his business and that he is interested only in scientific problems. He cannot safely treat his foreign colleagues as hired employees, people who collect data for him, and who are fairly recompensed by virtue of being paid. This attitude will not be acceptable when these countries have to conserve what limited resources they have for purposes that are of national significance to them and to which they have deep commitments.

So while I would object to any professional association legislating "guidelines," still I agree that there are a number of principles which follow from the general principle that overseas research must reflect the concerns of the hosts. Publication in the host country is usually very important so that people in that country can obtain the results of the study. Publication abroad is preferable at the same time or earlier. Also very important is that the activity result in institution building within the host country.

For a scholar with a certain amount of sensitivity and caution and with a real devotion to the principle that if you are asking people abroad to do things they have to be things that are meaningful to them, it is possible to work on almost any subject in the world, in almost any place in the world, but not (it must be recognized) by any methods in the world. I can illustrate this by my own experience. My own research tends to be in very sensitive areas. At the moment, as the Chairman said, I am working on the communications systems of the Communist countries. I have been engaged in this activity for a number of years. One of my decisions, made long before Camelot and any of the present review procedures for research in this area, was that under no circumstances would I use my Defense Department support to send anybody to a Communist country. It would be playing with that person's safety. Everything we are doing is open, published scientific research, but that may not be accepted by the Communists. I have, myself, visited Eastern Europe and have talked about my research, but I have done it on the invitation of an East European research organization. Increasingly the socialist countries are using social science to solve their problems and they are ready to collaborate with Western social scientists, but on what they see as their research. Their scientists cannot agree to be subjects.

Similar reactions are found around the world. Let me quote from a document.

The people of X had had a discouraging experience of exploitation by researchers, writers and politicians. These visitors had customarily breezed in with their own questions to answer, their own books to write, their own careers to promote. After establishing some relationships in the neighborhood, obtaining their materials, and making a few promises, they had moved on, leaving X essentially as it was before. Residents had been made indignant by the resulting labels that had been attached to X and by tourists who came to see and exclaim. Reactions ran high in X. The people of X wanted to be sure that there was going to be something in it for them this time. They wanted to be hired for whatever jobs were to become available. . . .

X happens to be 100th Street in Harlem. Sensitivity to being studied is not just an international problem.

Since Camelot, however, there have been some rather absurd reactions by social scientists to these sensitivities. Alarmed at the attacks upon themselves, they have looked for talismans that could protect them. Worst of all, a kind of neo-McCarthyism has raised its head in the academic community. There has arisen an attitude that claims the right to censor and restrict the kinds of research that one's colleagues choose to do. Specifically, the research that is being attacked by the witch hunters is that done for the U.S. government. There is going on now a lot of discussion, the tenor of which is that social scientists somehow should not be working for government agencies because such an association will corrupt them.

There are obviously wide differences of opinion among

social scientists as well as among citizens about government policies and that is as it should be. A social scientist should not work for an agency with whose basic purposes he is not in sympathy, but the claim that other scientists should not put their skills at the service of agencies of which they approve is an arrogant imposition. To serve policy with knowledge is their professional duty, to be praised not criticized.

Unfortunately some of the same destructive panic about social scientists and policy agencies has appeared in Congress and in some parts of the executive branch too. George Denney and I have debated the issue of regulation of overseas research on various occasions in the past when the State Department rules were still under consideration, so it is no surprise to him that we do not agree 100 percent. But I do not want to spend my time arguing over spilt milk. The President issued an order, regulations have been instituted under it, and I must say that the State Department has been doing an extremely good job in trying to implement what I consider to be an impossible assignment.

Let me conclude by explaining why I consider it an impossible assignment and why I regret personally that it was ever thrown onto the shoulders of the State Department, as ably as they may be handling it. One central objective seems to me to be reducing the degree to which sensitive social science research abroad has to carry the cachet of State Department or any U.S. government authority. Sensitive research should be as far as possible the personal responsibility of the person conducting it. Any system of review and approvals has the opposite effect. It means that a project, once approved, is the sanctioned activity of the U.S. government and of its foreign affairs agency, the Department of State. The decision to do the research and the mode of its conduct if reviewed represent a government decision. It is far better if the record is clear that all decisions derive from the individual scholar and that if he does anything foolish he has merely misused government funds that had been given him. He should be disownable.

A better move would have been to improve the communication processes within the government so that the State Department would have known very early what was going on in the research activities of other agencies. I don't think there is much doubt that if the Secretary of State or any of his staff, or any Ambassador were to go to another agency and say, "Look at the trouble you might make, look how bad this could be" he would be listened to with great, if anything, excessive respect. The chances of a responsible official of another agency going against this kind of advice would be very small indeed.

A system of regulations and review reduces the chances of the State Department getting the information needed to give advice. We all know how bureaucracies operate. If something must be reviewed, the description is written so that the person who has to review it knows as little about what he is reviewing as possible. That is an inevitable process. So the problem of maintaining State Department control would be much better solved by increasing the flow of communication to the State Department about what is going on, and by the State Department expressing itself through government channels when it felt mistakes were being made, better than by review. As Mr. Denney so well pointed out, no review process is going to prevent another Camelot. While it may help, many of the most important decisions in any overseas project are decisions of detail made as the project is under way in the field. Perhaps some individual is doing something that somebody else could do perfectly well, but is just incompetent at handling his interpersonal relations and steps on people's toes. A flow of information may help catch this as it is going on. A review process that has stamped a project O.K. some months before hinders control because it gives this man carte blanche. These are the reasons why I, for one, feel that the present system of controls is ill-advised. Nonetheless we have it, and it is being carried out by the State Department as well as human competence permits.

I have said that one desirable direction of movement is

improvement of communication within the government. Another one would be to give the State Department a large amount of money for the conduct of research. Any agency that is going to examine and evaluate research and have any sensible understanding of it has to be an agency that is doing research. Perhaps the most useful thing that could happen in improving the whole conduct of foreign area research in the U.S. government would be if INR in the State Department received say a $10,000,000 yearly appropriation for research.

It is absurd that the State Department, with the horrendous responsibilities it bears on its shoulders, should be one of the government's smallest users of research.

Over the coming decades, I suspect that in the United States there is going to be a great rush to call upon social scientists for all kinds of help for governments, not just on international affairs but also for urban development, the poverty program, and so on. We also need to use social science to make our foreign policy and other international activities more rational.

Johan Galtung

International Peace Research Institute, Oslo

After Camelot*

I. INTRODUCTION

Project Camelot is a study whose objective is to determine the feasibility of developing a general social systems model which would make it possible to predict and influence politically significant aspects of social change in the developing nations of the world. . . . The project is conceived as a three to four-year effort to be funded at around one and one-half million dollars annually. It is supported by the Army and the Department of Defense, and will be conducted with the cooperation of other agencies of the government. . . .
The U.S. Army has an important mission in the positive and constructive aspects of nation building as well as a responsibility to assist friendly governments in dealing with active insurgency problems. Another major factor is the recognition at the highest levels of the defense establishment of the fact that relatively little is known, with a high degree of surety, about the social processes which must be understood in order to deal effectively with problems of insurgency. Within the Army there is especially ready acceptance of the need to improve the general understanding of the processes of social change if the Army is to discharge its responsibilities in the overall counterinsurgency program of the U.S. Govern-

---

* I am indebted to Robert Angell, Kenneth Boulding, Alex Inkeles, W. J. Goode, and to Simon Schwartzman and many other former students at FLACSO for helpful comments and criticism, but the responsibility rests entirely with the author.

ment. Of considerable relevance here is a series of recent reports dealing with the problems of national security and the potential contributions that social science might make to solving these problems. . . .

These excerpts are from an official document (dated December 4, 1964) of the Special Operations Research Office (SORO) of American University, introducing Project CAMELOT.[1] The words are very clear and it is difficult not to take

[1] The major sources on Project Camelot are

Jessie Bernard, "To the Editor," *The American Sociologist*, 1965, pp. 24–25. Also see *The American Sociologist*, No. 2 (1965); No. 4 (1966), and *American Psychologist*, Vol. 21, No. 5 (May 1966).

Alfred DeGrazia, "Editorial on Project Camelot," *The American Behavioral Scientist*, Vol. 9, No. 2 (September 1965), p. 40.

"Feedback from our Readers," *Trans-action*, Vol. 3, No. 3 (March-April) 1966, pp. 2, 55–56.

Myron Glazer, "Field Work in a Hostile Environment: A Chapter in the Sociology of Social Research in Chile," *Comparative Education Review*, June 1966, pp. 367–376.

Myron and Penina Glazer, "Social Science Research and the Real World: *Chilenos y los gringos*," mimeographed, 1966.

Irving Louis Horowitz, "The Life and Death of Project Camelot," *Transaction*, Vol. 3, No. 1 (November–December 1965), pp. 3–7, 44–47.

"Letters," *The American Behavioral Scientist*, Vol. 9, No. 3 (October 1965), p. NS–12 and Vol. 9, No. 4 (November 1965), p. 32.

George E. Lowe, "The Camelot Affair," *Bulletin of the Atomic Scientists*, (May 1966), pp. 44–48.

Kalman H. Silvert, "American Academic Ethics and Social Research Abroad: The Lesson of Project Camelot," *Background*, 1965, pp. 215–236. (Actually, the whole issue of *Background* deals with the Camelot aftermath.)

Theodore R. Vallance, "Project Camelot: An Interim Postlude," *American Psychologist*, Vol. 21, No. 5 (May 1966), pp. 441–444.

John Walsh, "Social Sciences. Cancellation of Project CAMELOT After Row in Chile Brings Research Under Scrutiny," *Science*, September 10, 1965. Also see *The American Behavioral Scientist*, Vol. 9, No. 2 (September 1965).

U.S. 89th Congress, 1st session, House Committee on Foreign Affairs, "Behavioral Sciences and National Security." Report 4, together with part 9 of hearings on *Winning the Cold War: the U.S. Ideological Offensive*, by Subcommittee on International Organizations and Movements pursuant to H.R. 84, committee print, available only in Depository Libraries.

By far the most extensive analysis, with ample documentation of material from Project Camelot, conclusions of the Special Investigation Committee of the Chilean House of Representatives as well as the debate, is found in *Sesión 33ª, en jueves 16 de diciembre de 1965* República de Chile, Cámara de Diputados, Legislatura Extraordinaria, 384 pp. These *Records* also have extensive quotations from newspapers.

An important article from Chile is José Pablo López, "La Tenue Red del Proyecto Camelot," *Ercilla*, July 7, 1965, pp. 20–21, 31.

DeGrazia's editorial contains a sentence: "A Norwegian pacifist named Johan Galtung egged on a Chilean communist paper to agitate South American antiyanqui jingoism among a few professors etc.," which is a rather incorrect description of what happened. Although it is true that I am a pacifist, this is irrelevant: I see nothing wrong in general in Defense Department sponsored research and fully appreciate the role of the armed services in sponsoring important behavioral science research. Being Norwegian is more to the point: Project Camelot looks different from the point of view of a small nation than from the point of view of the top nation in one of the power blocs. What is completely untrue is that I "egged on a Chilean communist paper." What happened was that I (working in Chile as a UNESCO professor) had been invited by the late project director to participate in the project, rejected the generous offer because I had misgivings about it, received no satisfactory explanation from the project directors about the issues I raised (the same as the issues discussed in the present article), and only then made the information I had about the project available to Latin American colleagues. I can assure DeGrazia that more than "a few professors" were appalled by the project and refused indignantly to participate in it; in fact, there have probably been few issues that have united empiricists, phenomenologists and Marxists alike as effectively. That all this later (in fact almost two months later) reached a local communist paper (*El Siglo*) will surprise nobody, nor that it was exaggerated into accusations of deliberate espionage or almost military intervention. Also blatantly untrue is the assertion that the project was "supported by some of the best foreign scholars in Latin America."

What sounds like a good idea, however, is DeGrazia's suggestion to have the appropriate learned societies appoint a committee to look into all aspects of the rise and fall of Project Camelot.

Two inaccuracies in Horowitz' excellent article should also be pointed out in this connection. Horowitz writes that "Galtung was also deeply concerned about the possibility of European scholars being frozen out of Latin American studies by an inundation of sociologists from the United States." My concern was with the future of the social sciences in Latin America, particularly if Project Camelot had been permitted to stay alive for some years — and what happened after the details had been revealed seemed to confirm this feeling. Where European versus U.S.

them seriously, even if other presentations of the project sometimes look different.[2] The present article is an effort to analyze the cancelled project and some of its implications. In so doing no effort will be made to go through all the material about the history of the project. Many details will still not be known for some time, and other circumstances have been well clarified through the many articles that have already appeared.

Briefly stated, what happened was the following. The project was prepared in the United States by a committee of social scientists, and the final design of instruments was to take place in the summer of 1965. However, when the information just quoted was made available to Latin American social scientists their reaction was a rather indignant refusal to cooperate and the matter was brought to national attention in Chile and

---

sociologists are concerned my preference would, in general, be in the direction of the latter — but much more important is the equal participation of Latin American social scientists, especially in the study of their own affairs.

Horowitz also writes that "Simultaneously, the authorities at FLACSO turned over the matter to their associates in the Chilean Senate and in the left-wing Chilean press." In fact, FLACSO as such and its authorities did nothing in connection with the Camelot affair. Everything I did in this connection was done in private capacity, and neither FLASCO nor its sponsor UNESCO bears any responsibility for it.

[2] Thus, Jessie Bernard's presentation (*op. cit.*, p. 24) reads quite differently from the memorandum quoted: "There was wide consensus that political rather than military solutions were needed. Could the conditions that made for violence be foreseen? Could the goals sought by violence be achieved by nonviolent means? These were among the questions requiring attention." However, a close scrutiny of the material available on the project does not warrant the conclusion that the project was well designed for this purpose. The emphasis seemed rather to be on how to forecast and avoid any revolution than to bring about social change by nonviolent means. The aim as stated by Dr. Bernard is also hard to reconcile with the wording of the memorandum. Besides, who in the developing countries has acknowledged that "The U.S. Army has an important mission in the positive and constructive aspects of nation building as well as a responsibility to assist friendly governments in dealing with active insurgency problems"? Moreover, why should the military sponsors reserve their right to classify some of the reports and findings?

then to international attention. The result was that the project was canceled on July 8 by the office of the Defense Secretary, and an order by the U.S. President was issued on August 5 to see to it that "no government sponsorship of foreign area research should be undertaken which in the judgment of the Secretary of State would adversely affect the United States foreign relations." Thus, the affair attained a certain celebrity last year and was much discussed at the meeting of the professional social science associations (particularly by the anthropologists).

But that does not mean that the essential lessons have necessarily been drawn from it, nor does it mean that it is entirely clear what these lessons might be.[3] More particularly, to the present author it has often been distressing to see how little many U.S. social scientists seem to understand of the complexities of emotions and arguments in an affair of this kind. Rather, what happened tends to be regarded as a technical difficulty one may encounter in "foreign area research," a difficulty that can be overcome if one is only clever enough. The excerpts quoted are explained as the price one has to pay for a six-million-dollar contract, the biggest sum ever made available for a social science project. Or what happened is interpreted as an expression of bad administration by SORO,[4] of rivalries between more and less traditionally military factions in the Pentagon, of rivalries between the Department of Defense and the Department of

---

[3] This point is made by virtually all who write on the subject, particularly in Silvert (*op. cit.*, p. 218) and Horowitz (*op. cit.*, p. 44).

[4] A good example is found in a quote from a distinguished U.S. political scientist: "Wasn't the naïveté of the Camelot project — the really massive naïveté of the project — that a project called by code name was sent through the mail to dozens of scholars in this country with the justification of counter-insurgency, in a sense bringing the whole of social sciences under the heading of counter-insurgency? Was that massive naïveté the consequence of the fact that in the planning of this project the social sciences that were used were not those which had some built-in political sensitivity?" (*Background*, 1965, p. 196). It is difficult to escape the conclusion that the speaker feels the project could have been saved with a little bit more secrecy, keeping the intentions, just not making them public.

State, of the dubious and unauthorized behavior by one particular person associated with the project,[5] of the "hostility of one invited social scientist,"[6] and so forth. In other words, the tendency has been, as so often in conflicts, to disregard the fundamental and look for some accidental characteristics of the situation.

The present article is an effort to analyze some more fundamental aspects of social science research abroad. In so doing, we shall use Project Camelot as an illustration. But our personal inclination is to regard the project as an unfortunate sidestep, and to direct the attention toward better future patterns of research abroad, not toward analysis and condemnation of what happened in the past.

II. THE POLITICAL NATURE OF PROJECT CAMELOT

What, then, was essential in this project? Certainly its political nature, which we shall comment on first. But the question is: Precisely what makes a project of this kind political? When would one say that the admixture of politics to a scientific project becomes too heavy?

Obviously, as most authors seem to agree, the criterion is

[5] However, it is too easy simply to discount this as the bad conduct by one particular man, who can then serve as a whipping boy. Thus, the Glazers write about a meeting at Princeton University October 1964 with a team of Camelot researchers: "Having just returned from Chile, we related how closely we had come to failure. The burden of military support for a project dealing with the causes of revolution, we stressed, would be unbearable. Neither Chileans, nor other Latin Americans would gracefully cooperate with North Americans under contract from the Pentagon, intent on learning about the techniques of insurgency. The response from one of the Princeton participants clearly implied that sophisticated investigators could well handle such a simple technical problem by disguising the source of support." Glazer and Glazer, *op. cit.*, p. 32.

[6] "The hostility of one invited social scientist precipitated the diplomatic incident which led finally to the cancellation of Project CAMELOT." Bernard, *op. cit.*, p. 24. Perhaps there were some reasons for being hostile located in the project itself?

not that the project is sponsored by the government nor that it is sponsored by the military establishment. This would be "guilt by association" and also serve to acquit highly politically biased research sponsored by private organizations.

Nor can one use as a criterion the circumstance that the project has *political implications* that favor one point of view rather than another, in other words, that policy directives can be derived from it. For this would eliminate most good social research to the extent that it permits prediction and/or manipulation of "politically significant aspects," to quote the Camelot document. To require, implicitly or explicitly, that policy research should somehow favor both or all camps is meaningless; research with political implication is, by definition, a political act that changes the political balance. Moreover, all nonclassified findings can be used by good people as well as bad people for good as well as for bad purposes, for if they contribute to knowledge about how a social condition may be obtained, then they implicitly also tell how it can be impeded, as pointed out very well by Jessie Bernard.

Should one then accept as a criterion that the results of the research are *classified*? To many this seems to be a good basis for judging. Often it is a good indicator since it may imply monopoly over the recipes that could result from the research. At any rate, classified research will lead to suspicion, but it should not be forgotten that there may also be other reasons for classifying a research report: The publication of the results might hurt some persons or some groups; it may be impossible to preserve anonymity; the results may cause unwanted conflict and make further research impossible; classification makes the report (and the agency behind it) look more significant, and so on. So this is not an infallible criterion.

Neither is the *purpose or intention*: An agency may want to design research for its political purpose and simply fail, and others with no such intentions may be blind to the political nature of their research.

Hence, we would prefer to use as a criterion the *design of the project itself*. What kind of perspective on the political system studied is implicit in the design? Is this perspective one that expresses one political view rather than another so that it is already built into the design that findings can be used in favor of one political course of action rather than another? And, of course, if *in addition* the sponsorship is political and even military, the purpose is political and the project is launched in a secretive manner — then we feel there is little doubt about the political nature of the project.

To clarify this very general problem using Project Camelot as an example imagine that a person has a model of Latin America as being run by essentially friendly, democratic although imperfect governments of the Leoni-Belaunde-Frei types threatened by Castro-Moscow-Peking-inspired insurgency movements — and that he sympathizes with the former and not with the latter. In that case, Project Camelot, apart from its considerable scientific interest, becomes an important potential weapon that might have pointed to softer ways of handling, say, the "insurgency" in the Dominican Republic. Then imagine a person has the view that Latin America is run by "puppets of Yankee imperialism installed to exploit the masses," under various guises — and that the only hope is an overthrow of these governments by the popular forces through internal wars. In that case Project Camelot becomes a weapon designed to crush such revolts.

Although these two models of Latin America are adhered to by very many, no serious student of these nations would maintain such simplified views. Rather, one would analyze nations in terms of mixed perspectives, since there are obviously cases where both may be applicable. But that does not detract from the basic issue: that this project was extremely asymmetric in its conception of Latin America, being far too close to the first model. It would have been easy, in principle, to supplement it with a study of patterns of "oligarchic dominance and exploitation" to use Marxist parlance — but it is hard to see how Project Camelot would have included research on how to "assist friendly insurgency movements in dealing with dictatorial governments" and still have retained the contract. In short: the project was a clearly political one, defining the problems of the world in terms extremely close to exactly what people of the Left, all over the world, feel to be the U.S. perception of world problems.[7] That the project also had considerable potential scientific value and that parts of it were brilliantly designed does not detract from this circumstance. Nor is it possible to accept the idea that the project was judged prematurely since the design was not yet completed; a vast investment had already been made, and the general direction was unmistakable.

People who have been conditioned to feel that the first model mentioned here is almost self-evident will easily fail to see the political nature of the project. People who always adhere to the second model will equally easily fail to appreciate its scientific nature. But that social scientists, systematically trained in seeing an issue from many angles, should fail to grasp the immense political implication of the project is strange. Particularly tragic is the failure to use the good old principle of looking at the problem from the point of view of the antagonist.[8]

[7] That this is not the only U.S. attitude in official circles is seen from Senator Fulbright's comments on the project: [it can be characterized as] "reactionary, backwardlooking policy opposed to change. Implicit in Camelot, as in the concept of 'counterinsurgency,' is an assumption that revolutionary movements are dangerous to the interests of the United States, and that the United States must be prepared to assist, if not actually participate in, measures to repress them." Quoted from Horowitz, *op. cit.*, p. 3. Also see his analysis on p. 6.

As an amusing account of how misplaced the official U.S. perspective on Latin America may be, see J. Mayone Stycos, "A New Look in Latin American Relations," *Human Organization*, Vol. 18, No. 2 (Summer 1959), pp. 149–151.

[8] This is very openly expressed by M. C. Kennedy: ". . . what is the real knocker-upper is the bottomless stupidity of most sociologists. They all talk about taking the role of the other, but few of them indeed seem capable of doing so. In short, we do not need ethics, but the kind that will protect us from the stupidity first and foremost of our colleagues." (*Trans-action*, Vol. 3, No. 20 [March-April 1966], p. 2.)

The social sciences are now rapidly developing in the Soviet Union and Eastern Europe. Imagine that the Soviet Defense Ministry launched a sociological/anthropological project to inquire into the nature of unrest in Hungary, Poland, and East Germany, say, early 1953 or early 1956. The task would be to find out something about how the Soviet Army could best help friendly governments "in dealing with active insurgency problems." Might one not have thought that some other problems in that sphere would also have been worth investigating and that the project had a taste of political manipulation? One may reject the example, saying that East-West relations are not symmetric, that what is right in the West may nevertheless be wrong in the East because our values are right, theirs not; or that what is wrong in the South may nevertheless be right in the North for a similar reason. But this is a position which is not generally shared by people in the countries that were the targets of the Camelot operation: there is no consensus that the most commonly found U.S. perspective is valid.

In short, from most Latin American points of view, outside of some very special circles, participation in Project Camelot was a clearly political action, raising all the problems of the role of social scientists relative to their governments. Some may object that in times of war these problems are not raised and point with pride to what *The American Soldier* and other pieces of wartime social science meant in the development of U.S. social science. But for this parallel to be valid the relationship to insurgent groups in Latin America and other places will have to be defined in a warlike way and as a war against the United States. This is a heavily politicized, egocentric, and partisan attitude, whether one agrees or disagrees. At any rate, it means buying one political perspective rather than another.

This was very clearly expressed in the Chilean House of

Representatives by the chairman of the special investigation committee to look into Project Camelot, Andrés Aylwin:[9]

It is important to point out something more. In this project one pretends to make an analysis of the problems of man, of hunger, of unemployment, etc. However, these vital problems are not studied because of the significance they have in themselves but only insofar as they can be causes of rebellion or revolution. Said in other words, in Project Camelot one does not analyze unemployment to find its causes and study its solutions, it is not a question of studying human needs to try to satisfy them. Social problems are only important insofar as they can lead to tensions. In short, this project has not been conceived to try to solve the problems of hunger in Latin America, only to avoid revolution.

However, it may be objected that social science research, or any research for that matter, is impossible without a perspective, and that in social affairs such perspectives should not be ruled out just because they coincide with the political views of a scientist. In fact, political perspectives may be the most interesting ones. It is only when this bias is built into the design of a project that points directly to lines of political control — *in casu* to the Pentagon — that the political nature becomes very clear. For the scientific bias of the project is closely coordinated with the political bias of the Pentagon — which brings us right to the old problem of "managerial sociology," this time at the international level. In earlier periods, one generation of sociologists ago, employers saw better than the employees the potentialities of sociology as a tool, and the whole trend of worker-oriented industrial sociology started. Recipes for change were always to be found in the workers, for instance by aligning the informal and formal systems of work. This time the world's richest nation sees better than anyone else the potentialities of research and engages in the same at the international level. It singles out for a six-million-dollar attention that aspect of

[9] *Records*, p. 3335. All translations from Spanish are mine. Also see, Irving Louis Horowitz, "Life and Death of Project Camelot," *Transaction*, Vol. 3. No. 1 (November–December 1965).

developing nations that is significant for itself for study, with obvious control purposes and implications.

The many U.S. social scientists of world renown who participated in this project might protest at this description. They would point to other aspects: the emphasis on non-military rather than military approaches to these problems, the possibility of supporting the "softs" rather than the "toughs" in the Pentagon by giving them a social science software that could serve as a substitute for their traditional military hardware, etc.[10]

There is no reason to doubt the sincerity of these people. There might be some reason to doubt their sense of realism, since politicians and bureaucrats are usually much more able to manipulate academic people than vice versa (it is part of their profession, and academic people will be more concerned with showing how clever they are than in selling their knowledge for political concessions that the bureaucrats may neither be able, nor willing, to give).

But the major objection is that even "software manipulation" by forces external to the target nations is a kind of intervention and as such objectionable. In fact, the present author heard many comments in Latin America to the effect that "we prefer military intervention to this sneaking kind of manipulation, for we know at least what it is." This aspect seems to have been almost completely overlooked: "By what right does the U.S. feel it is entitled to intervene in any way, hard or soft?" was the typical question.

Imagine now for a moment that the project had not been exploded at an early stage but had been launched more or less as intended, with the cooperation of prominent U.S. and Latin American social scientists. This would have happened only if the attempts to deceive, as explained by the faculty of the Catholic University, Santiago, Chile, in a letter to the

[10] For good expression of these intentions, checked against private communications with this author, see Jessie Bernard, *op. cit.*, and Horowitz, *op. cit.*, pp. 46–47.

President of the International Sociological Association, had been successful:[11]

> In fact, Dr. Hugo Nuttini, professor in the Department of Anthropology at the University of Pittsburgh, who came to Chile to establish contact with Chilean sociologists to make them interested in participating in Project CAMELOT, affirmed both in writing and orally that the project was financed by the National Science Foundation when in reality it was financed by the Army of the United States and the Department of Defense of that country. Moreover, in the copy of the Project Design that he gave to Chilean sociologists all references to the Army had been meticulously erased. Finally, efforts were made to make us believe that it pursued purely scientific interests when in reality it was intended to serve as a basis for the counterinsurgency politics of the United States.

Imagine further that findings from Project Camelot found their way to policy makers, as indeed was the intention, and were applied with the general perspective in mind, for instance, to keep military juntas in power by better timing and distribution of measures to satisfy population needs so that frustrations did not accumulate up to the point of active insurgency. *Not a single word in the many documents of Project Camelot rules out the possibility, for instance, of keeping a Batista or an Imbert in power;* the idea seems only to be that it should happen with more graceful means than U.S. military missions or direct military intervention.

[11] Quoted from the *Records,* p. 3348. It should be emphasized that Nuttini probably was not really authorized to do this recruitment in Chile since Chile is said not to be on the original list of target nations for the project. The fact is that Nuttini behaved as if he were authorized, as if Chile were on the list of nations to be studied, and as though his trip to Chile were partly paid for out of Project Camelot funds. What actually happened before this should probably be reviewed by some public or private judicial body to clear the air. Incidentally, that Chile was not included in the design cannot be used to imply that Chileans had no reason to react. Anybody in the modern world has a right to react in connection with something that takes place in other nations, particularly if they are close to his own and he identifies with them. Latin American sociologists all know each other very well, and Latin Americans in general have a wide basis of solidarity when it comes to relationships with the United States.

Imagine that only then had the document of December 4, 1964, been published, revealing the sponsorship and the purpose of the project. What would have been the consequences?

For one thing, some people would have been badly deceived, as they already were for some weeks or months in the Spring of 1965. But let us leave that aside.

Second, it would have been the end of Latin American social science for, say, ten or twenty years — for this would have confirmed the suspicions the radical Left has always entertained in Latin America as to the true nature of non-Marxist sociology: a design to perpetuate the capitalist system internally and the imperialist system externally. Even with the development that actually took place, the project seriously affected intellectual and to some extent also political confidence between North and South America. But let us leave even this aside and say that it is mainly the concern of the social scientists, and particularly of those who have the task of promoting social science in that region.

What remains is the problem of participation in political action when one believes that one is acting as a social scientist. This is more than merely deception. This is to make people responsible for actions they may want no responsibility for, even actions with far-reaching consequences. One might risk being quoted as the advocate of a scientific type of "solution" to a "problem" that one might have defined differently oneself, there would be the risk of co-optation into political control processes without even having been asked. And that places the social scientist in a situation not too different from that which the natural scientist has been in for a long time: his activities may have far-reaching implications if not in terms of life and death at least in terms of justice and freedom.

Then imagine that there had been no attempt to deceive, that the project had been launched quite openly as the combination of political and scientific venture it was. In that case, it would have been an honest affair: those who favor that perspective on U.S./Latin American affairs could have participated, and those against it could have abstained; it would have been a matter of political taste and interest. In Latin America, that would have ruled out both the quantity and the quality of social scientists; in the United States, possibly not — so the staffing of the project would have been even more problematic. But then one might also argue that it should have been requested of the U.S. scientists that they better understood the problems and the sentiments of the countries they wanted to investigate — and one just wonders what kind of scientific value could have come out of a project when its designers revealed such gross ignorance of the very same nations they were about to study.[12]

III. THE ASPECT OF "SCIENTIFIC COLONIALISM"

Let us now turn to another and equally serious aspect of Project Camelot which we shall refer to as "scientific colonialism." This is indeed an emotionally loaded term. We might have used a neutral term like "asymmetric patterns of research," but hesitated to do so since the stronger term in a sense expresses better what we are aiming at.

By "colonialism," in general, we mean a process whereby the center of gravity of a nation is no longer in that nation itself but in some other nation, the colonizer. Best known is *political colonialism*, where the center of gravity for crucial decision making is located with the colonizer, not in the colony. Number two is *economic colonialism*, whereby the center of gravity for crucial economic transactions is located outside

[12] As a matter of fact, that the project was essentially a political and even military operation is taken almost for granted by many who comment on it. The left-wing press in Latin America never described it otherwise: "espionaje yanqui." To the Cuban Weekly *Bohemia* (September 24, 1965, p. 86), Rex Hopper has become "un ex agente de la CIA." Upon his death, *The New York Times* (June 23, 1966, p. 6) describes Project Camelot as "a $4 million program in the social sciences aimed at discovering the causes of internal war in Latin America and other developing areas." And DeGrazia in his editorial writes very openly about the political value Project Camelot might have had.

the country. What is lost is usually referred to as political autonomy and economic autonomy — the latter not to be confused with self-sufficiency, which very few nations possess in today's interlocking world economic structure. Both patterns are well known, even though political colonialism of the classical type is out and economic colonialism is bitterly resented. Both of them would last longer if it had not been for the strong reaction against them among the people in the colonies.

By *scientific colonialism* we shall refer to a process whereby the center of gravity for the acquisition of knowledge about the nation is located outside the nation itself. There are many ways in which this can happen. One is to claim the right of unlimited access to data from other countries. Another is to export data about the country to one's own home country for processing into "manufactured goods," such as books and articles. As has been pointed out by the Argentinian sociologist Jorge Graciarena,[13] this is essentially similar to what happens when raw materials are exported at a low price and reimported as manufactured goods at a very high cost. The most important, most creative, most entrepreneurial, most rewarding, and most difficult phases of the process take place abroad.

Then there is the well-known pattern referred to as the "brain drain," whereby young scholars are invited on fellow-

[13] Jorge Graciarena, "Algunas consideraciones sobre la cooperación internacional y el desarrollo reciente de la investigación sociológica en América Latina," paper presented at the Conferencia Internacional sobre investigación social comparativa en los países en desarrollo, Buenos Aires September 8 – 16, 1964. It may be objected that when data are exported the country does not become poorer and may in fact be enriched if the data are made public afterward. Thus, both parties may gain: it is a positive-sum rather than a zero-sum game. And this may, of course, also apply to the export of raw materials: both parties get more capital out of the process. But even though this may be correct in absolute terms, it is not valid in relative terms. Even if both earn more, the rich country is likely to earn most: even if both get more knowledge, the advanced country is likely to get most. Only one of them can be no. 1 — so in relative terms the process is still a zero-sum game.

ships and then lured to stay on by the attractions of the richer country until most of their time is surrendered to contract work, whereupon they may, or may not, be re-exported, often as research bureaucrats, to the developing nation or to an international organization. This is done under the general heading of technical assistance.

And then, most importantly, there is the biased distribution or accumulation of personally acquired knowledge about the "colony." At present, this is expressed in terms of the high number of Ph.D. theses, journals, and institutes specializing in area studies (Latin American studies, African studies, studies of the "capitalist world"), found in the scientifically most developed nations of the world (among other reasons because this mirrors the structure of their foreign ministries). The foci of knowledge are precisely how these social and political systems function, so that the institutes can better serve such needs as bilateral diplomacy, technical assistance, and trade (and receive prestige and fundings in return). And here the point is not only that very little of this is done the other way — that few comprehensive studies of the colonizer are carried out by people in the colony — but also that scholars from the *scientifically powerful nations often know more about other nations than these nations know about themselves.* True, their knowledge may be of a stereotyped and old-fashioned kind, and above all about aspects of the "colony" that the people there are less interested in — for instance, because they belong to the past or to the atypical (as when most modern studies of the Lapps in Norway are carried out by foreigners). But in recent times, studies have tended to be extremely adequate and relevant, and often quoted by nationals of these nations as the best ones available.

But is this not to be commended, is it not a great favor to these nations that others contribute to their self-image? In one sense, it is, and in another, it is not. Knowledge is known as a good thing, but in human affairs it is not immaterial how that knowledge was acquired. Thus, we usually place high value on adolescents' efforts to discover themselves, to go through the painstaking trial-and-error of working out a reasonable self-image. If this image is too full of illusions, it may be corrected by others in interaction processes. Likewise with nations: to be told by "grown-ups" complete formulas as to who they are and how they are often has adverse effects. Not to be told so is also wrong. There has to be a balance, an exchange, as quickly as possible on equal terms. If there is always an adult around answering the questions about "Who am I?" and "What am I to do?" a sort of depersonification is likely to take place, a kind of self-alienation. Whether the purposes are benevolent or malevolent, the net result is an increase in the general possibility of manipulation of the young by the adult, whether they be individuals or nations. Two situations from Ghana a couple of years ago may serve to illustrate this better than more theoretical elaborations.

The first one relates to the activities of the U.S. Peace Corps in its first year in Ghana. Not that they did anything wrong, only that what they did was almost too good. Excellently trained by David Apter (*Gold Coast in Transition*), they knew so much more about Ghana than many of the local teachers that it was rather painful to watch. Knowledgeable, charming, youthful, *magna cum laude* students right out of college, pitted against the often stale and ritualized teaching done by Ghanaeans and British expatriates — is it strange that the Ghanaeans could feel despair and the British anger?

The second situation relates to a painting that used to be in the anteroom of former president Kwame Nkrumah. The painting was rather enormous, and the main figure was Nkrumah himself, fighting, wrestling with the last bursting chains of colonialism. The chains are yielding; there is thunder and lightning in the air; the earth is shaking. And out of all this, three small figures are fleeing toward the frames of the painting. They are white men, with a sickening, pallid color, — rather disgusting and unattractive. One of them is the capitalist: he carries a briefcase. Another is the priest or missionary — he carries the Bible. And the third is a lesser figure — he carries a book entitled *African Political Systems* — this is the anthropologist, or social scientist in general. So if the chains symbolize political colonialism, the fleeing men symbolize economic, cultural, and scientific colonialism, respectively.

To those who would object that we all know what happened to Nkrumah, it might be retorted that both stories are nevertheless rather representative of sentiments of despair, alienation, and anger in the new nations on which social scientists of the older nations feed. He who doubts should only take a careful look himself. He will find people in these nations insisting beyond any justification that "only he who is himself born in Latin America can ever understand Latin America," "you have to have Indian blood in your veins to understand India," "you have to be a native to really grasp the subtleties of the language," and so forth. In other words, people clinging to purely ascriptive criteria as a last barrier against the flood of knowledge-seeking scholars unleashed upon them.

It should be noted that scientific colonialism is different from mixing politics and science. The big power may study very innocuous aspects of the life in the small power, aspects that are of no or little political significance, and still contribute to this tremendous lopsidedness in knowledge. And politics and science may certainly be mixed also when two nations that know about equally as much about each other launch social science projects against each other.

But it is also obvious that the two can easily be combined, with Project Camelot as the most glaring example. Social science knowledge about a small nation in the hands of a big power is a potential weapon and contributes to the asymmetric patterns already existing in the world, because it contributes to manipulation in the interests of big powers.[14]

[14] One is reminded of the comments made in the Editorial, *Human Organization*, Vol. 17 (1958), criticizing an important aspect of the Burdick and Lederer book, *The Ugly American*. Essentially what Colonel

A major aspect of scientific colonialism is the idea of unlimited right of access to data of any kind, just as the colonial power felt it had the right to lay its hand on any product of commercial value in the territory. Project Camelot is a good example in this respect, and the indignation it led to is well expressed in the documents and debate published by the Chilean House of Representatives:

To denounce Project Camelot as an instrument of intervention by the Defense Department of the USA, as an attack against the dignity, sovereignty and independence of nations and peoples and against their right of self-determination, guaranteed by Interamerican Law.[15]

.   .   .   .

Nations, like homes or other institutions, have their proper individuality and intimacy. Nobody can enter and investigate what goes on in the home without the consent of the head of the family. Neither can foreign powers or institutions look into the most personal and intimate details of what goes on in another nation, its Armed Services, its Judiciary, its trade unions, its public administration, its institutions, without the explicit authorization by the Government[16]

Illustrations of how unreasonable this assumption is — that in the name of social science access to data abroad should be (close to) unlimited — are easily found. Most of us would, as don Andrés, usually not accept prying into the affairs of individuals without their consent; and when this is done, as

---

Hillendale does is to "know the local language and culture, [and then] trick people into doing what you want them to do." "A program aimed at outwitting and outmaneuvering our supposed friends may win temporary successes, but we are fearful of its long-run consequences. Sooner or later — and probably pretty soon — people find out that they are being fooled and they lose all confidence in those who are doing the fooling. We hope therefore that those who serve us overseas [will not use this] model for the effective American." However, there is a fallacy in this argument too. The editor does not say that such action may be wrong in itself, only that it is wrong if its long-run consequences are wrong, which means adverse to the United States.

[15] First point in the denunciatory conclusion by the Special Investigation Committee, *Records*, pp. 3325–3326.
[16] *Records*, p. 3340, quoted from the speech by don Andrés.

often in political and police matters and sometimes in social science, there is either an outburst of protest or efforts at justification in terms of major social or scientific values that are served. In general, we respect a sphere of privacy around individuals, to be penetrated only with the deliberate consent of the individual himself.[17]

That this also applies to nations is very easily seen by turning the stage somewhat. How would the United States react to a commission of Soviet social scientists to investigate the assassination of President Kennedy? Or to investigate the roots of the Cuba invasion? Or the interests behind the Santo Domingo intervention? All the time under the same assumption as Project Camelot that the government of the nation that is the object of the study is not even asked but hears about the project via others?

In a sense, this is a question of simple human decency but also of fundamental human rights; and at the international level, it is a question of national dignity and national autonomy. It must be understood that social science is today a potential political tool of great significance, which means that the entry of social scientists into another country is a potential political action. And that poses the dilemma of reconciling the values of accumulating knowledge with the values of decency and autonomy. For there is no doubt that there is a strong value-conflict here. A government that does not want any outsider to study the internal affairs of the nation, including attitudes and behavioral patterns of private individuals, can use such values as dignity and autonomy as pretexts to protect its own monopoly on information. There is an element of paternalism in don Andrés' idea quoted above, that "nobody can enter — without the consent of the head of the family," and this type of paternalism writ large is called an authoritarian system.

[17] The American social scientist will think of the debate over the publication of *When Prophecy Fails,* by Leon Festinger, Henry Riecken, and Stanley Schacter (Minneapolis, Minn.: University of Minnesota Press, 1956).

At this point, the distinction between governmental and private research abroad, although by no means a sharp one, is useful. It seems reasonable to require that a government, if it wants to do research on foreign territory, should launch the projects through appropriate diplomatic channels, obtain the consent of the individuals approached as well as the consent of the government. It is not equally obvious that this should be required of private research organizations; the consent of the individuals and organizations explored should be sufficient in open societies. The moment governments are given rights to interfere, research will, by definition, be interpreted as governmental research — and this is an unfortunate consequence of the Camelot affair for U.S. social scientists. Research should be carried out man to man, in a community of scholars, in an atmosphere of openness.

IV. SOME SUGGESTED REMEDIES

Much more challenging and much more important than the analysis of what happened is the effort to find workable solutions to the problems raised by the Camelot affair. Essentially, there are only these two problems: the *problem of combination of scientific and political goals* and the *problem of scientific colonialism*. Whether governments should ever sponsor scientific research is not a problem — they do so by maintaining state universities in most countries as well as in other ways; and it is difficult to argue that there is anything intrinsically wrong in government-sponsored research without denouncing the greater portion of research that has ever been carried out. Whether military agencies should ever sponsor research is not an issue either: they do so for military purposes, which one may like or dislike, or they may do so for nonmilitary purposes, which should then be evaluated on their scientific merits. Another aspect is that the borderline is not that sharp and that sponsorship of good scientific research always adds to the prestige of the sponsor. It then becomes a matter of ordinary value conflict whether one dislikes the sponsor sufficiently to deny it sponsorship of a study one actually likes.

Nor is the issue one of dishonesty: Most people today will probably subscribe to (if not live up to) an ethical code whereby lies are only permitted under conditions of extreme *force majeure*, in matters of life and death, and would not include the operation of a research project under this heading. Moreover, since scientists are presumably engaged in the pursuit of truth, lies seem antithetical as means. But many of the social science techniques for launching a project come dangerously close.

To start with the problem of mixing politics and science, it is difficult to see any end to this or any way of easing the tensions that may arise from it. However, some principles can be suggested.

First of all, there is the idea of *frankness where purpose and sponsorship are concerned*. No *bona fide* social scientist should ever present a project without being willing to declare purpose and sponsorship. If he is not, then he is no longer a *bona fide* social scientist. He may be an excellent consultant to the intelligence services of this or that nation, but should no longer be known only as a scientist. Rather, he is to be compared to the vacuum cleaner salesman who enters a house under the pretext of carrying out a survey, and leaves it with the door slammed behind him with or without a contract in his hand.

Of course, there is little reason to doubt that governments and others will ever abstain from using social science to further their political goals and that people who identify with those goals and/or with the salaries and other conditions offered will join, be they social scientists or not. Hence, the rules in this field should be as clear as possible.

Second, it might be required of *bona fide* social science projects that they be *unclassified*, with the obvious limitations due to rules of anonymity, general considerateness, and so on. But, as mentioned earlier, we feel that much too much emphasis has been put on this condition, probably because it is easily understood and relatively unproblematic, both to implement and to circumvent.

Third, and this is less trivial: one should see to it that *the tools of social science are more equally distributed,* that this political weapon does not become the monopoly of one group or one nation to be used against others. This is not only a question of free access to theory and methods and effective technical assistance but also a question of devising social science methods that are so good and so cheap that they can be used by anybody with a sufficient level of training. Thus, at present the costs of large-scale projects of the Camelot type are prohibitive for all but the bigger nations of the world. Realistically, all these technical assistance efforts should be seen not only as measures to diffuse social science *but also as measures of self-defense for the nations in the periphery of the world.* In part, the tools would allow all nations to understand better what happens when the social science searchlight is turned against them; and in part, they would enable the nations to turn the searchlight the other way — as will be developed in the following section.

Fourth, as pointed out by Ulf Himmelstrand when this general issue was debated at the Sixth World Congress of Sociology (Evian, 4–11 September 1966), it is naive just to refer to the general availability of research results — that they are there for everybody to read. The foreign researcher should also define it as part of his responsibility to help create the possibilities for local personnel to get such access. This may be by presentation of the results in a comprehensible form locally, by facilitating dissemination of research results, or by promoting the type of training that would make technical reports accessible. Of course, today this is done, to a large extent, under bilateral and multilateral, private and governmental sponsorship.

Fifth, much research of a politically touchy nature should preferably not be handled by the parties to the conflict but by third parties or by international institutes.

Finally, one should have more openness about the entire

problem, above all be willing to see and to admit the political aspect of such research and not be lured and distracted by too much talk about the freedom to do research. We all believe in the value of science, but not at all costs; to do so, would be to put knowledge higher than, say, freedom, autonomy, dignity, life, and death. Therefore, let us face these problems with more openness and less mystique — this will serve us all better.

Let us now turn to the problem of *scientific colonialism*, the key to which is asymmetry, and the cure of which is to introduce as many elements of symmetry as possible in the projects. Of course some asymmetry will always remain. The trivial aspects of this have to do with the organization *of the single project*, although it has taken the social sciences a long time to realize this and to do something about it. The epitomized asymmetric project is carried out by the social anthropologist. The design is his own; he himself carries out the data collection although he may hire natives to do some of the prospecting for data for him and to function as interviewers, interviewees, or informants; the data are then carried home and the processing, the analysis, the theory-formation, and the final write-up are all his. He leaves his country with the design, collects his data abroad, and comes back with his suitcase filled with extracted data, to be processed at home. More often than not he does not even inform his subjects as to his findings prior to the publication, and not afterward either.

To this it will be objected that he does not have much of a choice. He is studying primitive peoples who have been discovered by social science but have not themselves discovered social science, so that they cannot possibly participate on an equal level, let alone carry out their own projects in the country of the social anthropologist. But this objection becomes increasingly invalid as the social sciences are developing around the world. To this, in turn, the objection would be that few, if any, of the social science research milieus around the world can foster the sophistication of U.S. social science so that they would not be equals as collaborators. And to this again it may be said that this type of argument could serve — and has served — as an argument to deny nations, for instance, their independence. One is dealing here with a very basic and — it seems — inalienable right: the right to participate actively and consciously, when knowledge about oneself is to be acquired; or at least to have been offered such participation.

The recipes for symmetric organization of a research project initiated by social scientists in A to study conditions in B, hence, would be as follows (in addition to asking appropriate authorities and individuals for the permission to carry out such projects):[18]

1. *Participation of scholars from B in the design of the project* and the drawing up of instruments etc., preferably from the very beginning, so that the project does not have a prehistory that is used to argue courses of action ("we are used to doing it this way; we originally thought of doing it that way," etc.).
2. *Participation in the data collection* at all levels, not only as interviewers, etc.
3. *Participation in the data processing* at all levels, not only as coders, etc.
4. *Equal access to data analysis,* which often means equal access to IBM cards. The basic point here is to have the right, not necessarily to make use of it.
5. *Participation in theory formation,* and
6. *Participation in the write-up,* which may mean to be invited to become a coauthor.

Obviously, these conditions will have to be tempered by local circumstances, such as the degree of development of social sciences in nation B. Also, the rules would generally only apply to the bigger projects; it would be ludicrous to

[18] For more details, see Johan Galtung, "Some Aspects of Comparative Research," in *POLLS*, 1966.

start this complicated machinery just for the sake of some minor process of data collection.

All this looks attractive on the paper but may be less attractive in practice. Thus, social scientists in the developing countries are very often trained in developed countries and have acquired the perspectives of these countries, often in a simplified form that makes them "more Catholic than the Pope." Moreover, they often have an even more stereotyped perception of their own country than the outside social scientist who is at least protected by ignorance, and their limited social and geographical mobility may make them very myopic when it comes to perceiving the social structure of their own nation.

In addition to this, cooperation of this kind (which is now quite often practiced, wholly or partly) often serves to maintain a very unfortunate pattern, that social scientists in developing countries get used to studying the same problems as social scientists in developed countries study at home — as if the two types of societies were similar enough to warrant this. It is often pathetic to see how much the list of projects in the social science institutes in the world periphery is copied from the world center, with obvious political implications.

But most important is what we have alluded to earlier, that this part of the general problem as well as its solution has a flare of the obvious compared to the deeper problem. When scholars from A have carried out a number of projects according to this recipe in B, the result is symmetry in project organization but nevertheless a fundamental asymetry in knowledge accumulated. People in A know much more about B than people in B know about both A and B, and this knowledge is often presented in the idiom (not only the language) of A, and is of a kind that may facilitate tremendously A's manipulation of B — provided it is good social science.

Of the two possible ways of obtaining symmetry where this problem is concerned, that is, to discontinue A's research in *B* or to start *B*'s research in *A*, the latter is certainly to be preferred, In the Camelot case, this would mean a design that would have been expanded so as to include, for instance, a study of the conditions of military intervention by the United States, a study of the ramifications of the famous "military-industrial" complex alluded to by Eisenhower, a study of general attitudes toward developing countries, a study of the potentials for violent and nonviolent change in U.S. society, and so on, all to be carried out by mixed U.S. – Latin American teams. To colleagues from developed countries who feel that such projects are not serious and that they have a definite political tinge, it might be retorted that this was exactly the reaction of most Latin American social scientists to Project Camelot — which means that the examples are useful for heuristic purposes. It might also, with appropriate sponsorship, have become a fascinating project.

But such research would be extremely useful for other purposes as well. Just to mention some:

- it would give scholars from the world periphery — the developing countries — a chance to gain more thorough insight into the nature of the social and political systems they are emulating;
- it would enrich social science in the developing nations by forcing them to use other methodologies and theories — just as scholars from developed countries have to change their tools considerably when studying social and political systems in very different nations;
- it would give scholars in the developing countries a chance to get out of a certain self-centered frame of reference into a more global vision of mankind and get rid of the feeling that they alone are interesting and worth studying (a feeling played up to by scholars from the center wishing to launch their own project);
- it might force some viable patterns of cooperation on scholars from developing countries.
- it would contribute to insights about the "top dog" nations

of the world, since they would no doubt be studied from other angles by scholars from developing countries (as examples, think of what Tocqueville's and Myrdal's studies have meant to the self-images held by Americans);

• it would contribute to less ideological and more empirically guided debate about the center nations in the periphery nations — perhaps even take some aspects of the North-South debate out of its highly emotional setting and place it in a context more germane to finding solutions, not only ideological formulas;

• it would contribute to better social science by making it more universal and by exploiting more systematically the difference in research perspectives, and

• it would contribute to more equality in the international system by institutionalizing equality in nations' access to knowledge about each other, and, consequently, to a "balance of knowledge" as opposed to a "knowledge hegemony." This is at the same time a relatively cheap and relatively effective corrective to existing asymmetric power structures, since knowledge is, at least in principle, more easily diffused than property and means of violence.

Thus, the potential gains are many. Yet, in conversations with social scientists from the developing countries it has repeatedly come out how uninterested they are in such studies, except as parts of more comprehensive, comparative projects where their own nation would be included. In a sense, this is national since it is an expression of deep concern and interest, of joy at discovering one's own nation. There is a feeling of urgency in connection with national problems, a feeling that scarce resources for research should be allocated to studies that could foster socioeconomic development. But there is also an element of egocentric provincialism in all this, not unlike adolescents' concern with themselves rather than with the welfare of their parents. However, this may change rapidly and such studies may become fashionable overnight. In fact, foundations would make an important contribution if they would start allocating money to scholars from the periphery who are able to and want to study nations in the center and not only be concerned with sponsoring research done by the center on itself, by the periphery on itself and, of course, by the center on the periphery. It might, simply, contribute to a richer and more interesting world to let all nations enjoy the privilege of having other nations contribute to their self-image.

Thus, what we have called scientific colonialism has two aspects (the organization of the single project and the distribution of all projects) and two relatively simple recipes for their solution (symmetry in either case) — at least on the surface. But imagine one could only solve one of them, which one should one then try to solve? We would argue for the latter since it is by far the most important, but also the most difficult. To have an asymmetric organization of any single project may affront the dignity of local social scientists and be a disgrace to the national prestige since they feel bypassed. But to continue with the heavily skewed distribution of research experience in other nations is a way of perpetuating the generally feudal structure of the world and thus a politically heavily loaded act. Of course, nobody will deny that both quantitatively and qualitatively there is more literature available about the developed and powerful part of the world even though it is written by nationals of these countries. But that is not the same as the kind of empathy direct research experience gives.

On the other hand, it is easy to profess a preference for one value rather than the other, not so easy to institutionalize solutions that correspond to these principles. Thus in order to have good studies of the center carried out by the periphery, the periphery has to know the techniques. And this is one more reason why symmetry in organization takes precedance in practice: it is one of the simplest forms of diffusion of technical knowledge, since personal participation is recognized as one of the best learning mechanisms. And once at least the fundamentals of social science theory and methodology have been sufficiently diffused and absorbed, one may be reasonably certain that the second phase will follow as a matter of course: One's own nation will simply not be sufficient to satisfy the curiosities of the social scientists from the developing countries.

It should be noted that truly international research institutes have great advantages when it comes to implementing both of these principles: symmetry in project organization and symmetry in the project. First of all, efforts can be made in such institutes to staff all projects in a symmetric manner, and to see to it that the accumulation of knowledge is relatively evenly spread over the groups of nations of the world. This would be a heavy argument against the area institutes — unless they stand in an exchange relation with institutes that can complement them: an institute for the study of underdeveloped nations should ideally relate itself to an institute for the study of overdeveloped nations, and so on.

Second, international institutes may get around the whole issue simply by defining the project as *international* sponsored neither by nation A nor by nation B. Several kinds of symbolism can be invoked to bring this about. There is the idea of having the study carried out mostly by people from a third nation. Then the staff may be highly mixed. And there is the possibility that the institute is already recognized as not only *inter*national but *super*national so that there is little suspicion as to national bias, regardless of the nationality of the researchers. One way of obtaining this enviable status would be to tie the institute to a supernational organization such as the United Nations, but then the difficulty is that the United Nations may itself be a party to what one wants to study (and there are other difficulties, such as the problem of doing nontrivial scientific work for 117 masters who may have highly discordant tastes).

V. CONCLUSIONS

Thus, Project Camelot opens for many possibilities of debate about the structure and organization of social science once it transcends the borderlines of one nation. It is to be hoped that this debate will now be oriented toward the future rather than the past.

But it is also to be hoped that the fate of Project Camelot can serve as a warning to those who still feel such projects may be legitimately launched in the name of social science,[19] and to those who may become the targets of such projects, that they are not blind to their political overtones and able to react toward them accordingly.[20]

[19] Thus, there are persistent rumors about Camelot-type projects, and it is difficult to get precise information about them. Horowitz reports that Project Revolt, designed to study the French Canadian separatist movement, was canceled "somewhat prior to the demise of Project Camelot" (*Trans-action*, March – April 1966, p. 56). *Correio da Manha* in Rio de Janeiro and other sources mention the suspicion of a camelot-type operation at the Minas Gerais University in Belo Horizonte. In the Chilean debate, there are references to other projects called "Operación Simpatico" and "Operación Colonia," in Colombia and Peru (p. 3370). According to the Lima newspaper *El Comercio*, June 17, 1966, the "Simpátic" project encountered no resistance in Colombia, and was concerned with the civic programs of the armed forces and how the people reacted to it. Similarly, Project Numismático is carried out in "selected countries," whereas Project "Reasentamiento," designed to study Peru was cancelled at the request of Peru's government.

[20] In *Trans-action*, July – August 1966 and in *The American Sociologist*, August 1966, five U.S. social scientists specializing in research in and on Latin America call for a debate, not only between the people concerned in the United States but also with Latin American colleagues. They hold Project Camelot to be scientifically and ethically irresponsible, with a list of seven arguments – all of them valid in our mind. It is interesting to note how much better the analysis of Project Camelot becomes when it is carried out by people with expert knowledge of the region concerned. On the other hand, it might also be interesting to know how these arguments are weighted: would Project Camelot still have been objectionable with only six, five, four, etc., of them valid? In other words, what is essential and what is accidental in the Camelot debate?

Robert A. Nisbet

University of California at Riverside

Project Camelot and the Science of Man*

I

Project Camelot may well be the worst single scientific project since King Canute dealt with the tides: the worst conceived, worst advised, worst designed, and worst executed. But this much has to be said for it. Never has one project in the social sciences aroused interest so broad, so diverse and in such high places of the national government. More important, never has one project produced, or at least stimulated, results so momentous (and possibly beneficial) in the long run to government policy with respect to the social sciences.

Reading through the multitude of reactions and comments aroused by Project Camelot, one is irresistably reminded of the ancient tale of the three blind men and their individual descriptions of an elephant. For *The Washington Evening Star*, whose political reporter, Walter Pincus, first broke the story, Camelot was another episode in the unending conflict between the Departments of Defense and State. For the

* Published in *The Public Interest*, Fall (November) 1966, and reprinted with permission of the editor.

United States Army, under whose auspices Camelot had been conceived, it was a research project concerned with conditions of social unrest, riots, and insurrection, that would, in the words of General Dick, "help us to predict potential use of the American Army in any number of cases where the situation might break out." For more than a few Chileans, in whose country Camelot first came to international light, it was a flagrant and odious intervention in the domestic affairs of a country with which the United States was at peace. For Senator Fulbright, Project Camelot was one more indication of the generally reactionary character of the modern behavioral sciences with their consecration to methodology and repudiation of values. Secretary Rusk saw Camelot as a less than brilliant intrusion by the Army into the always delicate sphere of Latin American foreign relations. Most members of the House Subcommittee on International Organizations and Movements saw Project Camelot as a sad consequence of the dispersed, unfocused, and inadequate role of the behavioral sciences in the Federal Government. (This view, as we shall see, comes perhaps the closest to the whole elephant and it is, of all reactions, the one with greatest long-run implications to the social sciences.)

For many social scientists, at first sight at least, the most conspicuous feature of Camelot was its summary cancellation by the Army, an act widely held to reflect yet another chapter in the government's discrimination against the behavioral sciences. (This view, as we shall see, was perhaps the most self-serving, the least founded in reality.) For methodologists and computerologists, the death of Project Camelot could be righteously taken as the retribution that must befall projects not conceived by those pure in design. For some university administrators across the country, and also a few behavioral science project tycoons, the reaction to Camelot was, or might have been: "There but for the grace of God go I." For American social scientists at work in the field abroad, especially in those political areas where national patriotisms tend normally to be on trigger, Camelot was dynamite that might easily spell disaster for future foreign-area research everywhere.

It was not, however, Chilean but Washington reaction to Camelot that proved decisive and of great long-run significance to the behavioral sciences. Our Ambassador to Chile, Ralph Dungan, stung by his ignorance of something that (given U.S. Army sponsorship) understandably seemed part of his proper business, sent a sharp cable to Rusk after reading the details of Camelot in Chilean newspapers. Rusk went to LBJ, LBJ went to McNamara, McNamara went down gracefully (and gratefully, no doubt), and out of it — in one of the fastest actions ever recorded in official Washington — came a Presidential directive prohibiting *government-sponsored* foreign-area research that in the opinion of the Secretary of State would adversely affect United States foreign relations. Without the loss of measurable instant, Defense put Camelot to rest; or, to stay within the lovely imagery of it all, sentenced its inhabitants to return to the world of reality. "How dead," asked one of the investigating Subcommittee members at one point in the hearing, "is the project now, General?" The answer from Army Chief of Research and Development, General Dick was: "Camelot, as it was conceived up to the moment of cancellation, is totally dead."

II

Camelot's real importance in the history of the social sciences begins, indeed, with its death. As nothing in the life of Charles I of England was said to have become him as did his manner of ending it, so nothing in Camelot's life was as fertile to the social sciences, as pregnant with issue, as its corpse; the corpse that was ordered exhumed for Congressional autopsy almost before its last breath. From the hearing conducted on Camelot by the House Subcommittee on International Organizations and Movements came a report, and I can think of nothing more edifying for social scientists than a reading of this two-hundred page document; edifying and flattering. If any further medicine is needed to wash away the minority-group syndrome that still characterizes the self-evaluation of so many of us in the social sciences, that still leads us to feel despised, discriminated against, and disliked by society and government, it is to be found, free, in this little report. Let it be trumpeted far and wide: The federal government, starting with the subcommittee whose job it was to look into Camelot's coffin, and going all the way across town to Secretaries Rusk and McNamara, love the behavioral sciences; love them not despite but, apparently, because of their sins.

In fact, one discovers, as he reads through the text of the Report, the behavioral sciences are miraculously found free of sin. The Military's *use* of the behavioral sciences is not free of sin, but that, as we shall see, is a different story. Twice only could I find, in comments of individual members of the subcommittee on the behavioral sciences, undercurrents of the ironic, but these were prompted by testimony on the behavioral sciences that has to be read to be believed. Let me cite the two instances. At one point, the Director of SORO (the administrative structure within which Camelot was hatched) was explaining to subcommittee members the importance of American behavioral science know-how being exported to the underdeveloped nations; his illustration is the account given him by a friend who, while traveling in Africa, had once seen an automobile on an African highway stopped because of a flat tire, with its occupants standing about helplessly, as it seemed. To this one of the subcommittee members could only gently recommend that the Director drive down any American highway. The second example was offered by a representative of the military. (Note to all behavioral scientists: Judging from the Report, the military's confidence in, and dollar support of, the behavioral sciences is great!) He pointed, when pressed by the subcommittee, to behavioral science's discovery that the Viet Cong frequently travel in village groups, with women and children along, and that they eat their meals at fixed times of the day. This intelligence, he noted, has made possible easier exterminatory actions by the American forces. One of the subcommittee members, patience by now somewhat tried, wondered why batteries of behavioral scientists and computers were required to discover what presumably would be within the powers of any scouting detail, something that Julius Caesar had found out through simple legionaries in his Germanic campaigns. But these, I emphasize, are the only examples I can find in the subcommittee report, and their real butt was not the behavioral sciences but, rather, the military and its use of them.

Reading the report, one finds himself, as a social scientist, almost literally holding his breath as he progresses through the testimony. Far from caricature or hostility, there is only respect, courtesy, and seriousness of interest in the contributions of the behavioral sciences and in their proper status in the federal government. After all, where else in a congressional document (or professional document, for that matter) can one find the behavioral sciences characterized as "one of the vital tools in the arsenal of the free societies," and with a concluding recommendation made that funds for their subvention be greatly increased and their official status honored by inclusion in the Executive Office of the President as well as in a national foundation.

III

Not once in the subcommittee hearing was the matter of professional ethics raised with respect to the behavioral scientist participants of Project Camelot. It was, however, in Chile, where apparently a different standard of conduct is expected of academic scholars. Reading the Chilean Select Committee report and some of the expressions of opinion in Chilean newspapers, one finds little if any of the censure of the American military that our own subcommittee confined itself to, for in Chile, as in Latin America generally, nothing but the worst is usually expected from the military. What bothered, still bothers, Chilean social scientists was, first, the fact that American academics could have allowed themselves to become involved in something like Camelot and, second, that no acts of censure toward Camelot social scientists had been taken, or even voiced, by American social science organizations. From Chilean perspective it seemed incredible that social scientists could have loaned themselves in the first instance to a project under the auspices of the U.S. Army involving research into "the most intimate details" of Latin American institutions and personal lives; equally incredible that in their earliest communication with Chilean social scientists, American social scientists had camouflaged Army sponsorship by vaguely referring to private foundation and NSF support. To this day, there are Chilean and other Latin American social scientists who believe it the responsibility of American academic professional organizations to render apology in some form, even to register censure for the conduct of the Americans. But anyone who knows the reluctance of American professions, medical, legal, or academic, to voice censure of their own kind knows that the Chileans will wait a long time.

The ethical aspects of Camelot have received some attention by American social scientists, but it has been chiefly in the form of letters to the editor of one or other journal, and these seem on the whole superficial and tangential, frequently self-serving, with the military and the State Department made the scapegoats, largely concerned with the question of whether or not the behavioral sciences have any business working for the military. The last seems to me a baseless question, except on grounds of personal ideology. I happen to believe that there was a major ethical responsibility that Camelot's technicians flouted by acceptance in the first place of the nature of the assignment. But this has nothing to do with what would appear to me to be the unquestionable, the almost axiomatic, propriety of the behavioral sciences entering into professional engagements with the military.

If the behavioral sciences are what their prime representatives say they are — nonideological, objective, bodies of hypotheses and conclusions drawn from dispassionate and controlled study of human behavior — then there is nothing intrinsically wrong with their conclusions being used by or given to the Army.

Ideology aside, why should not the behavioral sciences contribute to military and foreign policy as they contribute to community organization, urban renewal, race relations, and other areas of society? Whether behavioral scientists make this contribution to the military directly — as employees on a military-designed project — or through quasi-autonomous foundations or universities is, as I shall emphasize later, a matter of profound operational and organizational significance. But it is hardly a matter of ethical nature.

The right of the individual — whether he be a sociologist, chemist, or engineer — to hold back from the military, to the best of his abilities, the efforts and contributions he has made as a scientist is, I should suppose, incontestable, however vain and illusory it might be. But the grounds for this have nothing to do with the nature of the sciences and everything to do with personal moral values. I do not see how we can argue on the one hand that the behavioral sciences are *sciences* — that is, bodies of knowledge that reach beyond individual caprice and moral preference to the level of empirically validated conclusions — but that on the other hand their principles should not be given to the military or some other established, recognized part of American society and government.

Where the issue of professional ethics entered most significantly in Project Camelot, it seems to me, was in the initial acceptance of the mission of the project by social scientists *acting in their role as social scientists*. Let us, for sake of emphasis of this one point, dismiss the feelings of the Chilean social scientists and others who felt put upon by the Americans; it is always difficult to prove who said what when. Let us, for the same reason, dismiss the ethical matter of the motives Professor Horowitz's interviews uncovered among principals of Camelot, motives which, I have to confess, shock in me what I had thought was an unshockable sense of propriety; for, motives, after all, are elusive, tenuous, and probably irrelevant.

But what cannot be overlooked is the fact that a group of American social scientists, acting as social scientists, allowed the American military to believe there was nothing *scientifically* wrong in an American social science project, under American Army sponsorship, entering the historically sensitive areas of Latin America for the express purpose of discovering, through every possible penetration of culture and mind, the conditions of social unrest, conflict, and insurgency.

Here is a cross-cultural consideration that one might justifiably assume to be understood by every sophomore in an introductory sociology or anthropology course, one that might occur to any lay American who has been reading the news over the past decade or two. Was there no one in the administrative organization of SORO, no one among the social scientists who was appointed as a *professional* man, not as a simple technician, to say in effect to Lieutenant General William Dick, Chief of Research and Development, Army: "Your objective is your business and no doubt admirable from the point of view of the Army; as behavioral scientists we desire to be of such help as we can but everything we know as behavioral scientists suggests the monumental, possibly catastrophic, unwisdom of such a project"?

Not five minutes would have been required to acquaint the General with the most elementary aspects of Latin American ethnocentrism, especially where the American military is involved. Was not such a question necessary and fundamental? I do not mean "ideologically" fundamental but professionally, *scientifically,* fundamental. Is not the physician *as physician* ethically bound to refuse even the order of a patient to prepare a compound that medical knowledge tells the physician is injurious? Does any sociologist believe that the physician can properly take refuge in the implicit statement: "I am a behavioral scientist and if my sponsor orders it, it is not my role to reason why"?

Putting the matter bluntly, are behavioral scientists, simply *because* they are behavioral scientists, entitled to blot from their lay, if not scientific, memories the facts of history? History and also contemporary international reality; a reality in which, like it or not, the image of America is frequently that of a military behemoth, a political juggernaut. To say that the social scientists have no right, as scientists, to question a mission, even to refuse (still as scientists) co-operation, is not only to miss the nature of professional ethics but to be blind to the view that has come to prevail in the larger scientific community today, where the scientist's duty to pronounce on matters of policy, pronounce as a scientist, is not only unquestioned but, as Don K. Price has documented in admirable detail in his *The Scientific Estate,* a matter on which Congressional and Executive opinion has come to depend.

But this, from all I have been able to read, was not a consideration, either ethical or technical, in the minds of the behavioral scientists of Camelot or their consultants. Theirs not to reason why, theirs but to do or die — an epitaph more fitting, however, for cavalrymen than for professional scientists from whom judgment of feasibility is a recognized part of any contract.

IV

If the behavioral scientists and the military never saw the underlying, constitutive question, the members of the House subcommittee assuredly did. Over and over during the hearings, the question was raised by one or other member as to the propriety of the military undertaking the kind of research contained in Camelot's objective. No one asked the question more tersely and pointedly than Representative Roybal: "Wouldn't the mere fact that the Army was heading the project itself create a problem in many countries?"

That is indeed the question. Nor was Mr. Roybal alone in identifying it as the crucial one. Representative Fraser put it in this fashion:

The question I have is, why is the military in this? If I can use the kind of crude example that I have used on other occasions, if we have a political problem in one of our States, we don't send out a military man or economic aid, but people who know about politics, how to organize people and do things that make people act and react. How does the military get into this act: Why should it be in these developing countries?

To this General Dick replied that when American soldiers go into a foreign area it is useful for them to know about the mores, customs, and also possible internal conflicts of that area; hence the Army's long-standing custom of issuing handbooks to its entering troops. But this was hardly an answer to Mr. Fraser's real question, which pertained not to handbooks issued soldiers in areas in which the United States maintained troops but the multimillion dollar "basic science" project that was Camelot. Mr. Fraser conceded the necessity of handbooks in a Vietnam or Korea.

"But," he went on, "when you try to create a model of a developing society for purposes of predicting what is going to happen in that society for purposes of trying to figure out what kinds of things can be done to affect decision making and the social processes, I do not see the Army in the game."

Nor would a good many other persons, but so far as one can infer from a reading of the transcript, neither Dr. Vallance, representing Camelot's behavioral scientists, nor General Dick and Mr. Seymour Deitchman, representing the Army, ever got it into his head that some gross impropriety or — looking at the matter "methodologywise" — some scientific anomaly lay in the U.S. Army having, as it were, commissioned behavioral scientists to go into Latin American countries like Chile. It was not a behavioral scientist connected with Camelot but, once again, Congressman Fraser who uttered the following words — this time following some rather pious testimony from Dr. Vallance.

> [T]here is throughout your whole presentation a kind of — an implicit attitude or relationship that this country bears to the rest of the world which, if I were not an American, I would find perhaps not highly offensive, but it suggests somehow we are the ones to find out the dynamisms that are at work in these countries for the benefit of our Military Establishment. If I were a Latin American, I wouldn't find this a particularly happy arrangement.

With Camelot to spur them, conceivably subcommittee members could have entered into the record that just as war has long been held too important a matter to be left in the hands of the generals, the behavioral sciences are too important to be left in the hands of project titans.

But the subcommittee did not. With the kind of luck that, as Arthur Guiterman described it many years ago in his famous jingle, God grants to children, fools, drunkards, and citizens of the United States of America, the behavioral sciences emerged from this potentially devastating hearing with their luster untarnished, their prestige, if anything, higher. Social scientists were treated in the subcommittee report to something that they could rejoice in almost to the degree of their pleasure in seeing the military made the scapegoat. This was the spectacle of the State Department being told by the subcommittee to commence making more use of the behavioral sciences in the formulation of foreign policy.

It is an old story that between State Department policy sections and the American academic community there is, and for long has been, distrust founded upon the State Department's lack of confidence in the concrete results of social science research and the academic community's belief — best expressed by Professor Gabriel Almond to a reporter for *Science* — that the State Department is a "conservative institution dominated by a foreign service which is trained largely in the law, in history, in the humanistic disciplines. They believe in making policy through some kind of intuitive and antenna-like process." According to official estimates gained by *Science*, of the $25.3 million spent by government agencies on social science research abroad during the fiscal year 1966, the State Department spent only $200,000. The Defense Department spent $12.5 million or half the total.

Despite his generally candid and impressive testimony before the subcommittee, Secretary Rusk did not appear eager to go into reasons for this disproportion. When pressed by Representative Frelinghuysen as to why, given the large amount of money that Defense got from Congress for behavioral science research, State received, and asked for, only pennies, and, more to the point, why such research as that represented by Camelot was not in State's hands rather than the military's, Rusk indicated only that he preferred not to get into the "question of criteria by which one or another Department might accept responsibility for certain types of research." To be sure, Secretary Rusk did, at this juncture, make the important point that such research "might be better left even to private agencies." I shall return to this in the final section of my article, for it is probably vital to the future of foreign area research by American scholars.

But if Secretary Rusk did not choose to explain the gulf between the State Department and the academic community, others with equal experience in both the foreign service and the universities have. Louis J. Halle, writing in *The Virginia Quarterly Review* (Winter 1964) has put the matter illuminatingly.

There was a period after the [Second World] War when various departments of the Government tried to marry themselves to the universities. This worked in the case of the Pentagon and the faculties of science and technology, a wartime precedent having already been established at Oak Ridge and Los Alamos. In the case of the State Department it did not work. Professors of diplomatic history, professors of Latin American history, professors of economics and of sociology were brought to Washington for meetings at which the men in the State Department tried to explain their troubles. But the gulf could not be bridged. The professors tended to confine themselves to the general nature of the problems that the officials hopefully set before them, often speaking about the need to maintain the traditional idealism of our international conduct. When confronted by the direct question, "What shall we *do*?," they fell silent. They could answer every question up to that last, but that last was the one question for which the men in the State Department had to have an answer. The experiment, abandoned at last, left the State Department men in a mood of disenchantment tinged with bitterness, such as often follows a frustrated courtship or a broken engagement.

One guesses, however, that in the future the State Department, under the prodding of the subcommittee (formal prodding, contained in its official recommendations), will engage more actively in research partnered with social scientists. Not the kind that is expected to produce an answer to each ad hoc question that crosses a desk during a State Department day but a kind that, when carried on long enough and, hopefully, with a degree of discrimination lacking in Camelot, could be the context or seedbed of decisions of policy.

I cannot conclude discussion of Camelot's impact on the State Department without reference to one development that for awhile led to considerable agitation in the social science world. This was the memorandum from President Johnson, following immediately upon the heels of Camelot's disclosure in Chile, directing the Secretary of State henceforth to screen all government-sponsored foreign area research for its possible adverse effects upon U.S. foreign relations. Heaven knows, given the blunders of Camelot, there was every good reason for such a directive. But the first response of social scientists, including those who had been involved in Camelot, was to cry censorship. By what right, it was asked, did one department of government take to itself the function of scrutinizing research projects sponsored by other government departments in which American social scientists were participating?

The answer could have been stated simply. By the same right under which today, though still imperfectly, the State Department screens "projects" of American industry that involve entry into Latin American countries. The once odious spectacle of American business men entering the banana republics of Central America and then calling for the Marines when the going got difficult should not be repeated, it would appear obvious, when it is large-scale social science projects that are involved. Despite the myth of Immaculate Conception that obtains among American behavioral scientists — under which the most aggressively intimate forays into human privacy are held miraculously pure — the rape of national dignity by American academic enterprise is as repugnant to foreign feeling as rape by American business or government. The Chilean Select Committee Report makes this very plain indeed!

On a hot day one can chill himself by reflecting on what might have happened in Chile — or any of the countries marked by Camelot for invasion — had the Project had "good" luck, had it been "successful," had not unforeseen exposure led to premature death. How the *Fidelistas* would have loved us! Several regiments of Marines would have been necessary to salvage American research capital and protect American lives.

The wonder is, given all the considerations of national dignity involved, considerations that, as the Chilean Select Committee Report specifically emphasized, could not be waived "under the pretext of the scientific character of Camelot," that the President's directive did not — rashly, unwisely, tragically — include *all* foreign-area research. For what can be more important than preservation of good feeling in Latin America, good feeling that for years was jeopardized by American commercial arrogance and that American academic arrogance jeopardized in 1965.

But the President's memorandum did not make this mistake. It properly confined itself to *government-sponsored* research. It excludes altogether from its scope private research — of universities, foundations, and of individuals. Secretary Rusk made this emphatic in his testimony before the subcommittee. Almost equally important, the Foreign Affairs Research Council that was established by the State Department to give effect to the President's memorandum, has, in practice, excluded also from its jurisdiction domestic grants of the National Science Foundation, the National Institutes of Health, the National Defense Education Act, and the Fulbright program. The council's range is thus restricted to federal departments — Defense, Commerce, Treasury, and so on — in the more customary sense.

Considering the specific exclusion of private agencies, as well as NSF, NIH, and similar scientific agencies of the government, it is difficult to understand what the executive officer of the American Psychological Association had in mind when, according to *Science* (8 July 1966) he declared that the new risk-review procedures "have eroded confidence in the government's understanding of how science goes about its business. . . . You would prefer that your peers look at your work. This is the way science is advanced, by having your critical colleagues look over your shoulder."

Such words are as irrelevant as they are pious. Returning to Camelot, it may be assumed that dozens of scientific consultants looked over the shoulders of dozens of Camelot principals. But if there is any record of their having looked critically enough to get at the core — diplomatic as well as ethical — of this monumental blunder, I have been unable to find it. To talk serenely about the holy ground of science in the aftermath of Camelot, a project that, above anything that has ever happened, has weakened the confidence of Latin American intellectuals in the *American academic and scholarly community,* is a little like talking about the rights of free private enterprise in the predatory contexts of dollar diplomacy.

The members of the Chilean Select Committee (censoring Camelot) were unmoved by the "scientific" objectives of Camelot. It is useful to quote the words of the Committee report: "We wish to say that this foreign intervention in our internal affairs may not be defended on the pretext that the social investigation which was proposed has a scientific character." In other words, rape is rape by whomever conducted. I shall have more to say later of the mounting implications to American foreign policy of large-scale, corporate research in search of foreign areas. Here it suffices to emphasize only that when a major federal department — be it Defense, State, or Commerce — *sponsors* a scientific project, even one composed of dues-paying psychologists and sociologists, it is elementary that not even the elixir of scientific method is sufficient to wipe away the fact of sponsorship.

V

We come now to what are surely the most far-reaching episodes in the aftermath of Camelot: the Congressional hearings and bills which, if approved, will result in a National Social Science Foundation and an Office of the Behavioral Sciences in the Executive Office of the President — not to mention a White House Conference on the Behavioral Sciences. I do not mean to imply that Camelot was the sole cause of these momentous events. After all, proposals along their line have been in the minds of social scientists for years.

Whether a National Social Science Foundation is desirable at this juncture in the history of the social sciences is debatable. Unfortunately we do not have, so far as I know, official, considered statements of policy from the professional social science associations, though there has been ample time during recent years for the kind of systematic consideration so momentous a development now deserves.

The major difficulty would come, I believe, from the heavy likelihood that the federal government, which already tends to be largely and increasingly "mission-oriented" in its conception of science, would place upon such a federally sanctioned office responsibility for massive policy questions and problems that the social sciences neither can nor should be expected to answer.

Over the past generation, the social sciences have made

contributions of considerable value to society and to social policy. This is incontestable. That, given current tendencies, they will make even greater contributions in the future is almost certain. But this is not the essence of the policy problem. The essence is whether, given the monumental policy *expectations* of the social sciences that would be created by establishment of such agencies as those envisioned in Representative Fascell's bills, the social sciences (or, for that matter, *any* sciences) could meet them in a way not leaving a gulf between expectation and reality so wide as to promote disillusionment in government and society at a time when the social sciences have already achieved a high level of esteem. Stating the matter briefly, the danger consists, it seems to me, in the ever-present temptation of government to see the social sciences as physicians — called upon to answer *ad hoc* questions today, yesterday if possible — when they are, at their best, *physiologists*, still concerned with vital matters of the nature of human behavior. The root is still man, and one of the most fascinating and encouraging of all tendencies today in the behavioral sciences is the synthesizing of strains of social, psychological, and physiological (and, who knows, physical in the next generation) research in the study of man. If there is anything that makes the elusive term "behavioral sciences" different from the term "social sciences," it is the closer concentration, it would seem, upon *human behavior*, as the rigorous point of departure, in contrast to the plethora of problems, issues, values, and ideologies that the long history of moral philosophy and the social sciences has bequeathed to us. There are vital problems that are neither social nor biological in character but both — problems on which important research is now being conducted. To seek, in effect, through separate funding and design of problems, to disengage the social from the biological would be to reverse present healthy trends.

It seems to me that it would be far better to widen, through appropriate legislation, the present social science area of the National Science Foundation. (A bill now before Congress proposes exactly this.) Experience of recent years with this agency has certainly been encouraging from the viewpoint of the social sciences. Having for years protested, as many of us have, the arbitrary distinction the public makes between "science" and "social science," why seek to institutionalize this distinction now, risk perpetuating it forever through establishment of a foundation?

In short, at a time when everything suggests the accomplishment of a long-hoped-for liaison among the sciences, when a significant and spreading amount of research in the social sciences is, in the judgment of everybody, as "scientific" as anything to be found in the natural sciences, this would appear to be a time for integration, not segregation.

VI

Important as it is, the matter of a new foundation may be of less vital relevance than still another question — one also dramatized by Camelot — and that is the continued usefulness of the whole "project system" that has been in vogue in the Federal government's relation to the sciences ever since the years just following the Second World War when a group of outstanding scientists in Washington were able to give it the wise guidance and control that the project system so plainly needs. But such wisdom cannot be taken for granted. The opportunities, on the one hand, for bureaucratic direction and misdirection of scientific research and, on the other, for political (I mean intrascientific politics as much as other) considerations to govern are all too rife. There is much to be said for the abandonment or at least sharp cutback of a system that not only permits but encourages scientists to go to Washington as individuals or in small groups and receive grants for projects with scrutiny too hurried and too much governed by pecking-order considerations. The system, moreover, promotes disaffection within universities.

Dr. Frederick Seitz, President of the National Academy of Science, has recently uttered some important words to this effect. "I think that the whole process of supporting academic research with federal funds would be improved substantially if a larger fraction of the money granted by the government came to universities in the form of institutional grants that were handled on the basis of decisions made jointly by university administration and faculty."

Dr. Seitz makes clear that one of the primary reasons for his recommendation of this change in policy is that of restoring strength to the inner governments of universities — to department chairmen, to deans, but also to constituted faculty committees and councils — strength they have lost under a project system in which such governments are either bypassed altogether or reduced to mere clerical or clearinghouse status by individual scientists whose own power and mobility are guaranteed by project wealth and the independence of their project from the university in which their primary identity (and tenure, high salary, and perquisites) is rooted. (As Dr. Seitz emphasizes, such independence forms much of the root of the kind of disintegration of academic community on a campus that Berkeley exemplified two years ago.)

The second reason Dr. Seitz gives for his recommendation is the fatal affinity that seems to lie between the project system and *size* of projects that take residence on university campuses. No bureaucracy likes to administer funds for an infinity of small, individual projects. It is so much easier to grant one distinguished man large sums of money in a single project. Knowing this, scientists submit applications accordingly. Add to this the fact that Congress can most easily be pleased, on the occasions of its examination of how funds for science have been spent, by projects that are "mission-oriented," that have a high degree of applied flavor. The result of this is to encourage proliferation of types of scientific projects of a practical or applied nature that could as easily be handled by nonuniversity bodies — federal, state, or private — and a subtle but puissant downgrading of appeal of those smaller, more open-ended, even amorphous "projects" that fall in the basic or theoretical areas of science.

There would be, it is clear, still another gain, and that is to the steadily enlarging field of American foreign-area research. If Project Camelot teaches anything, it is the crucial importance of *sponsorship* when a team of American social scientists goes abroad to conduct inquiries into social structure, culture, and values which, by their very nature, run the risk of offending foreign sensibilities. There is, among many foreign scholars — quite apart from government officials and citizens — a certain suspicion of not only the United States government and its agencies but government agencies in general: a suspicion founded upon frequent conflicts between their own governments and the intellectual communities in these countries — especially in the new and underdeveloped areas.

Universities, on the other hand, would appear much less susceptible to such suspicion or charges, especially when their research enterprises abroad are based, from the start, upon full cooperation with universities in the areas to be studied. In almost all countries of the world, the university is, and is most likely of all institutions to remain, trusted. One need think only of the large numbers of scholars, scientists, and public servants in the Latin American, Asian, and African countries whose higher educations have been gained in whole or part in American universities — quite apart from a generally distinguished record of American university scholars in these foreign areas.

It can be said, of course, that Camelot is evidence of the contrary. After all, this project was conceived within SORO which is itself administratively connected with American University. But from all one can gather SORO has virtually independent status; it would appear to be only nominally a part of the university; in it but not really of it; its ties with the Army come closer to being those of RAND's to the Air Force. It is, in fact, a research center of the Army that for various reasons which must once have seemed good to officials of American University is housed there instead of in the Pentagon.

This is surely a very different thing from university sponsorship as we generally and rightly understand it. And if Latin American scholars were, unhappily for us all, justified in placing some of the odium on a university in the United States, sober analysis nevertheless requires the differentiation I am making. But there is a hard lesson nevertheless in Camelot. If the system of block-grants to universities should be adopted by government foundations in preference to the present project system, then much is properly owing these government foundations by the universities in the way of *guaranteed administrative machinery* within the universities through which all such block-grants will be handled. Federal foundations should insist upon, at a minimum, proper academic-administrative bodies of review within the universities composed of faculty members, as well as of administrators, which would have something of the same over-all responsibility for research conducted under these block-grants that faculty-administrative councils and committees have immemorially had over curriculum, courses, and internally financed research in the universities.

VII

No matter what the "infrastructure" of American foreign-area research, it would be naïve to suppose that the future can be made free of the threat of impact upon foreign relations that Camelot represented in so egregious a way. Even if Camelot had never happened, there would still be what Camelot assuredly intensified: the problem of retaining (not to mention increasing) the hospitality of foreign nations toward American research in the behavioral sciences.

It is well to be reminded that some of the animus toward Camelot found in the Chilean Select Committee Report has to do with the basic type of problem that was buried beneath the Project's more manifest absurdities. From the

Chilean point of view, there was gross impropriety in the fact that, irrespective of Army sponsorship, Project Camelot proposed (I am quoting almost verbatim here) to investigate not only isolated and innocuous aspects of Chilean life but to make an x-ray of the nation, including the most intimate aspects of human beings: what they think, feel, believe, or hope. And all of this without the consent or authorization of either Chilean government or universities.

It is a fact worth stressing that personal and institutional privacy is still taken more seriously in Latin American and many other countries in the world than it is in the United States. Even under the military dictatorships of Latin America, a freedom of individuality and of personal privacy is known and cherished that we in the United States may be beginning to forget.

There is a further reason for possible distrust among intellectuals and social scientists abroad of American foreign-area projects involving the intimacy contained in Camelot's design. That is the slightly uneven record of preservation of research confidence by individual American social scientists. There have been instances, as is well known, in which full entry into a community, a sect, a club or gang, or a file of documents was granted a social science project *only* under the guarantee of absolute confidentiality and anonymity of respondents: confidentiality and anonymity which were ruthlessly violated by one or more individuals of the self-same projects acting, despite the best efforts of the principals to restrain such violation, under the cloak of individual freedom to publish the truth, however gained. The recent cancellation by the U.S. Air Force of a project funded by the Air Force Office of Scientific Research but administered at the University of Wisconsin is possibly a case in point. Although the Air Force gave no official excuse for cancellation, there is reason to believe that when some of the detailed and intimate questions that were to be asked of selected Air Force officers were examined, the conclusion was reached that such a questionnaire would be inimical to service morale, given the ever-present possibility of future leaks of community, group, or individual identity. Here again, as with so many of the issues raised by Camelot, the immediate, instinctive, reaction of the academic research community is a curious one to say the least. We find one professor declaring that the prime lesson to be learned from the Air Force cancellation is that we, the social scientists, must educate the public into understanding that the same kind of personal intimacy of question is to be expected and accepted from social scientists as has long been accepted from physicians and lawyers. But at least two aspects of the matter render this comparison decidedly suspect. In the first place, the physician's "intimacy" stems solely from diagnosis designed to cure. Intimacy of the social scientist stems from research designed for publication. There is, second, the matter of responsibility and sanctions. A physician found guilty of broadcasting or leaking the identity of a patient with, say, a venereal disease or advanced case of alcoholism or nymphomania would be broken professionally. There are no such sanctions in the academic profession. It is possible indeed to be promoted and to draw excellent royalties in the behavioral sciences for actions that would lead to suspension from the legal or medical professions.

This may seem a tangential matter. I am suggesting, however, that what is an increasingly complex and uneasy matter for American conscience is bound to be, given the less than perfect record that the behavioral sciences have for preservation of confidentiality, a matter of considerable moment when the subjects are Chilean or French instead of American. As I noted earlier, one of the responses of the Latin American academic and intellectual community to Camelot has been precisely that of asking what acts of censure have been taken by American social science associations toward the individuals involved in Camelot.

More important, however, to the future of American foreign area research even than type of research project and question is its potential volume. Here we have something that can, not inexactly, be put in Malthusian terms. The number of foreign areas will increase (through dropping of barriers) only *arithmetically*, but the population of American behavioral scientists with questions to ask of foreign areas will increase *geometrically*. Where once American foreign-area research was confined to a tiny handful of anthropologists and geographers — who learned the hard way the exceeding importance of tact, trust, honesty, and limits to questions when dealing with foreign peoples and who went in as individuals, not as members of formidable projects — such research now, as we know, engulfs all the behavioral sciences. Given its rising popularity among social scientists who once could not have found their way to a passport office, given the shrinking (in the sense of diminishing returns) domestic market of political attitudes, religious beliefs, social aspirations, dreams, orgasms against the voracious requests of domestic behavioral science titans for ever-enlarging masses of subjects, and given, finally, the hordes of graduate students writing dissertations, junior professors on the make, senior professors in struggle for Project Titanship, not to mention the tens, the hundreds of millions of dollars for such research that will inevitably come from formalized federal assistance, given all this, it could hardly be a matter for wonder if more and more foreign governments (and also foreign academic communities) began to take the hostile stance toward American social scientists that was once reserved for American businessmen. The bland and righteous belief among American academics that any degree of invasion of privacy, any degree of public exposure of the human psyche, is justified so long as it is in the name of science rather than, say, the TV industry, is no more likely to win popularity in the long run than did the medieval Inquisition, which defended its invasions in the name of piety and protection of the faithful.

I mention these considerations because of the possible importance in the near future of our somehow channeling, if not actually limiting, the growing demand for foreign "markets." To assume that all will be well if only investigation of natives abroad is done by an American NSSF or a university is, I fear, naïve. There will be, all too certainly, other considerations — of foreign relations, national policy and so on — when the American knowledge industry really gets tooled up for foreign markets and its production rolling.

Does such language offend? We had better get used to it. The relevant model of behavioral science research is fast ceasing to be the scholar — he of "furrowed brow in bookish corner" — and fast becoming the brisk executive, equally at home in institute, business, and government. We still use the beguiling image of the scholar and his natural right to freedom of inquiry. It is to today's large-scale, corporate research what the image of the small individual businessman and his natural right to profit is to corporate industry: a compound of honest nostalgia, guilty conscience, and camouflage. The structure, the incentives, and even the language of contemporary large-scale research have more in common with business than with the academy. And it matters little, substantively, whether we have reference here to "academic" or "nonacademic" research.

It is possible, I think, to apply to today's knowledge of industry what Berle and Means wrote thirty years ago of the modern corporation: "Just what motives are effective today, in so far as control is concerned, must be a matter of conjecture. But it is probable that more could be learned regarding them by studying the motives of an Alexander the Great, seeking new worlds to conquer, than by considering the motives of a petty tradesman of the days of Adam Smith." Substitute "petty scholar" for "petty tradesman" in the foregoing words and the relevance is immediate.

Foreign-area research is bound to become massive and potentially invasionary. If one were a Marxist-Leninist he could say that the American research industry is just beginning to enter its imperialist phase. Diminishing returns, a falling rate of profit, are encountered in the American market. Smalltown, Midcity, Big City have been entered too often; the middle, upper, and lower classes are beginning to be sucked dry; American marriage and divorce (God knows!) have little yield left in their sweated ranks; WASP, Catholic, Jew, Negro, Pole, and (soon) Mexican have been nearly exhausted of domestic return on capital; religious belief, political preference, reading taste, sex life, coloration-response of organism cannot, in the American population, hold up much longer. New worlds are needed for conquest if the already frenzied competition for returns within the United States is not to result in civil war. (A sometime business executive, now financial vice-president of a great university, said recently: "Nothing I saw in fifteen years of business compares with the gut competition, the dog eat dog, that I see in the university. God help the natives abroad when the academics get at them in full force.") There must be, at this moment, literally tens of thousands of American behavioral scientists — Ph.D. aspirants in search of dissertations, professors of all ranks, not to mention the hordes of nonacademic researchers in business and government — poised, computers oiled and ready, troops of technicians waiting to be employed, for the Big Leap across all oceans.

Irving Louis Horowitz

Washington University

*Social Science and Public Policy: Implications of Modern Research**

Economics, sociology, psychology, and the other social sciences have in recent times begun to play a new and problematic role with respect to national and international policy. The problem of social policy has become acute precisely to the extent to which social science has become exact. Legitimation of policy recommendations from social scientists emerges in this period and not in previous periods because of a demonstrable feasibility of putting social science and social theory into a framework of political action. Demand for operations research analysts, tactical data systems, war gaming and simulation experts now rivals the search for basic engineering personnel. There is a paucity of exact information on how this transvaluation took place, due in part to the novelty of the situation and in part to the novelty of self-examination in the social sciences. What is at stake as a result of this newly acquired influence is not the feasibility of social science but the credibility of social scientists.

Any discussions of villains and values, which inevitably is what the study of social science and public policy boils down to, involves two distinct areas. One is the empirics of present

* Originally published in *International Studies Quarterly*, Vol. XI, No. 1 (Spring 1967), pp. 32–62.

relationships between social science and public policy, its formation and its execution. The other is the question of what the relationship between social science and public policy should be. In connection with both what it is and what should be, there are two variables. The first is the utilization of social science in the formation of public policy; the second involves the *relation* between social scientists and policy makers. The fact that an ever increasing number of individuals can with some legitimacy claim both scientific and policy-making statuses tends to blur the lines between these issues.

1. THREE STYLES OF POLITICAL EXHORTATION

The first problem we come upon concerns the factual issues in the character of the relationship between social scientists and the policy makers, that is, how this relationship differs in various social structures. What is the relationship of sociologists to society in a totalitarian State? Or in a welfare State? Or in a *laissez faire* State or system? What are the stresses and strains upon the social scientists and policy makers in each type of national system?

Most social science disciplines require open-ended conditions for their functioning. Invariably and almost necessarily, established dogmas about society must be challenged. In this sense, sociology has been as much a problem for the socialist ideology as astronomy was for seventeenth-century Catholicism. For example, do women go to church more often than men in the Soviet Union? From the point of view of Marxism, this is a ridiculous question. Men and women are equal by definition. Only historical antecedents are considered in accounting for differential sexual responses to religious practices in a socialist nation. Therefore, the sexual variable itself tends to be suppressed as a legitimate area of inquiry for Soviet researchers despite the noticeable difference in church attendance between male and female, not only in the Soviet Union but in many countries displaying similar political structures and levels of industrialization.

This discrepancy between fact and theory leads to the conclusion that in a pure command structure the relationship of social science to public policy is not much of a problem because the social sciences, aside from their technical vocabularies, are suppressed. The ideology of science is harnessed to the ideology of the State. This is done by celebrating only the "pure" and the "natural" sciences. Applied social sciences may exist, but what does not exist is an analysis of the whole society. To the extent that meaningful data contradict the established order, the social sciences are suspect. Not accidentally, the more exaggerated the totalitarian system, the less available for public inspection is the social scientists' information. The degree to which the development of the social sciences is permitted within a nation operates as a twentieth-century index of freedom. And the extent to which the development of an independent social science is stifled provides a measure of political stagnation. Allowing myself an *ex cathedra* judgment, I do not think anyone can participate in social research and fail to see a high correlation of good social science and a good society.

The evidence provided by the Soviet Union on this score is illustrative. While the research and academic personnel in the Soviet Union engaged in the arts, history, humanities, and social sciences continues to grow numerically — from 620,600 in 1956 to 740,400 in 1960 — this represents a downward percentile trend with respect to the physical and engineering sciences — from 27.9 to 24.0. If this figure is broken down further, it is found that only 3.9 of the scientific personnel are engaged in what would in the West be called the social sciences — and these are gathered in the fields of economics and planning.[1] Undoubtedly, what occurs is a wide-

---

[1] See Nicholas DeWitt, *Soviet Professional Manpower: Its Education, Training and Supply* (Washington, D. C.: U.S. National Science Foundation, 1955); and more recently, his essay on the "Reorganization of Science and Research in the U.S.S.R.," in Norman Kaplan (ed.), *Science and Society* (Chicago: Rand McNally, 1965), pp. 303–321.

spread infiltration of social science findings through "alien" fields such as pedagogy, geography, jurisprudence, and even such refined areas as mathematical statistics. More recently, this subterranean approach has been replaced by an opening up of the social sciences at least to include sociology and psychology (the latter has always been available as part of the medical and biological sciences, and now is being thought of as a social science). This indicates a distinct movement in the Soviet Union from totalitarian to authoritarian modalities. That is to say, there is a distinct tendency away from political dominance and surveillance of all scientific products to a political exclusivity that demands relevance rather than conformity in the products of social research.[2]

In a welfare system, in contrast to a command system, the social sciences tend to have exceptionally close ties with policy-oriented sectors of the society. The two are joined functionally by the ministries of science, such as those which exist in England, France, and Germany. Policy makers, for their part, often think of the social sciences as a rationale required for any projected change estimated to be in the social interest. Before a major piece of legislation is introduced into the English Parliament, for example, the likelihood is that a survey has already been conducted providing a form of social science legitimation. Thus in England, while investment in social science is relatively smaller than in the United States, there is a high payoff for social science information.[3] The social scientist is not only listened to. His advice is frequently sought. Social science has become a recognized aspect of national investment. The welfare system has been a tremendous source for social science growth; and in turn, the social

[2] Allen Kassof, "American Sociology Through Soviet Eyes," and Talcott Parsons, "An American Impression of Sociology in the Soviet Union," in *American Sociological Review*, Vol. 30, No. 1 (February 1965), pp. 114–124.

[3] See Irving L. Horowitz, *The New Sociology* (New York and London: Oxford University Press, 1964), pp. 43–47.

sciences have reinforced the "socialist" tendencies within the societies they operate.

The character of the social science practiced in the welfare system tends to be of a strongly applied nature. England no longer produces the great theories about society; rather it paves the way for practices intended to reshape social policy.[4] Empiricism extends deep into the marrow of the policy orientation. Both the opportunities and the payoff are in such a direction. Furthermore, "pure" social science research involves a study and evolution of fundamental theories about man, and neither the pragmatism of the twentieth-century British party system nor the empiricism of the educational system places much faith in "fundamentals."

The linkage between the British political and educational systems may have delayed the evolution of an independent social science curriculum at the more traditional places of learning; but when the penetration did take place (by economics in the eighteenth century, administration in the nineteenth century, and political science in the present century), the situation was ready-made for the close cooperation between social science and social policy. And with the defeat of ideological Toryism (based as it was on "classical studies") by the close of the Second World War, the last shreds of opposition to social science vanished.[5] The impulses of British social science to welfare projects dovetailed neatly with the welfare projects outlined by the political apparatus. And the

[4] A new series of articles on "reshaping social policy" appearing in the English publication *New Society* is indicative of this trend. The articles deal with population pressures, urban design, professional practices, and immigration, all as they relate to England. See *New Society*, Vol. 7, Nos. 179–181 (March 1966).

[5] For a general outline, see D. S. L. Cardwell, *The Organization of Science in England: A Retrospect* (London: William Heinemann, 1957); and for a more specific essay, see Eric Ashby, "Science and Public Policy: Some Institutional Patterns Outside America," in B. R. Keenan (ed.), *Science and the University* (New York and London: Columbia University Press, 1966), pp. 13–26.

mutual suspicions of scientists and policy makers characteristic of an earlier epoch in British history dissolved into mutual reinforcement and even joint celebration.

In *laissez faire* consensus systems, the social sciences are compelled to compete with directly involved policy agencies. For example, in the United States executive policy makers have traditionally consulted those with training in diplomacy, law, and administration. But until well into the present century, little attention was given any of the so-called hard social sciences — psychology, economics, and sociology. Furthermore, not until the establishment of bureaucratic modes of social science performance have the social sciences been granted the kind of hearing they enjoy in the welfare State. The extent to which the *laissez faire* system becomes permeated with welfare elements, concerning itself with protecting and caring for the citizenry, to that degree is there a high penetration of the social sciences into the area of government policy.

There appear to be three distinctive factors accounting for the special role of social science in the formation of American policy. They explain not only the significance of social science in policy making but the dependence of American social science on policy agencies.

First, a strong social reform tendency developed early in opposition to general theories of change and revolution. American social science has been consciously, almost self-consciously, dedicated to issues of practical reform: elimination of poverty, integration of ethnic minorities, immigration and population issues, urban redevelopment schemes, etc. This has led major foundations and philanthropic agencies to lose interest in the direct alleviation of social problems through charity and to invest heavily in indirect means of alleviation: social science programs.

Second, development of a pluralistic educational system made room for many and diverse social scientific activities. This gainful employment in teaching, while it prevented some of the worst excesses of the German university system from being repeated in the United States — chauvinism, nationalism, anti-Semitism — weakened the status system in American higher education. Status tended to be conferred from the outside, especially from federal and private agencies who drew upon educational expertise as the only sources of nonpolitical opinion. This permitted the American social scientist to retain an independence from government no less than the policy maker to reserve judgment on the worth of the social sciences.

Third, an entrepreneurial spirit developed in Americal social science to accommodate growing government needs. Bureaucratic organizations served to mediate the claims of educational and political establishments, safeguarding both from detriment or disrepute. Social science middlemen emerged in all forms. Bureaus of social research blossomed at the major universities. Independent, nonuniversity agencies sprang up: the RAND Corporation, Institute for Defense Analysis, Aerospace Corporation, Peace Research Institute. Organizations geared to marketing research and national opinion surveys proliferated. These entrepreneurial responses to government needs meant the institutionalization of a buying and selling arrangement. And as is customary in such arrangements, the buyers perform superordinate and the sellers subordinate roles, except in special circumstances.[6]

Table I indicates the network of private military research agencies and their base of military support. Of this amount, it has been estimated that approximately twenty million are earmarked for the behavioral and social sciences directly.

The *laissez faire* consensus system is not an exact description of American society. The system of social science evolved in special circumstances of United States political and economic history. In effect, its political rhetoric remains

[6] See Don K. Price, *Government and Science: Their Dynamic Relation in American Democracy* (New York: New York University Press, 1954) and Warren O. Hagstrom, *The Scientific Community* (New York and London: Basic Books, 1965).

TABLE I
Private Military Research Agencies

Supported by Military	Contract Holdings in millions*
Air Force	
Aerospace Corporation	$76.2
System Development Corporation	51.6
Mitre Corporation	34.4
RAND Corporation	11.4
Analytic Services, Inc.	1.3
Navy	
Applied Physics Laboratory (Johns Hopkins)	54.9
Franklin Institute (Center for Naval Analyses)	11.5
Army	
Research Analysis Corporation	9.3
Defense Department	
Institute for Defense Analyses	2.1
Logistics Management Institute	1.0
Created at Suggestion of Military (Major Institutions)	
Lincoln Laboratory (M.I.T.)	49.4
Instrumentation Laboratory (M.I.T.)	47.0

* Net value of prime contract award, fiscal year 1964.
Source of Data: Defense Department.

steeped in consensus, while its economic characteristics have increasingly been subject to welfare elements. This is one central reason for the "schizophrenia" in applied social research.

As an over-all characterization, it could be said that: (1) In a command society, policy dictates both the character and the activities of the social sciences. Social science loses control over both the instruments and purposes of research. The operational aspects become so important with respect to what policy dictates that the social sciences can do little but "plug into" the going political system and hope for enlightened outcomes. To the extent that the sciences do so satisfactorily, they survive. (2) In a welfare system, policy and social sciences interact but without any sense of tension or contradiction between scientific propositions and the therapeutic orientations. The integration is so complete that there is a loss of identity at both the scientific and political poles. Spill-over between scientific propositions and therapeutic prescriptions is tremendous; all functions of social science are funneled into a social-problems orientation. The result is a decline of interest in the larger analysis of social systems or social forces. (3) In a *laissez faire* system, the social sciences tend to be independent and autonomous of political policy. However, to the degree they remain in this pristine condition, they are also weak in power and status. What takes place typically is an exchange system based on a reciprocal transference of information for money. But this reduces the amount of social science autonomy, which leads to a trade-off of high status for maximum power. This in its turn creates a source of inner tension within the social sciences as to the appropriate role of the social scientist in the forging of public policy.

II. SOCIALIZATION INTO SECRECY

Until now, we have considered the training of social scientists as a given. Here we must take note of their training as policy consultants or advisers. While most officials in government have a series of checks and balances to guide their behavior, few forms of anticipatory socialization apply to social scientists who advise government agencies. Since such social science advisers are asked for operational guidance on sensitive issues, they are often shielded from the consequences of their policy utterances. The anomaly arises that the more sensitive the policy question the less subject it is to public scrutiny.

Secrecy has been maintained about government scientists that is practiced elsewhere in Washington only on behalf of Central Intelligence Agents. As one commentator has recently pointed out: "Not only are the names of some two hundred P-SAC consultants kept secret, but so are those of other paid scientific advisers to government. Spokesmen for both the Air Force and the Arms Control and Disarmament Agency recently refused to divulge the identity of certain of their scientific advisers on the grounds that to do so would (1) expose them to pressure, (2) ensure that they would receive unwanted mail, and (3) put them under public scrutiny, which was exactly where they did not want to be."[7] Yet, since the purpose of research may have an effect on the judgment of social scientists, why should secrecy be either prized or praised?

The question of secrecy is intimately connected with that of policy because it is a standing assumption of policy makers never to reveal themselves entirely. No government in the "game" of international politics feels that its policies can be placed on the table for full public review. Therefore, operational research done in connection with policy considerations is bound by the canons of privacy. In its most basic form, the dilemma is as follows. Social scientists have a "fetish" for publicizing their information. However, policy branches of society have as their "fetish," as their essential method, private documents and privileged information. How else does one gain in the game of one-upmanship without privacy, without knowing something that the other side does not know? Therefore, a premium is placed not simply on gaining information but on maintaining silence about such information. A reversal of premiums and a transvaluation of values arises, leading to extreme tension. What often reduces such tension is the sacrifice of the social sciences, their yielding to considerations of policy.

Social scientists yield on such issues not simply because of a power imbalance between buyer and seller of ideas but because they prefer a recessive role. Social scientists may enjoy the idea of partaking of a secret order of things. There

[7] M. Greenfield, "Science Goes to Washington," in Norman Kaplan (ed.), *Science and Society* (Chicago: Rand McNally, 1965), pp. 415–429.

is something tremendously fascinating about being "in" and not being "out." The cost of this "inside dopester" role may be a heavy one — the institutionalization of a subordinate position. But in being privy to things of secrecy, the feeling of powerlessness is largely eliminated; the subordinate role with respect to political authorities may be more than counterbalanced by a superordinate feeling with respect to other social scientists.

One critical factor reinforcing the common acceptance of the norm of secrecy is the allocation of most government research funds for military or semimilitary purposes. As Table II indicates, approximately 70 percent of such funds have

TABLE II
Federal R & D Expenditures, Fiscal 1965, by program area

Program Area	Estimated Expenditure (in millions)
*Space research	$6,700
Military research	5,200
*Medical research	1,300
*Nuclear research	1,200
Agricultural research	179
*Oceanographic research	138
*Metereological research	108
*Water and transportation research	129
Educational research	24
Vocational rehabilitation research	19
Welfare administration research	7
Other (not allocable)	87
TOTAL	$15,287

* Program estimate by Bureau of Budget. Other items estimated by author.
Source of data: 1965 Federal Budget.

either a directly military or semimilitary basis. Under such circumstances, the real wonder is not the existence of a norm of secrecy but the relative availability of information.

Social scientists involved with research defined as secret or confidential can easily develop a self-definition of importance derived from their connections rather than the intrinsic merits or demerits of their work. They come to desire secrecy as much as their superordinates because they want to be shielded from public scrutiny of their work. Being publicly called to account in congressional committee hearings, for example, has a demeaning effect on status. If an economist or political scientist working for the Central Intelligence Agency filed a report to the government so erroneous that it helped pave the way for policy disasters, public availability of the report would reflect negatively on his standing in the academic community. Thus secrecy is a mutual advantage in the event of failure even more than in successful ventures. In this protected environment, the social science advisory competence becomes an unknown quantity. About the only surety available to the hiring federal agencies is to choose from the elite corps of social scientists and to offer financial rewards high enough to attract such an elite.[8]

The widespread acceptance of the canons of secrecy, no less than the commitment to policy as such, makes it extremely difficult to separate science from patriotism and hence to question the research design itself. The acceptance of the first stage, the right of the government to secrecy, often carries with it acquiescence in the last stage, the necessity for silence on the part of social scientists. The demand for secrecy has its most telling impact on the methodology of the social sciences. Presumably, policy personnel hire or employ social scientists because this group represents objectivity and honesty. The social scientists represent a wall of truth, off of which the policy makers can bounce their premises and practices. Social scientists are thought to provide information that

[8] This was clearly done in the case of Project Camelot. The consultants were drawn from the more eminent members of the social science community. See Committee on Foreign Affairs of the House of Representatives, *Behavioral Sciences and the National Security* (Report No. 4 together with Part IX of the Hearings on Winning the Cold War: The U.S. Ideological Offensive) (Washington, D. C.: U.S. Government Printing Office, 1965).

public opinion is not able (or willing) to supply. To some degree, social scientists are hired because they will say things that may be unpopular but nonetheless significant. For example, that the Chinese Communist system is viable and will not collapse is a difficult position to assert, unless one is a social science expert. Then such a statement can be made with relative impunity — even before a Senate Foreign Relations hearing.

The norm of secrecy overturns the scientific premise of publicity. Since the terms of research and conditions of work require an initial compromise with the methodology of social science, the lofty purpose of truth acquisition tends to be blunted. The social scientist is placed in a cognitive bind: He is conditioned not to reveal maximum information lest he become victimized by those who employ him; and yet he is employed precisely because of a presumed impartiality. Once the social scientist becomes gingerly and clever, then his value to social science *qua* social science is endangered. But once his scientific acumen interferes with policy, his "usefulness" to the policy maker may likewise be jeopardized. The social scientist engaged in policy research walks a tightrope, with secrecy as the invisible net lest he fall.

Social scientists think they have a good commodity for sale or for hire, and at least one large sector of society shares this estimate. Avid consumers of social science products such as government policy makers may come into direct competition for services with equally concerned but less affluent consumers of social science. There are people who think highly of social science information and others who think poorly of it. However, even those with a high opinion are not always in a position to pay for social science services. Thus, as can be seen in Table III, funds for research are, for all practical purposes, restricted to government, industry, and university sources.

TABLE III
Sources of Funds Used for Research and Development, by Sector, from 1953 to 1962 (millions of dollars)

Year	Total	Federal Government	Industry	Colleges and Universities	Other Nonprofit Institutions
1953–1954	$5,150	$2,740	$2,240	$130	$ 40
1954–1955	5,620	3,070	2,365	140	45
1955–1966	6,390	3,670	2,510	155	55
1956–1957	8,670	5,095	3,325	180	70
1957–1958	10,100	6,390	3,450	190	70
1958–1959	11,130	7,170	3,680	190	90
1959–1960	12,680	8,320	4,060	200	100
1960–1961	13,890	9,010	4,550	210	120
1961–1962	14,740	9,650	4,705	230	155

Source of data: National Science Foundation.

Because of the complex nature of social science activities and their increasing costs — both for human and machine labor — the government becomes the most widespread buyer. Government policy makers get the first yield also because they claim a maximum need. Private pressure groups representing corporate interests are the next highest buyer of social science services. The Bureaus of Social Research vaguely attached to universities service most nonfederal research needs. The role of foundations and universities is ambiguous. Theoretically they ought to be encouraging pure research, particularly if government agencies encourage applied research. In fact, rarely are they interested in pure research. If anything, they tend to be as concerned with applied problems as the public and business agencies, since they are concerned with justifying their worth precisely to business donors and government agencies. Further, big foundations and major universities are often policy extensions of federal agencies — if not directly, then through special laws and rules governing the taxation of philanthropic agencies and universities. The sources of funds for research tend to be exclusively concentrated in the upper classes. The fact that the President can indirectly participate in the selection process of major foundations indicates the intimacy that exists between federal and private controllers of wealth despite legal niceties. This fusion of government and corporate wealth makes it difficult to bring about a countervailing pluralistic system of power with respect to social science funding.[9]

There is a direct relationship between the ability to pay and belief in the utility of the social sciences. Who are the high users? The federal government, some state governments, basic industries, marketing industries. Who are the low users? Farmer-labor groups, the poor in general, minority groups (with the exception of highly sophisticated groups such as affluent religious organizations that spill over into the high-users category). In the main, racial and ethnic groups do not place much value on the uses of social science. Perhaps the use of social science research is itself a suave reflection of wealth. Those who wish to use social science agencies extensively are wealthy enough to afford them; those who disparage social science groups are often rationalizing their own lack of affluence.

The image of social science tends to be far less flattering in the attitude of the poorer classes than in that of the wealthier classes. Ultimately, the social scientists, to the extent that they become involved with policy-making agencies, become committed to an elitist ideology. They come to accept as basic the idea that men who really change things are at the top. Thus, the closer to the top one can get direct access, the more likely will intended changes be brought about.[10]

Two flies can be found in this particular ointment. First,

[9] For a defense and an acknowledgment of this, see Paul F. Lazarsfeld, "Reflections on Business," *The American Journal of Sociology*, Vol. 65, No. 1 (July 1959), pp. 1–26; and for a critique, see Irving L. Horowitz, "Establishment Sociology: The Value of Being Value Free," *Inquiry: An Interdisciplinary Journal of Philosophy and the Social Sciences*, Vol. 6, No. 2 (1963), pp. 129–139.

[10] See Robert Presthus, *Men at the Top: A Study in Community Power* (New York: Oxford University Press, 1964), especially pp. 3–63.

there is slender evidence that information bought and paid for is made the basis of policy in critical times. Indeed, there is just as much evidence for the conclusion that information is used when it suits policy makers and discarded when it does not "fit" political plans. Second, there is no evidence that the elitist model is uniquely cast to solve problems of social change. The model of elites changing the world is itself controversial. It may be flattering to think that involvement with elites enables one to determine the course of society. But if a Marxian or mass model is used, what happens to the relationship of the policy maker to the social scientist? The whole situation must then be perceived in terms of social forces. By minimizing any other historically derived model, such as a mass model, the social scientist leaves unexplored variables which ought to be examined and tested for their significance; these variables simply become heuristically manipulated as part of the ongoing ethos of social life.

An aspect of the norm of secrecy often alluded to informally but rarely publicly is: How is exact information obtained about potentially enemy or alien groups? In situations of relative insularity or isolation, whose judgments concerning the intentions of other nations, races, or groups can be relied upon? The character of the informants no less than the quality of the information itself has become a central problem in decision making. Nor is this merely a problem for foreign affairs. For example, in estimating the potential for mass violence of American Negroes, how valuable is information supplied by major institutionalized Negro associations? If the leadership of the Urban League is asked about the possibility of mass racial violence, will it provide the same kind of response as the Black Muslims or an opinion survey of the unorganized Negro? The tendency has been to rely upon institutionalized expressions for information concerning "spontaneous" crowd behavior, but reliance upon established organizations may easily distort our vision of a situation. There is a judgmental issue to be settled even before any sampling is undertaken. How serious this can be is reflected in the fact that at the very height of the Negro revolution, studies of crowd behavior and mass movements in the United States have practically faded from the work done by behavioral scientists.[11]

Even more complicated is the evaluation of foreign affairs. How are the military intentions of Communist China to be estimated? Are studies made in Hong Kong or information supplied by Taiwanese Army officers to be relied upon? Yet, if there is no direct access to the "enemy," whoever it may be at any time, how is exact information to be derived? The alternative to partisan bias would be to accept the rhetoric of the enemy society at face value. However, reading reports of major political and military figures of the enemy society from afar may create an approach akin to inspirational divinations of Biblical passages. Recent examples of multiple and conflicting interpretations abound. Consider the Chinese addresses that have been monitored concerning the politicalization of military cadres in North Vietnam. These remarks have been "interpreted" as indicating Chinese support for the war effort, Chinese distance and even withdrawal from the war effort, Chinese pleasure (and displeasure) with the National Liberation Front. Interpretation too easily becomes a function of policy perspectives rather than an objective study of foreign power intentions.

The filtering process, based as it is on the secrecy norm, leads to an abuse of what can be considered legitimate scientific inquiry. It minimizes possibilities of empirical and ethnographic surveys. Knowing what the "other side" is doing or planning in the main areas of government policy is absolutely necessary for the establishment of informational parity. But this runs squarely against policy rulings having to do with overseas travel, having to do with definition of the

[11] Paul F. Lazarsfeld, "Political Behavior and Public Opinion," in Bernard Berelson (ed.), *The Behavioral Sciences Today* (New York: Basic Books, 1963), p. 187.

enemy, and sometimes having to do with attitudes toward people considered to be less than human. The needs of policy are difficult to square with the needs of the social sciences. Policy may dictate *de jure* nonrecognition of a foreign power, but it is impossible for the social scientist to accept such policy recommendations as a *de facto* basis for research. He has to find a way of violating nonrecognition in order to serve in a scholarly capacity.

This unanticipated contradiction between science and policy cannot easily be resolved without redefining the enemy in nonpartisan terms or accepting the idea of partisanship as an institutionalized limit to scientific enquiry. But to do so would require a general redefinition of the role of social science in a democratic culture. What results in situations of high policy stress is low quality research. Conversely, when there is a low stress situation there can be high yield information. Democracy is linked to social visibility; hence we know a great deal about England and its society. But England poses no immediate threat, and therefore social scientists working in the area of English affairs are less than vital with respect to policy. The more important the subject the less likely is there to be access to critical information. As long as the political situation is defined exclusively in terms of policy needs, the possibility of a social science of operational worth remains seriously impaired.

The proud announcement in the early fifties of the policy sciences has given way to a profound skepticism of such a concept in the sixties. Perhaps the notion of a policy science is a contradiction in terms, not previously recognized as such only because of the enormity of federal and commercial needs for exact information in an age when mass participatory democracy has sharply declined. There can never be a policy science from the point of view of the polity because its needs have to do with sovereignty and with the protection of its citizens even if this involves secrecy, war, and deceitful forms of defense or attack. Whereas, from the point of view of the social scientist, the same concept of policy science must be challenged because in the final analysis the scientific community can never accept an exclusively therapeutic definition of social life. Social science can never take for granted the things that make for political sovereignty. Perhaps this contradiction is a creative tension. But I am not so optimistic. My own feeling is that this is a degenerative relationship. The negative features implied both for policy and for science cancel the pragmatic worth of a concept of policy science.

The value-free doctrine has been examined at too great a length to require additional commentary. Yet there is an aspect of the fact-value issue which deserves deeper analysis here, since it involves the connection of social science to public policy in a direct way. When translated into a personal ideological expression, this fact-value dualism can provide a rationale for selling information to the highest bidder. It can become a way of saying that facts are for public sale, while values are for private sensibilities.

Quite conceivably, the classical disjunction between fact and value may turn out to be a greater problem for distributors of "hard" science than for those who traffic in "soft" science. For if the doctrine of value irrelevance is taken seriously, it becomes a mandate for any values. Hence the complete separation of fact and value can jeopardize tough policy scientists quite thoroughly. Conventionally, advocates of the value-free doctrine have considered it to be a functional instrument safeguarding against any ideological infiltration of the social sciences. However, it is becoming uncomfortably plain that the notion of selling information to the highest bidder is not at all inconsistent with people who have no "higher" values at all, and not only those who refuse to express value preference in their social research.

The more expensive an originating research design turns out to be, the more differential access to the findings is demanded as the price for an initial expenditure of risk capital.[12] The policy sector demand for differential access may take various forms:

(1) The policy agency will insist upon a defined period of lead time before release of findings to the public.

(2) The results can be made immediately available only if they are initially cleared by the sponsoring agency so that no information of a "delicate" nature is revealed.

(3) This often leads to a more formal situation, in which the publication of an exoteric document is allowed, while a more complete esoteric document serves as a special payoff to the agency.

(4) Finally, by insisting that all research done under contract is private, the sponsoring agency settles all "problems" of publication. Often the distinction between "liberal" and "conservative" agencies is made on the basis of data released and has no general political moorings.

None of these four types of data processing represents a classical model of social scientific behavior with respect to publication. But the bureaucratic style has become increasingly generalized. New elements have entered into the policy game even at the level of publication. One sensitive issue, for example, is what constitutes publication. Is a mimeographed report an authentic publication? Reports in such nontypographical form appear regularly and have peculiar qualities. They are not available for public consumption. They are not copyrighted and hence not subject to public review. Even "official-looking" mimeographed reports released in bound form remain private documents. This raises not only questions of differential access but of arbitrary limits to access. It is not only who but how many people are in a position to read such documents. The norm of secrecy has become so much part of the character of social science publications that the general risks to unlimited diffusion of information have greatly increased.

[12] On this question see the contribution by Richard J. Barber, *The Politics of Research* (Washington, D. C.: Public Affairs Press, 1966), pp. 91–108.

The issues can be divided into sponsorship problems and ideological problems. At one level, the policy issue is who sponsors the research rather than the character of the research. At the other end of the spectrum, the scientific issue is the goal sought from any given research. More profoundly, as I have already suggested, the issue is the nature of sovereignty and the nature of privacy.

Nations are not often thought to be private entities. Rather we think of them as macroscopic and publicly available to investigation. However, sovereignty carries with it, if not explicitly then surely implicitly, a notion of restricted public access, that is, privacy. Sovereignty is a statement of the rights of citizens, and such rights impose restrictions upon noncitizens. Therefore, a sovereign, whether in its universalistic national form or a person, has a private side, a private self.

This might best be seen in legal terms of juror performance and jury room wire tapping. From the point of view of social science, the phenomenology of decision making in a closed setting represents a fascinating problem. How do people interact within "alien" restricted confines? Do the decisions they reach rest upon rational or irrational indicators? What is the character of personal interaction in a jury room? From the point of view of the sovereign, the elements of jury decision making require secrecy for their realization. The sovereign assumes that people in private interaction, untouched by public pressure, are in a position to make decisions that are more truthful and hence more useful than publicly debated decisions. This is an example of competing needs. The political requirement is different from the scientific requirement. Who is right? Would it be right to implant a microphone in a jury room for the sake of social science, running the risk ultimately of destroying confidence of jurors and potential jurors in a democratic legal system? Or is it right to preserve an irrational kernel of madness that may well be what a jury system is about, simply to maintain the myth of democratic processes?

There is no ready-made answer to this kind of dilemma. But raising this sort of problem gives an indication of the anxieties and disturbances felt by sovereign powers in the realm of foreign area research. For what is being tested by the study by one nation of the inner workings of another nation is nothing short of the right to remain private. The justification of such privacy may be quite shaky, based on custom and myth. At the moment, however, the problem is not the *origins* of sovereignty but rather the *rights* of sovereignty. From this point of view, anxieties concerning foreign area research have to be appreciated, irrespective of social scientific or policy claims.

The sponsoring agent of research may not be as important for the sovereign under scrutiny as for the individuals engaging in a field investigation. Whether sponsorship of foreign area research is under the aegis of the Department of Health, Education, and Welfare or the Department of Defense may dwindle in terms of how such research is perceived by the foreign government. But from either the public or the private viewpoint, visibility of research funds is significant. It may well be that openness of sponsorship is a determining element in how far access to a foreign sovereign may be pushed. To put matters directly: The reaction of the sovereign to an investigatory body in some measure depends on the premises and purposes of the investigatory body. This in turn may require a fresh look at the norm of secrecy — and understanding that such a norm affects sovereignty as well as science.

III. UNIVERSITY BUREAUCRACIES AND VALUE SYSTEMS

The social ecology of where various activities are performed leaves an imprint on the nature of the findings. Social scientific activities usually take place within a university context. The university, viewed as a social force, has strong feudalistic elements. Some people mistake this feudal ancestry for humanism, possibly because of the historical distance between our epoch and the founding of the university system nearly eight hundred years ago. The feudal core of university life is that a stratum of people is employed to engage in activities that may not be practical. They are paid to be nonfunctional. To put matters in a more exact form, the function of a university is to absorb the welter of nonpragmatic activities that go on within any viable society. University activities may or may not relate to the betterment of man, but pragmatic goals do not exhaust the scholarly role as such. This traditional nonfunctionality has begun to crumble under the impact of courses in basket weaving and jewelry making on one side and war gaming and systems designing on the other. Still, the great thrust of university life in America through the mid-fifties has been to keep the university a place of general theory and statements of fundamentals, to retain the European notion of *universitas*.

Policy-making activities, on the other hand, usually take place in a nonacademic or bureaucratic context. Policy as distinct from politics as such is a modern innovation, beginning as a mass enterprise in the industrial era. True, there was a specie of policy connected to political classes in ancient or medieval times where political structure was directly and organically related to class interests. However, policy making as an autonomous activity, linked to appointment based on expertise, is a twentieth-century phenomenon. The style of policy is antifeudal. It is based on premises having to do with function, operation, instrumentation, utility: premises converting theory into immediate practice. This differs radically from the traditional university bias toward separation and even suspicion of a ready conversion of theory into action.

The invasion of policy making into university life, in the form of direct capital expenditures no less than through contractual arrangements for specific purposes, transforms this traditional feudal-industrial dichotomy. Indeed, it undermines even the long-standing ties between university life and the business community that arose earlier in the present century. Table IV on behavioral contracts related to foreign areas is just one minuscule indicator of the degree to which the social sciences have furthered an interpenetration of social sciences and policy formation. The investigators are for the overwhelming part professors, and they are located at major university centers. This serves not only to pragmatize university research projects but also to supply financial support for graduate instruction, funds for administrative and office personnel, and funds for new and improved buildings and equipment.

The Air Force Office of Scientific Research, the Office of Naval Research, and the Special Operations Research Office of the United States Army each maintain separate funding arms. These are in addition to standard funding agencies such as the National Science Foundation and National Institutes of Health. The development of federal funding to universities has become so extensive and sophisticated that subcontracting is now commonplace. A government agency may provide a cover-all grant to the Smithsonian Institution or the Social Science Research Council, which in turn may parcel out the funds for private agencies and individuals. The total amount spent by the Department of Defense Establishment alone for one year (1965) came to $27,300,000. Table V indicates the distribution of these funds. It is abundantly evident that the disbursements of these funds are usually indirect, through university agencies; and only infrequently direct, through subagencies having direct responsibility to the government. And it is apparent to students of the sociology of science that universities are now faced with the alternatives of either maximizing or holding constant such government allocations of research contracts.

This is a problem not of universities in general but of social science in particular. The extent to which the social sciences are connected to university styles governs that extent to which they are concerned with issues beyond those of policy. The growth of bureaucratic mechanisms and institutes to funnel and channelize social science activities, while it has be-

Select Behavioral Science Contracts Related to Foreign Areas and Foreign Populations*

Title	Location	Description
1963 American Mount Everest Expedition.	Berkeley Institute of Psychological Research	Psychological aspects of stress behavior.
Changing values in Japanese, Americans, and Japanese-Americans	Institute of Advanced Projects, University of Hawaii	Analysis of how Japanese change their values as they come in contact with American culture.
International conflict (Israel and Egypt)	Stanford University	Analysis of relationship of opinions and writings of decision makers and the actual decisions rendered.
Foreign research symposia	Social Sciences Research Council	Meetings of American and foreign scholars in Europe on social psychology.
Persuasive communications in the international field	University of Wisconsin	How foreign nationalities react to various kinds of American communications.
Sociopolitical precursors to insurgency	Pennsylvania State College	Study of insurgency and causes related to it to determine role Navy plays.
Nationalism and the perception of international crises	University of Texas	Perceptions that people have of international crises and relating this to the psychology of the persons involved.
Group factors influencing creativity	University of Illinois	Discovering how a heterogenous group can establish a common communication system in order to be effective; some of these groups composed of individuals of different languages and cultural backgrounds.
Group equilibrium	Rutgers University	Studies made in U.S.A. on small group effectiveness have been replicated in Japan.
Role theory	University of Missouri	Theory of role structure. Work being done with collaborators in Australia and England.
Cross-cultural investigation of some factors in persuasion and attitude change	University of Maryland	Structure and mechanics of attitude change methods; research replicated with Japanese subjects to determine generality of findings.

* Source of data: *Behavioral Sciences and the National Security*, Report No. 4 (Washington, D. C.: U.S. Government Printing Office, 1965).

TABLE V
Budgeted Behavioral and Social Sciences Research Funds, 1965 (in thousands)

	Military Departments		ARPA*	Total		Grand Total
	(Contract)	(In-house)	(Contract)	(Contract)	(In-house)	
Selection and classification	$ 730	$1,900		$ 730	$1,900	$ 2,630
Training and education	4,150	1,480	$ 60	4,210	1,480	5,690
Job design	300	620		300	620	920
Human performance, engineering, and proficiency management	2,230	2,620	470	2,700	2,620	5,320
Manpower management (assignment, retention, etc.)	520	430		520	430	950
Group effectiveness	1,270		240	1,510		1,510
Psychophysiology and stress	1,650	470		1,650	470	2,120
Support of policy planning and strategic concepts	820		210	1,030		1,030
Studies of foreign countries, counterinsurgency, and unconventional warfare	1,79		3,070	4,860		4,860
Foreign areas information	870		250	1,120		1,120
Psychological operations and weapons	380			380		380
Military assistance and civic action	400			400		400
Decision making in military operations	110	260		110	260	370
TOTAL	$15,220	$7,780	$4,040	$19,520	$7,780	$27,300
PERCENT	66	34		71	29	

1965 Budgeted Behavioral and Social Sciences Research Funds (in thousands)
* Advanced Research Projects Agency

come increasingly important, still does not represent more than a distinct minority of social science staffing in the United States. For the most part, teaching remains the core occupation.[13] It is worth considering the degree to which the strain between social scientific activities and policy-making activities ought to be viewed as a conflict of rules between feudal, university-based and modern, state-based institutions. Recognizing the different origins and locales of the distinctive work styles inherent in science and policy will help account for present discrepancies. The strains that exist are not just transient or temporary, not reducible to financial allocations; they are basic differences in the way objects are studied, as well as what is considered worthy of study.

In examining contract social science research, two problems have to be distinguished: first, the sponsorship involved in any kind of research, and second, the nature and purposes of the research design. Both problems simultaneously involve methodological and moral dimensions. Methodological guidelines can do everything but answer the question: Why study a field? That is why the moral base of social science is directly involved in the nature of the investigatory proceedings.

Let us restrict ourselves to an issue raised, but not resolved, in the previous section of the paper — the issue of sovereignty. Sovereignty is an ultimate politically, but not scientifically. The investigation of another nation is no more but no less legitimate than the study of another person, for the problem of magnitude is not one of morals. It is hard to envision a situation in the immediate future when national studies, so long a part of social science, will vanish. The whole of the nineteenth century was taken up by Europeans studying the

[13] See National Register of Scientific and Technical Personnel, National Science Foundation, *Summary of American Science Manpower, 1964*, Washington, D. C., March 1966; and Committee on the National Science Foundation Report on the Economics Profession, "The Structure of Economists' Employment and Salaries, 1964," *American Economic Review*, Vol. 55, No. 4 (December 1965), Part 2, Supplement.

United States, from Alexis de Tocqueville to Harriet Martineau. The tradition has persisted into this century. Many of the so-called classics of the social sciences have a national character, including the work of men like Ostrogorskii and Weber. Indeed, anthropologists have made the nation a basic measure. They may have been accused of engaging in unfriendly acts, or in secular missionary roles, but they were not denied access to data.

The question is: Why has this traditional situation of tolerance not prevailed? First, in the past, social scientists were not working for a government. Therefore they were without special interest in bringing to light the private aspects of another nation. Second, the issue of sponsorship has become particularly acute at the present time because to define research in operational terms is necessarily to arouse a considerable amount of fear and trepidation. Operational or instrumental research has a goal beyond the research itself. Such latent political goals elicit fear and even hostility on the part of a "host" nation to the social science "vendors." Third, the problem has become acute because superordinate nations are interested not so much in the public side of life in the subordinate nations they study but in their private side. The subordinate nations are viewed not as objects of disinterested enquiry, but as objects of instrumental or operational worth.

IV. AUTONOMY AND RELEVANCE IN SOCIAL SCIENCE

Let us now turn to the connection that the social scientist should maintain with policy-making bodies. Should the policy maker continue to be a separate entity with a separate professional identity, or should he be a social scientist in government? Is it the role played or the functions performed that divide policy maker from social scientist? Before attempting to answer questions of advantages or disadvantages in various relationships of social scientists to policy-making bodies, we ought to look more carefully into the lines of relationships that presently obtain.

Dividing the "world" into four parts — basic social sciences and applied social sciences on one side, executive and legislative branches of government on the other side — reveals interesting relations. The basic social sciences (anthropology, political science, economics, psychology, and sociology) have government connections different from the applied social sciences (administrative sciences, education, law, planning, and social work). Let us divide the federal government into the presidential or executive government (White House staff and the cabinet-level officials) and the permanent or legislative government (career federal executives, the Congress, and federal judiciary).

The State Department and the Defense Department and the various cabinet-level executives are the ones who make the highest use of basic social sciences. The State Department, through its diplomatic functions, has long been associated with political science and anthropology. The White House, for its part, is directly linked to the economics profession through the Council of Economic Advisors. The State of the Union address institutionalizes the relation of the executive branch of government to economics as a social science. The Defense Department, perhaps because its own power is of more recent derivation, relies heavily upon the younger social sciences, especially psychology and to a somewhat lesser degree sociology. In sum, the basic social sciences are used primarily by the presidential staff and by the executive branch of government as a whole.

The area of applied social science is more often called upon by the congressional and legislative branches. Education, administrative sciences, social work, and particularly law are themselves areas of professional competence for many congressmen. Thus the legislative relationship to applied social science fields is not only one of utility but an organic relationship. The pragmatic base of enacting legislation having to do with changing relations between men ensures a continuing demand for applied researches among legislators.

The gap between applied and basic models of social science that obtains in most American universities is paralleled by lines of influence in the government.[14] Policy making cannot be considered a unified science or a unified role. Quite the contrary, the tendency is for policy-making groups within the executive branch to be related to the social sciences differently from policy-making bodies within the congressional sphere. While it is true that definitions of "basic" and "applied" social sciences vary, there is enough consistency to reveal this differential policy pattern.

What then are the supposed advantages of fusing social science and social policy? The basic advantage is said to be a higher sense of responsibility for the social sciences and a greater degree of training for policy-oriented personnel. This has, at any rate, been the classical rationale for a tighter linkage between policy making and social science.

What has prevented this amalgamation from occurring is not simple negligence or sloth. On the contrary, to judge by the amount of federal funds dedicated to bringing about such a union — *de facto* if not *de jure* — the wonder is how slight the steps toward amalgamation have been. The reason is that it is quite impossible to think of therapeutics being the same as science. In order to get a fusion of social science and policy, there would have to be a complete disruption of the present notion of social science as sharply different from reform therapy. While applied social science may be the expression of practical reason in the twentieth century, an applied

[14] The judiciary itself makes little direct use of social science findings. If it employs such findings at all, it is through the law journals and periodicals relating to the legal profession. Insofar as social science permeates law journals, to that degree the judiciary reacts to trends in social science. This may be one factor in the length of time it takes for judicial decision concerning Negro-white relations. The access system between the judiciary and social sciences is often so blocked that important social science issues escape the attention of the judiciary for a longer span than any other federal group.

social science cannot dictate the character of social science findings. The notion of basic science requires a distinct separation of its functions from policy-making functions. That high-level policy implies a recognition of this distinction can be seen by the extensive use they make of "basic" findings and theories. On the other hand, the more practical the level of policy making (legislative activities are typical), the more closely linked they are to applied researches. The realities of the situation are such that the utility of the social sciences to policy-making bodies depends upon some maintenance of the separation of the social sciences from the policy situation.

Essential to understanding the present dilemmas about the relationship of science to policy are the radically different conceptions that government officials and social scientists have of that relationship. What concerns social scientists is not only making available the most important findings for "intelligence" needs but the methods by which the policy process gets put into motion and the results of the study of policy for general scientific theory. What concerns government policy makers is not so much social science but social engineering. The ready-to-hand bureaucratic research institutions set up at major universities and in the giant corporations provide both the institutional support and the ideological props with which to pursue these engineering "systems" ends with great vigor.[15]

The government in the present period has sought to resolve its staffing problems on key agencies and committees by attracting people whose conceptions of social science extends to construction but not to criticism. In contrast to the types of men solicited for marginal advisory roles, decision makers have been chosen from the fields of business administration and urban planning rather than from the hard social sciences.

The "constructive" policy-science approach was actually begun in the administration of Herbert Hoover and continued

[15] See Robert Boguslaw, *The New Utopians: A Study of System Design and Social Change* (Englewood Cliffs, N.J.: Prentice-Hall, 1965).

at an accelerated rate by Franklin Delano Roosevelt. Hoover had a deep engineering commitment. In fact, his image of the presidency often bordered on that of the great engineer, the social engineer. The President's Research Committee on Social Trends (1930–1932), which Hoover created, inaugurated the difficult relationships between social science and social policy that have now come to plague American policy. The degree to which this early effort was a mutually felt need is reflected in the fact that the Social Science Research Council, with its support stemming from the Rockefeller-dominated Spelman Fund, underwrote the President's Research Committee on Social Trends. The demands of social science professionalization coincided with the crisis in the American economy — a crisis profound enough to generate demands from within the policy to seek out support even from previously ignored, if not feared, intellectual currents.

Given the enormous significance of the "generation of the thirties" in founding relations between public officials and social scientists, it might be instructive to single out three important intellectual figures who assisted in the creation of these relations: Charles Merriam, Luther Gulick, and Louis Brownlow. Merriam, a founder of the American Political Science Association and of the Social Science Research Council, was the only one of the three who qualified as an academic figure. Even he had stronger ties to government officials, regional planners, and managers than to other social scientists. Brownlow was Merriam's closest associate at the University of Chicago; his main contribution was as Director of the Public Administration Clearing House. He was, in effect, the chief manager of the nation's city managers. Brownlow had been a city manager in Washington, D. C., Knoxville, and Petersburg (Va.) long before he came to join Merriam at Chicago. Gulick was a different kettle of fish. Like the Dulles, Kennan, and Davies families, he came out of the milieu of the American (Congregational) Foreign Mission Society. John Foster Dulles was, in fact, an aide to Gulick's father. He entered government planning service not by way of the social sciences but through the auspices of the New York Bureau of Municipal Research, which also had the support of large capital (the Harriman banking interests).

These were the men who comprised the Committee on Administrative Management under Franklin Delano Roosevelt and under Herbert Hoover. They provided government officials with an early indication of what was to become the dominant "policy-making style," that is, an unconcern with politics, or at least a strict division between politics as a mass activity (with which the policy-making social scientists were unconcerned) and policy as an elite activity (with which they were intimately concerned).[16]

Their highest achievement was to draft the Executive Reorganization Act of 1939, which foreshadowed many of the changes which took place in the postwar executive regimes of Truman, Eisenhower, and Kennedy. The Council of Economic Advisors was, for instance, an early fruit of this reorganization plan. This in turn led to the Council of Scientific Advisors. The men who established the institutional and organizational patterns of social science to social policy were by training and inclination engineers, managers, and planners. When they did link up to a social science, it was invariably to political science — a field which in its successful attempt at rapid professionalization chose alignment with federal interests rather than criticism of such interests as its high road to success.

The dominant view of the relationship of social science to social policy was consequently that social science should fulfill an ancillary function to social engineering — no less, but certainly no more. The policy makers sought to answer the question "knowledge for what?" in a pragmatic and

[16] See Barry Dean Karl, *Executive Reorganization and Reform in the New Deal: The Genesis of Administrative Management, 1900–1939* (Cambridge, Mass.: Harvard University Press, 1963). I would like to acknowledge the suggestions offered by Thomas M. Hill on the critical importance of the New Deal period in establishing the present relationships between the behavioral sciences and government policy-making echelons.

direct way: Harold Lasswell sought to answer Robert Lynd's defiant stance by asserting the need of knowledge for augmentation and operationalization of federal policies in the areas of health, welfare, and war. During the period between 1930 and 1945, the growth of social science organizations was fused to their increasing acceptance of a professional ideology. This combination of organizational advancement in the social sciences and ideological commitment to the political system served to cement the relations with policy-making branches of government by removing the last vestiges of ideological mistrust.

These new developments deeply affected the autonomous character and growth of the social sciences. Standards of methodological precision were raised, a wider set of people from diverse class and ethnic backgrounds began to permeate the social sciences, and professionalism itself served to both unite and to distinguish between the tasks confronting social science and those of government. The very growth of work styles in the social sciences that were both accessible and amenable to policy makers also served to raise anew the doubts as to the worth of such a fusion.[17]

This brings us face to face with the relationship of autonomy to involvement. This issue is especially significant in the light of the large number of government contracts and policy-making demands upon the time, energies, and capabilities of social scientists. This is not simply a contrast of citizen responsibility and professional roles but a question of the nature of the discipline itself — over and beyond the way in which the social scientist perceives institutional affiliations. The autonomy of the social sciences was rarely doubted until the present. The same cannot be said for the autonomy of policy-making sectors of government. Since the latter are

[17] See S. M. Lipset and Mildred A. Schwartz, "The Politics of Professionals," in H. W. Vollmer and D. L. Mills (eds.), *Professionalization* (Englewood Cliffs, N.J.: Prentice-Hall, 1966, pp. 299–309; and Irving L. Horowitz, "Professionalism and Disciplinarianism," *Philosophy of Science*, Vol. 31, No. 3 (July 1964), pp. 275–281.

openly involved in operational research, they make slender pretenses toward autonomy.

The problem now arises on two fronts in the federally supported research situation. What are the lines of independence, and what are the lines of responsibility from the "vendors" to the "funding agency?" The autonomy of a social science is directly linked to the very existence of each field. The most powerful argument for the maintenance of a distinction between public policy and social science is that without such a distinction the very concept is severely jeopardized. Admitting the risk of inviting dilettantism or "idle speculation," to transform all research into command performances is far riskier. There is no science that does not have an element of autonomous growth. Indeed, a great deal of time and energy in any social science is spent arguing and worrying not about the social world in general but about people occupying critical roles or command positions in the world of social science. Nor is such self-reflection and constant autoexamination to be lightly dismissed, since it accounts precisely for the sorts of improvements in the functioning of a scientific theory that provide operational worth to begin with. In other words, the autonomous realm is not incidental either to the formation of the social scientist or to that which makes him truly scientific in his behavior.

The great failing of a policy science approach is that it has not recognized that the price of rapid professionalism and integration is high. By raising the banner of "the policy sciences of democracy" this approach minimizes the autonomous and critical aspects of social scientific development.[18] Without this autonomic aspect to science, one cannot really speak either of a profession or of an occupation. There are standards in a social science and levels of performance within each science that link its practitioners apart from their actions or reactions toward policy questions. When a breakdown of

[18] See, for example, Harold D. Lasswell, "The Policy Orientation," in Daniel Lerner and Harold D. Lasswell (eds.), *The Policy Sciences* (Stanford, Calif.: Stanford University Press, 1951), pp. 3–15.

autonomy occurs, when policy questions or ideological requirements prevail, the deterioration in the quality of the social science is a certain consequence. Policy places a premium on involvement and influence; science places a premium on investigation and ideas. The issue is not so much what is studied or even the way an inquiry is conducted but the auspices and the purposes of a study.

Finally, the introduction of the relationship of social science to public policy as a question reflects first and foremost the belief (at least among the practitioners of social science) in the efficacy and the feasibility of scientific activities in social life. It is no longer either fashionable or particularly profound to ask: Are the social sciences really sciences? This is a naïve question, a meaningless question. The efficacy of social science is firmly established. Were this not the case, the issues herein dealt with would never have arisen in the first place. But precisely at that point in scientific history where efficacy is established beyond any doubt in the minds of both policy personnel and social scientists, the question of the aims of social science loom large. This issue of purpose was not raised when the social sciences were really little else than a specie of literature or belles lettres When an individual pontificates about the nature of the world or the nature of man in society, one man's platitudes may be another man's poison. But when someone offers a plan for redesigning the world and proceeds to do so in a more or less anticipated way, he can be ridiculed and reviled but not easily ignored. The recognition of this has been so widespread that the value demands upon the social sciences have become central, with decisions as to the performance of the science becoming directly linked to the goals set for the society.

What we witness in the present generation from the point of view of the social sciences is the breakup of the functionalist ideology with its value-free orientation. Because the peculiar autonomous aspects of each social science generate a special internal history, the breakup occurs differently in each discipline.[19]

From the point of view of policy makers, the breakup of the old way of doing things has been equally profound. Perhaps the largest shock that they have undergone is the recognition that there is probably no such animal as a policy scientist. There has been no definition of a policy maker that can legitimize his role as a social scientist — basic or applied. Policy makers in one agency have slender connection with policy makers in other branches of government. Increasingly, the policy maker is being confronted with the fact that he is not so much an applied social scientist as he is a representative of the State Department or a representative of Health, Education, and Welfare. In other words, what defines his role is not the policy-making activities but rather the requirements of the agency for which he works. In effect, what he is engaged in is ideology, not policy.[20] Therefore, unless one is willing to speak of the science of ideology, which is a contradiction in terms, it is not possible to legitimately deal with the social sciences exclusively from a policy point of view.

The social sciences are challenged and tested as never before by their involvements with policy organs. This association increases the chances for meaningful research and knowledge scientists may acquire about the workings of the world. It also makes possible the corruption of social science on a scale hitherto unimagined — through the submerging of tasks of inquiry into contract fulfillments. The drive shaft of government agencies' demands upon social scientists is ideo-

---

[19] N. J. Demerath III and R. A. Peterson (eds.), *System, Change and Conflict: Functionalists and Their Critics* (New York: The Free Press of Glencoe, 1967).

[20] See Irving L. Horowitz, "The Life and Death of Project Camelot," *Trans-action*, Vol. 3, No. 1 (November — December 1965) and Kalman H. Silvert, "American Academic Ethics and Social Research Abroad: The Lesson of Project Camelot," in *American Universities Field Staff Reports* (West Coast South American Series), Vol. 12, No. 3 (July 1965).

logical; and yet the larger needs of such agencies are, as never before, a wider understanding of the shape of societies around the world. Perhaps the main problem therefore is not so much the relation of policy to science — a common challenge for social scientists and policy makers that must be answered in separate and distinct ways — but answered it must be.

Irving Louis Horowitz

Rutgers University

The Pentagon Papers and Social Science*

Today, no major political event, particularly one so directly linked to the forging of American foreign policy as the publication of the Pentagon Papers by the *New York Times* and the *Washington Post*, can be fully described without accounting for the role of the social scientist. In this case, the economists clearly performed a major role. From the straightforward hawkish prescriptions offered in 1961 by Walt W. Rostow to the dovishly motivated release of secret documents on the conduct of the war in 1971 by Daniel Ellsberg, the contributions of social scientists were central. As a consequence, it is fitting, nay imperative, that the import of these monumental events be made plain for those of us involved in the production and dissemination of social science information and insight.

The publication of the Pentagon Papers is of central importance to the social science community in at least two respects: social scientists participated in the development of a posture and position toward the Vietnam involvement; and at a more abstract level, the publication of these papers provides lessons about political participation and policy making for the social sciences.

We live in an age in which the social sciences perform a

* Reprinted from *Transaction* (now *Society*), Vol. 8, No. 11 (September 1965).

special and unique role in the lives of men and in the fates of government, whatever the status of social science theory. And because the question of laymen is no longer "is social science scientific," but "what kinds of recommendations are offered in the name of social science," it is important that social scientists inquire as to any special meaning of the Pentagon Papers and documents, over and above the general and broad-ranging discussions that take place in the mass media. Thus, my effort here is not to be construed as a general discussion of issues, but rather a specific discussion of results.

I. FINDINGS

The Pentagon's project director for a *History of United States Decision-Making Process on Vietnam Policy* (now simply known as *The Pentagon Papers*), economist Leslie H. Gelb now of The Brookings Institution, remarked: "Writing history, especially where it blends into current events, especially where the current event is Vietnam, is a treacherous exercise." Former Secretary of Defense Robert S. McNamara authorized this treacherous exercise for a treacherous conflict in 1967. In initiation and execution this was to be "encyclopedic and objective." The actual compilation runs to 2.5 million words and 47 volumes of narrative and documents. And from what has thus far been made public, it is evident that this project was prepared with the same bloodless, bureaucratic approach that characterizes so much federally inspired social science and history. The Pentagon Papers attempt no original hypothesis, provide no insights into the behavior of the "other side," make scant effort to select important from trivial factors in the escalation process; they present no real continuity with past American foreign policy and in general eschew any sort of systematic survey research or interviewing of the participants and proponents. Yet, with all these shortcomings, these materials offer a fascinating and unique account of how peace-keeping agencies became transformed into policy-making agencies. That this record was prepared by 36 political scientists, economists, systems analysts, inside dopesters and outside social science research agencies provides an additional fascination: how the government has learned to entrust its official records to mandarin types, who in exchange for the cloak of anonymity are willing to prepare an official record of events. An alarming oddity is that, in part at least, the chronicle was prepared by analysts who were formerly participants.

For those who have neither the time nor the patience to examine every document thus far released, it might be worthwhile to simply summarize what they contain. In so doing, it becomes clear that the Vietnam War was neither a Democratic nor a Republican war, but a war conducted by the political elite, often without regard to basic technical advice and considerations, and for reasons that had far less to do with curbing communism than with the failure of the other arms of government in their responsibility to curb executive egotism. The publication of these papers has chronicled this country's overseas involvement with a precision never before available to the American public. Indeed, we now know more about decision making in Vietnam than about the processes by which we became involved in the Korean War. For instance, we have learned that:

1. The United States ignored eight direct appeals for aid from Ho Chi Minh in the first half-year following World War II. Underlying the American refusal to deal with the Vietnamese leader was the growth of the cold war and the opposition to assisting a communist leadership.

2. The Truman administration by 1949 had already accepted the "domino principle," after the National Security Council was told early in 1950 that the neighboring countries of Thailand and Burma could be expected to fall under communist control if Vietnam were controlled by a communist-dominated regime.

3. The Eisenhower administration, particularly under the leadership of Secretary of State John Foster Dulles, refused to accept the Geneva accords ending the French-Indochina war on the grounds that it permitted this country "only a limited influence" in the affairs of the fledgling South Vietnam. Indeed, the Joint Chiefs of Staff opted in favor of displacing France as

the key influence rather than assisting the termination of hostilities.

4. The final years of the Eisenhower administration were characterized by a decision to commit a relatively small number of United States military personnel to maintain the Diem regime in Saigon and to prevent a détente between Hanoi and Saigon.

5. The Kennedy administration transformed the limited risk gamble into an unlimited commitment. Although the troop levels were indeed still quite limited, the Kennedy administration moved special forces units into Vietnam, Laos and Cambodia—thus broadening the conflict to the area as a whole.

6. The Kennedy administration knew about and approved of plans for the military coup d'état that overthrew President Diem. The United States gave its support to an army group commited to military dictatorship and no compromise with the Hanoi regime.

7. The Johnson administration extended the unlimited commitment to the military regime of Saigon. Under this administration between 1965 and 1968, troop levels surpassed 500,000 and United States participation was to include the management of the conflict and the training of the ARVN.

8. After the Tet offensive began in January 1968, Johnson, under strong prodding from the military Chiefs of Staff, and from his field commanders, moved toward full-scale mobilization, including the call-up of reserves. By the termination of the Johnson administration, the United States had been placed on a full-scale war footing.

Among the most important facts revealed by the Papers is that the United States first opposed a settlement based on the Geneva accords, signed by all belligerents; that the United States had escalated the conflict far in advance of the Gulf of Tonkin incident and had used congressional approval for legitimating commitments already undertaken rather than as a response to new communist provocations; and finally that in the face of internal opposition from the same Department of Defense that at first had sanctioned the war, the executive decided to disregard its own policy advisers and plunge ahead in a war already lost.

II. DECISIONS

Impressive in this enumeration of policy decisions is the clinical way decisions were made. The substitution of war game thinking for any real political thinking, the total submission of the Department of State to the Department of Defense in the making of foreign policy, and the utter collapse of any faith in compromise, consensus, or cooperation between nations, and the ludicrous pursuit of victory (or at least nondefeat) in Vietnam, all are so forcefully illustrated in these Pentagon Papers, that the vigor with which their release was opposed by the Attorney General's office and the executive branch of government generally, can well be appreciated.

Ten years ago in writing *The War Game* I had occasion to say in a chapter concerning "American Politics and Military Risks" that "a major difficulty with the thinking of the new civilian militarists is that they study war while ignoring politics." The recent disclosure of the Pentagon Papers bears out that contention with a vengeance; a kind of hothouse scientology emerges, in which the ends of foreign policy are neatly separated from the instruments of immediate destruction. That a certain shock and cynicism have emerged as a result of the revelations in these papers is more attributable to the loss of a war than to the novelty of the revelations. The cast of characters that have dragged us through the mire of a bloody conflict in Southeast Asia, from Walt W. Rostow to Henry A. Kissinger, remain to haunt us and taunt us. They move in and out of administrations with an ease that belies political party differences and underscores the existence of not merely a set of "experts," but rather a well-defined ruling class dedicated to manufacturing and manipulating political formulas.

The great volume of materials thus far revealed is characterized by few obvious themes: but one of the more evident is the utter separation of the purposes of devastation from comprehension of the effects of such devastation. A kind of Howard Johnson sanitized vision of conflict emerges that reveals a gulf between the policy makers and battlefield soldiers that is even wider and longer than the distance between Saigon and

Washington. If the concept of war gaming is shocking in retrospect, this is probably due more to its utter and contemptible failure to provide battlefield victories than to any real development in social and behavioral science beyond the shibboleths of decision theory and game theory.

III. "SCIENTISTS"

A number of researchers as well as analysts of the Pentagon Papers were themselves social scientists. There were political scientists of considerable distinction, such as Morton H. Halperin and Melvin Gurtov; economists of great renown, such as Walt Rostow and Daniel Ellsberg; and systems analysts, such as Alain C. Enthoven. And then there was an assorted group of people, often trained in law, such as Roger Fisher and Carl Kaysen, weaving in and out of the Papers, providing both point and counterpoint. There are the thoroughly hawkish views of Walt Rostow; and the cautionary perspective of Alain Enthoven; and the more liberal recommendations of people like Roger Fisher. But it is clear that social scientists descend in importance as they move from hawk to dove. Walt Rostow is a central figure, and people like Carl Kaysen and Roger Fisher are at most peripheral consultants—who, in fact, seem to have been more often conservatized and impressed by the pressurized Washington atmosphere than to have had an impact on the liberalization or softening of the Vietnam posture.

The social scientific contingency in the Pentagon, whom I christened the "new civilian militarists" a decade ago, were by no means uniform in their reactions to the quagmire in Vietnam. Poiltical scientists like Morton Halperin and economists like Alain Enthoven did provide cautionary responses, if not outright criticisms of the repeated and incessant requests for troop build-ups. The Tet offensive, which made incontrovertible the vulnerability of the American posture, called forth demands for higher troop levels on the part of Generals William C. Westmoreland and Maxwell Taylor. Enthoven, in particular, opposed this emphatically and courageously:

Our strategy of attrition has not worked. Adding 206,000 more U.S. men to a force of 525,000, gaining only 27 additional maneuver battalions and 270 tactical fighters at an added cost to the U.S. of $10 billion per year raises the question of who is making it costly for whom. . . . We know that despite a massive influx of 500,000 U.S. troops, 1.2 million tons of bombs a year, 200,000 enemy killed in action in three years, 20,000 U.S. killed in action in three years, 200,000 U.S. wounded in action, etc., our control of the countryside and the defense of the urban areas is now essentially at pre-August 1965 levels. We have achieved stalemate at a high commitment. A new strategy must be sought.

Interestingly, in the same month, March 1968, when Enthoven prepared this critical and obviously sane report, he wrote a curious paper on "Thomism and the Concept of Just and Unjust Warfare," which, in retrospect, seemed to be Enthoven's way of letting people like myself know that he was a dissenting voice despite his earlier commitment to war game ideology and whiz-kid strategy.

As a result of these memoranda, Assistant Defense Secretary Paul Warnke argued against increased bombing and for a bombing pause. He and Assistant Secretary of Defense for Public Affairs, Phil G. Goulding, were then simply directed to write a draft that "would deal only with the troop issue," hence forcing them to abandon the internal fight against an "expansion of the air war." And as it finally went to the White House, the report was bleached of any criticism. The mandarin role of the social scientists was reaffirmed: President Johnson's commitments went unchallenged. The final memo advocated deployment of 22,000 more troops, reserved judgment on the deployments of the remaining 185,000 troops and approved a 262,000 troop reserve build-up; it urged no new peace initiatives and simply declared that a division of opinion existed on the bombing policy, making it appear that the division in opinion was only tactical in nature. As the Pentagon Papers declared:

Faced with a fork in the road of our Vietnam policy, the working group failed to seize the opportunity to change directions. Indeed, they seemed to recommend that we continue rather haltingly down the same road, meanwhile, consulting the map more frequently and in greater detail to insure that we were still on the right road.

One strange aspect of this war game strategy is how little

the moves and motives of the so-called "other side" were ever taken into account. There is no real appreciation of the distinction between North Vietnam and the National Liberation Front of South Vietnam. There is not the slightest account taken of the actual decisions made by General Giap or Chairman Ho. The Tet offensive seems to have taken our grand strategists by as much surprise as the political elites whom they were planning for. While they were beginning to recognize the actual balance of military forces, Wilfred Burchett had already declared, in 1967 to be exact, that the consequences of the war were no longer in doubt—United States involvement could not forestall a victory of the communist factions North and South. Thus, not only do the Pentagon Papers reveal the usual ignorance of the customs, languages and habits of the people being so brutally treated, but also the unanticipated arrogance of assuming throughout that logistics would conquer all. Even the doves like George W. Ball never doubted for a moment that an influx of a certain number of United States troops would in fact swing the tide of battle the way that General Westmoreland said it would. The argument was rather over tactics: is such a heavy investment worth the end results? In fact, not one inner circle "wise man" raised the issue that the size of the troop commitment might be basically irrelevant to the negative (from an American viewpoint) outcome of the Southeast Asian operations. One no longer expects good history or decent ethnography from those who advise the rulers, but when this is compounded with a heavy dose of impoverished war gaming and strategic thinking in the void, then the question of "science for whom" might well be converted into the question of "what science and by whom."

All of this points up a tragic flaw in policy making by social science experts. Their failure to generate or to reflect a larger constituency outside of themselves made them continually vulnerable to assaults from the military and from the more conservative sectors of the Pentagon. This vulnerability was so great that throughout the Pentagon Papers, one senses that the hawk position is always and uniformly outspoken and direct, while the dove position is always and uniformly ubiquitous and indirect. The basis of democratic politics has always been the mass participation of an informed electorate. Yet it was precisely this informed public, where a consensus against the war had been building, that was cut off from the policy planners and recommenders. Consequently they were left in pristine isolation to pit their logic against the crackpot realism of their military adversaries within the bowels of government.

IV. DISCLOSURES

Certain serious problems arose precisely because of the secrecy tag: for example, former Vice President Hubert Humphrey and Secretary of State Dean Rusk have both denied having any knowledge whatsoever of these papers. Dean Rusk went so far as to say that the research methodology was handled poorly: "I'm rather curious about why the analysts who put this study together did not interview us, particularly when they were attributing attitudes and motives to us." (*New York Times*, Saturday, July 3, 1971.) Perhaps more telling is Dean Rusk's suggestion that the Pentagon Papers have the characteristics of an anonymous letter. Along with Dean Rusk, I too believe that the names of the roughly forty scholars connected with the production of these papers should be published. To do otherwise would not only prevent the people involved from checking the veracity of the stories attributed to them but, more important, would keep the social science community from gaining a clearer insight into the multiple roles of scholars, researchers, professors and government analysts and policy-makers. The nature of science requires that the human authorities behind these multi-volumes be identified, as in the precedent established by the identification of the authors of the various bombing surveys done after World War II and the Korean War.

One serendipitous consequence of the Pentagon Papers has been to provide a more meaningful perspective toward the proposed "Code of Ethics" being advanced by so many social science professional associations. They all deal with the sanctity of the "subject's rights." All sorts of words guarding privacy are used: "rights of privacy and dignity," "protection of subjects from personal harm," "preservation of confidentiality of research data." The American Sociological Association proposals, for example, are typical:

> Confidential information provided by a research subject must be treated as such by the sociologist. Even though research information is not a privileged communication under the law, the sociologist must, as far as possible, protect subjects and informants. Any promises made to such persons must be honored. . . . If an informant or other subject should wish, however, he can formally release the promise of confidentiality.

While the purpose of this code of ethics is sincerely geared to the protection of individuals under study, if it were taken literally, a man like Daniel Ellsberg would be subject to penalty, if not outright expulsion, on the grounds that he was never allowed by the individuals concerned to make his information public. What so many professional societies forget is that the right to full disclosure is also a principle, just as significant as the right of the private subject to confidentiality, and far more germane to the tasks of a social scientific learned society. The truly difficult ethical question comes not with the idea of maintaining confidentiality, but with determining what would be confidential, and when such confidentiality should be violated in terms of a higher principle. All social science codes of ethics presume an ethical standpoint which limits scientific endeavor, but when it is expedient to ignore or forget this ethical code, as in the case of the Pentagon Papers, the profession embarrassingly chooses to exhibit such a memory lapse. The publication of the Pentagon Papers should once again point the way to the highest obligation of social science organizations: to the truth, plain and simple, rather than the preservation of confidentiality, high and mighty. And unless this lesson is fully drawn, a dichotomous arrangement will be made between making public the documents of public servants whose policies they disapprove of and keeping private the documentation on deviants whom supposedly the social scientists are concerned with protecting. This is not an ethical approach but an opportunistic approach. It rests on political and professional expediency. The need therefore is to reassert the requisites of science for full disclosure, and the ethics of full disclosure as the only possible ethics for any group of professional scientists. If the release of the Pentagon Papers had done nothing else, it has reaffirmed the highest principle of all science: full disclosure, full review of the data, full responsibility for what is done, by those who do the research.

V. SECRETS

Another area that deeply concerns the social scientist and that is highlighted in the Pentagon Papers is the government's established norms of secrecy. While most officials in government have a series of work norms with which to guide their behavior, few forms of anticipatory socialization have applied to social scientists who advise government agencies. The professionalization of social scientists has normally been directed toward publicity rather than secrecy. This fosters sharp differences in opinion and attitudes between the polity and the academy, since the reward system for career advancement is so clearly polarized.

The question of secrecy is intimately connected with matters of policy, because the standing assumption of policy makers (particularly in the field of foreign affairs) is not to reveal themselves entirely. No government in the game of international politics feels that its policies can be candidly revealed for full public review; therefore, operational research done in connection with policy considerations is customarily bound by the canons of government privacy. But while scientists have a fetish for publicizing their information as a mechanism for professional advancement no less than as a definition of their essential role in the society, the political branches of society have as their fetish the protection of private documents and privileged information. Therefore, the polity places a premium not only on acquiring vital information, but also on keeping silent about such information precisely to the degree that the data might be of high decisional value. This leads to differing premiums between analysts and policy makers and to tensions between them.

Social scientists complain that the norm of secrecy oftentimes involves yielding their own essential work premises. A critical factor reinforcing an unwilling acceptance of the norm of secrecy by social scientists is the allocation of most government research funds for military or semimilitary purposes. Senate testimony has shown that 70 percent of federal funds targeted for the social sciences involve such restrictions.

The real wonder turns out to be not the existence of the secrecy norm but the relative availability of large chunks of information. Indeed, the classification of materials is so inept that documents (such as the Pax America research) designated as confidential or secret by one agency may often be made available as a public service by another agency. There are also occasions when documents placed in a classified category by sponsoring government agencies can be gotten without charge from the private research institute doing the work.

But the main point is that the norm of secrecy makes it extremely difficult to separate science from patriotism and hence makes it that much more difficult to question the research design itself. Social scientists often express the nagging doubt that accepting the first stage—the right of the government to maintain secrecy—often carries with it acquiescence in a later stage—the necessity for silence on the part of social researchers who may disagree with the political uses of their efforts.

The demand for government secrecy has a telling impact on the methodology of the social sciences. Presumably social scientists are employed because they, as a group, represent objectivity and honesty. Social scientists like to envision themselves as a wall of truth off which policy makers may bounce their premises. They also like to think that they provide information which cannot be derived from sheer public opinion. Thus, to some degree social scientists consider that they are hired or utilized by government agencies because they will say things that may be unpopular but nonetheless significant. However, since secrecy exists, the premises upon which most social scientists seek to work are strained by the very agencies which contract out their need to know.

The terms of research and conditions of work tend to demand an initial compromise with social science methodology. The social scientist is placed in a cognitive bind. He is conditioned not to reveal maximum information lest he become victimized by the federal agencies that employ his services. Yet he is employed precisely because of his presumed thoroughness, impartiality, and candor. The social scientist who survives in government service becomes circumspect or learns to play the game. His value to social science becomes seriously jeopardized. On the other hand, once he raises these considerations, his usefulness to the policy-making sector is likewise jeopardized.

Social scientists believe that openness is more than meeting formal requirements of scientific canons; it is also a matter of making information universally available. The norm of secrecy leads to selective presentation of data. The social scientist is impeded by the policy maker because of contrasting notions about the significance of data and the general need for replication elsewhere and by others. The policy maker who demands differential access to findings considers this a normal return for the initial expenditure of risk capital. Since this utilitarian concept of data is alien to the scientific standpoint, the schism between the social scientist and the policy maker becomes pronounced precisely at the level of openness of information and accessibility to the work achieved. The social scientist's general attitude is that sponsorship of research does not entitle any one sector to benefit unduly from the findings—that sponsorship by federal agencies ought not place greater limitations on the use of work done than sponsorship by either private agencies or universities.

VI. LOYALTIES

A major area that deeply concerns social scientists is that of dual allegiance. The Pentagon Papers have such specific requirements and goal-oriented tasks that they intrude upon the autonomy of the social scientist by forcing upon him choices between dual allegiances. The researcher is compelled to choose between participating fully in the world of the federal bureaucracy and remaining in more familiar academic confines. He does not want the former to create isolation in the latter.

Thus, he often criticizes the federal bureaucracy's unwillingness to recognize his basic needs: (1) the need to teach and retain full academic identity; (2) the need to publicize information; and above all (3) the need to place scientific responsibility above the call of patriotic obligation—when they may happen to clash. In short, he does not want to be plagued by dual or competing allegiances.

The norm of secrecy exacerbates this problem. Although many of the social scientists who become involved with federal research are intrigued by the opportunity to address important issues, they are confronted by some bureaucracies which oftentimes do not share their passion for resolving social problems. For example, federal obligations commit the bureaucracy to assign high priority to items having military potential and effectiveness and low priorities to many supposedly idealistic and far-fetched themes in which social scientists are interested.

Those social scientists, either as employees or as consultants connected with the government, are hamstrung by federal agencies which are in turn limited by political circumstances beyond their control. A federal bureaucracy must manage cumbersome overgrown committees and data gathering agencies. Federal agencies often protect a status quo merely for the sake of rational functioning. They must conceive of academicians in their midst as a standard bureaucratic type entitled to rise to certain federal ranks. Federal agencies limit innovating concepts to what is immediately useful, not out of choice and certainly not out of resentment of the social sciences but from what is deemed impersonal necessity. This has the effect of reducing the social scientist's role in the government to that of ally or advocate rather than innovator or designer. Social scientists begin to feel that their enthusiasm for rapid change is unrealistic, considering how little can be done by the government bureaucracy. And they come to resent involvement in theoryless application to immediacy foisted on them by the "new utopians," surrendering in the process the value of confronting men with the wide range of choices of what might be done. The schism, then, between autonomy and involvement is as thorough as that between secrecy and publicity, for it cuts to the quick well-meant pretensions about human engineering.

The problem of competing allegiances is not made simpler by the fact that many high ranking federal bureaucrats have strong nationalistic and conservative political ideologies. This contrasts markedly with the social scientist, who comes to Washington not only with a belief in the primacy of science over patriotism but also with a definition of patriotism that is more open-ended and consciously liberal than that of most appointed officials. Hence, he often perceives the conflict to extend beyond research design and social applicability into one of the incompatible ideologies held respectively by the social scientist and entrenched Washington bureaucrats. He comes to resent the proprietary attitude of the bureaucrat toward "his" government processes. The social scientist is likely to consider his social science biases a necessary buffer against the federal bureaucracy.

VII. ELITISTS

The publication of the Pentagon Papers sheds new light on political pluralist and power concentrationist hypotheses. When push finally did turn to shove, President Nixon and the government officials behaved as members of a ruling class and not as leaders of their political party. President Nixon might easily have chosen to let the Democratic party take the burn and bear the brunt of the assaults for the betrayal of a public trust. Indeed the Nixon administration might have chosen to join the chorus of those arguing that the Democratic party is indeed the war party, as revealed in these documents; whereas the Republican party emerges as the party of restraint—if not exactly principle. Here was a stunning opportunity for Mr. Nixon to make political capital on a no risk basis: by simply drawing attention to the fact that the war was constantly escalated by President Truman, who refused to bargain in good faith with Ho Chi Minh despite repeated requests; by President Kennedy, who moved far beyond anything President Eisenhower had in mind for the area, by making the fatal commitment not just to land troops but to adopt a domino theory of winning the war; by President Johnson, whose role can well be considered as nefarious: coming before the American people as a peace candidate when he had already made the fatal series of commitments to continuing escalation and warfare. That the president chose not to do so illustrates the sense of class solidarity that the political elites in this country manifest; a sense of collective betrayal of the priesthood, rather than a sense of obligation to score political points and gain political trophies. And that too should be a lesson in terms of the actual power within the political structure of a small ruling elite. Surely this must be considered a fascinating episode in its own right: the reasons are complex, but surely among them must rank the belief that Mr. Nixon behaved as a member of the ruling elite, an elite that had transcendent obligations far beyond the call of party, and that was the call of class.

One fact made clear by the Pentagon Papers is the extent to which presidentialism has become the ideology and the style in American political life. The infrequency of any reference to the judicial situation with respect to the war in Southeast Asia and the virtual absence of any reference to congressional sentiments are startling confirmations of an utter change in the American political style. If any proof was needed of the emerging imbalance between the executive and other branches of government, these papers should put such doubt to rest. The theory of checks and balances works only when there are, in fact, groups such as senators or stubborn judges who believe in the responsibility of the judiciary and legislative branches to do just that, namely, establish check and balance. In the absence of such vigor, the war in Southeast Asia became very much a series of executive actions. And this itself should give pause to the advocates of consensus theory in political science.

The failure of the Vietnam episode has resulted in a reconsideration of presidentialism as the specific contemporary variant of power elite theory. The renewed vigor of Congress, the willingness, albeit cautionary willingness, of the Supreme Court to rule on fundamental points of constitutional law, are indicative of the resurgence of pluralism. In this sense, the darkest hour of liberalism as a political style has witnessed a liberal regrouping around the theme of mass politics. Even the domestic notions of community organization and states rights are indicative of the limits of presidentialism—so that Mr. Nixon, at one and the same time, is reluctantly presiding over the swan song of presidentialism in foreign affairs, while celebrating its demise in domestic affairs. The collapse of the Vietnam War and the trends toward neo-isolationism are in fact simply the reappearance of political pluralism in a context where to go further in the concentration of political power in the presidency would in all likelihood mean the upsurge of fascism, American style. If the concept of a power elite was reconfirmed in the Pentagon Papers, so too, strangely, was the concept of political pluralism in the public response to them. The countervailing influence of the Supreme Court was clearly manifested in the ringing affirmation of the First Amendment, in the denial of the concept of prior restraint and prior punitive actions, and in the very rapidity of the decision itself. This action by the judiciary, coupled with a show of muscle on the part of the Senate and House concernng the conduct of the war, military appropriations, boondoggles, and special privileges for a select handful of aircraft industries in their own way served to underscore the continued importance of the open society and the pluralistic basis of power. Even executives, such as Hubert H. Humphrey, have declared in favor of full disclosure and reiterated the principles guiding the publication of the Pentagon Papers.

Power elites operate behind a cloak of anonymity. When that cloak is lifted, an obvious impairment in the operational efficiency of elites occurs. What has happened with the release of the Pentagon Papers is precisely this collapse of anonymity, no less than secrecy. As a result, the formal apparatus of government can assert its prerogatives. This does not mean that the executive branch of government will be unable to recover from this blow at its prestige, or that it will no longer attempt to play its trump card: decision making by executive fiat. It does mean, however, that the optimal conditions under which power elites operate have been seriously hampered. The degree of this impairment and the length of time it will obtain depend exclusively on the politics of awareness and participation, no less than the continuing pressures for lowering the secrecy levels in high level international decision making.

Probably the most compelling set of reasons given for President Nixon's bitter opposition to the release of the Pentagon Papers is that provided by Melvin Gurtov, one of the authors of the secret Pentagon study and an outstanding political scientist specializing in Asia affairs. He speaks of three deceits in current American Vietnamese policy: "The first and most basic deceit is the Administration's contention that we're winding down and getting out of the war." In fact, Vietnamization is a "domestic political ploy that really involves the substitution of air power for ground power." The second deceit is that "we're truly interested in seeing the prisoners of war released." Gurtov notes that "as far as this administration is concerned the prisoners of war are a political device, a device for rationalizing escalation, by saying these are acts that are necessary to show our concern for the prisoners." The third deceit "is that under the Nixon Doctrine the United States is not interested in making new commitments in Asia." In fact, the administration used the Cambodia coup "as an opportunity for creating for itself a new commitment in Southeast Asia, namely the survival of a non-Communist regime in Pnompenh." This outspoken position indicates that the defense of the power elite of the past by President Nixon might just as well be construed as a self-defense of the power elite in the present.

VIII. CONSPIRACIES

The Pentagon Papers provide much new light on theories of power elite and power diffusion and also provide an equal measure of information on conspiracy theory. And while it is still true that conspiracy *theory* is bad theory, it is false to assert that no conspiracies exist or are not perpetrated by the government. It might indeed be the case that all governments, insofar as they are formal organizations, have secrets; and we call these secrets, conspiracies. From this point of view, the interesting question is how so few leaks resulted from an effort of such magnitude and involving so many people as setting policy in the Vietnam War. Rather than be surprised that these papers reached the public domain four to six years after the fact, one should wonder how the government was able to maintain silence on matters of such far-ranging and far-reaching consequence.

Cyrus Eaton, American industrialist and confidant of many communist leaders, indicates that the Vietnamese almost instantaneously were made aware of United States policy decisions. But I seriously doubt that they actually had copies of these materials. Rather, like the American public itself, they were informed about the decisions but not the cogitations and agitations that went into the final decision. Perhaps this is the way all governments operate; nonetheless, it is fascinating—at least this once—to be privy to the process and not simply the outcome, and to see the foibles of powerful men and not just the fables manufactured for these men after the fact.

These papers tend to underwrite the common-sensical point of view that governments are not to be trusted, and to undermine the more sophisticated interpretation that governments are dedicated to the task of maintaining democracy at home and peace abroad. As bitter as it may seem, common-sense cynicism has more to recommend it than the sophisticated, well-elaborated viewpoints which take literally the formal structure of government and so readily tend to dismiss the informal response to power and pressure from men at the top. The constant wavering of Lyndon B. Johnson, his bellicose defiance of all evidence and information that the bombings were not having the intended effect, followed by shock that his lieutenants like Robert McNamara changed their position at midstream (which almost constituted a betrayal in the eyes of the president) were in turn followed by a more relaxed posture and a final decision not to seek the presidency. All of this forms a human drama that makes the political process at once fascinating and frightful; fascinating because we can see the psychology of politics in action, and frightful because the presumed rationality is by no means uniformly present.

The publication of the Pentagon Papers, while a considerable victory for the rights of a free press and of special significance to all scientists who still uphold the principle of full disclosure as the norm of all political as well as scientific endeavor, is not yet a total victory for a democratic society—that can only happen when the concept of secrecy is itself probed and penetrated, and when the concept of undeclared warfare is finally and fully repudiated by the public and its representatives. The behavior of the government in its effort to suppress publication of the Pentagon Papers cannot simply be viewed as idiosyncratic, but rather as part of the structure of the American political processes in which the expert displaces the politician, and the politicians themselves become so beholden to the class of experts for information, that they dare not turn for guidance to the people they serve. For years, critics of the Vietnam War have been silenced and intimidated by the policy makers' insistence that when all the facts were known the hawk position would be vindicated and the dove position would be violated. Many of the facts are now revealed—and the bankruptcy of the advocates of continued escalation is plain for all to see. It is to be hoped that this will strengthen the prospects for peace, and firm up those who, as an automatic reflex, assume the correctness of the government's position on all things military. It is also to be hoped that the principle of democracy, of every person counting as one, once more becomes the source of fundamental decision making and political discourse.

POSTSCRIPT (1974)

The publication several years ago of the Pentagon Papers suggests that what may have first appeared as a small, idiosyncratic aspect of the American social science community, namely its growing intimacies with American foreign policy, especially in sensitive wartime conditions and areas, has become a large-scale and central concern of the social science world. It is the singular merit of the release of these papers that it has shown that the "two cultures" of social science and practical politics have grown closer in recent years. The list of economists, political scientists, psychologists, and sociologists involved in the making and manufacture (they are not the same thing) has grown in legion and in legend. And this is not simply a matter of the Kissingers and the Moynihans, but of the exponential rate of growth in numbers of behavioral scientists working directly within the governmental apparatus—in everything from policy making to evaluation research.

And how could it be otherwise? The United States has become a society in which the gap between policy making and electoral politics has grown wide and deep enough to occasion a "constitutional" crisis. Social scientists, who have proven notorious failures at electoral politics (with but the rarest of exceptions) have, quite the reverse, proven to be ravishing successes at the policy level. That this is clearly the case derives from the "platonic" or "genteel" sort of fascism or elitism or conservatism that has come to characterize American politics. Under conditions such as these, the social scientists, long on engineering recommendations and short on populist sentiments, have found themselves drawn to the apparatus that makes decisions—the spin-offs and shake-downs of the executive branch of government. And before one gets off on the holier-than-thou track, it might be advisable to recall Rabbi Hillel's explication: if not you then who, if not now then when? Or more simply, under conditions of elite dominion, do not the social scientists with their congenital liberalism and abiding concern for evidence stand a better chance at a rational ordering of society than other would-be salvationists?

The absurdity in leaping forth with fire and brimstone condemnations of social scientists who participated in the past and participate in presently operational federally sponsored projects indicates the complexity of the issues involved. Basically we are faced with problems in the moral foundations of social science and how such foundations affect the conduct and rationalization of foreign policy. If social scientists have become more prudent, as a result of Project Camelot and its exposure, and have in fact demanded a much more careful documentation of the sources of sponsorship and the purposes of the research than they ever have in the past, this is not quite the same as either resolving or eliminating problems of participation and withdrawal from federally sponsored research. The relationship between men of knowledge (or presumed knowledge) and men of power (or presumed power) may have reached a higher stage of parity, but it would be the height of naiveté, not to mention plumbing the depths of ignorance, to think that such parity has done anything more than neatly disguise the issues posed so bluntly and even awkwardly in the Project Camelot affair. Perhaps that very blunt quality, that very angularity in which the problems were focused a generation ago, itself is a significant reason for the republication of this volume at this critical juncture in American political history, not to mention the raging turmoil within the inner history of the behavioral sciences.

If the fundamental issues remain very much the same as they were when the Camelot affair first broke in the pages of *Transaction/Society* in 1965 and as an MIT Press publication two years later, the fact also remains that this "exposé" served as a hallmark in social science self-criticism and as a benchmark in the self-realization that social science is not just fun, games, and nonsense, but is downright dangerous precisely to the degree that it is skillfully employed by its practitioners.

In one area of research after another, leaders of the field have come to grips with problems first opened by Camelot. It was a veritable Rorschach test for the behavioral researchers as a whole. Since the project involved admittedly lower and middle echelon professional troops in field after field—from anthropology to psychology to sociology—it became an essential element in the officer corps of each discipline to come to terms with what was happening. With the bestowal of professional status for service to country and to party, rather than to university and to occupation. From conservative deans to radical graduate students, the cry went out: no more work for the United States government. But this categorical imperative soon became eroded: would work for other governments or other nongovernment agencies be acceptable? Would work for congressional or senatorial "radicals" be viewed in the same light as work for the Department of Defense? Further, if social science was not really scientific, as many of the radical critics were claiming, then just what difference did participation or nonparticipation of socal scientists make?

That Project Camelot, and, specifically, the series of essays mounted in this volume focused directly on this series of problems served to undermine the functionalist and systemic paradigms of bygone epochs in social science. That it did not automatically render a brand new paradigm is hardly surprising. It is quite sufficient that in the very act of exposure the potential for reconstruction existed. Out of the ashes of the past will come the social sciences of the future. Not as full-blown monsters with perfectly articulated theorems and paradigms; but as sensitive researchers who will never again assume an automaticity in the dualism and dichotomy of empirical facts and moral values.

I. L. H.

Subject Index

Note: Index does not include material on pp. 377–399.

Abt Associates, 147, 147n, 149, 149n
Agency-directed research, 157–159, 163–165, 209, 210
   corrupting influence of, 167–172, 375–376
   and ideology, 159–163, 287, 375–376
   and social science, 156, 157, 159, 162–167, 173, 208, 287, 302, 375–376
   versus university research, 209–210, 302, 332
   see also Science
Air Force (U.S.), 9, 108, 109
Airlie House (Virginia), 47
Alliance for Progress, 86, 199, 200
American Anthropological Association, 71n
American (Congregational) Foreign Mission Society, 370
American Revolution (1776), 201–202
American Universities Field Services (AUFS), 90n
American University, 24–25, 47, 89
   see also Special Operations Research Office (SORO), at American University

Applied social science, *see* Pure versus applied social science
Armed Forces (U.S.)
   defense against Communist subversive warfare, 187, 188
   and foreign policy research, 189, 316
   and social science research, 188, 217
   see also Army (U.S.)
Army (U.S.), 5, 7, 8, 9, 10, 12, 17, 18, 48, 49, 52, 53, 119, 209
   opposition to Project Camelot, 26–27
   Research Office, 110, 205, 209
   and social science research, 186, 205, 217, 316, 321, 322–323
   see also Armed Forces

Basic social science, *see* Pure versus applied social science
Black Muslims, 354
Bolshevik movement, 272

Canada, French, 16
Catholic University (Santiago de Chile), 88, 292
Center for International Studies of M.I.T., 271

401

Central Intelligence Agency (CIA), 19, 72, 73, 120, 215, 270, 271, 275
Chile, -ans, vi, 11–12, 14, 37, 38, 84, 88, 89
  Congress of, 87
  left-wing press of, 13
  Santiago de, 11
  Senate of, 13, 229–231
  social scientists of, 318
Chilean Select Committee Report, 326–328, 333–334
China (Red), 197, 254
  U.S. policy toward, 199, 249, 254, 355
Classified research, 216, 217, 287, 303–304, 347, 348–355, 356, 357, 358
Colombia, 16
Colonialism, and social science, 295–302, 305–311
Communism, 197, 198, 199, 200, 201
  anti-, 197
  U.S. policy toward, 199, 200, 201, 276, 277
Conflict, 135–142, 147–151, 152
  and ideology, 142–143
  see also Game (theory)
Congress (U.S.), 18, 20, 21
Consensus, *see* Laissez faire consensus system
Counterinsurgency, *see* Insurgency
Cuban Revolution, 231

Deductive approach, 151
Defense Department (U.S.), 4, 5, 7, 9–10, 14, 17, 75, 179, 184, 209, 215, 219, 268–269, 275, 367
  versus State Department (U.S.), 18, 19, 21–22, 190, 224, 226
  see also Department of the Army
Department of the Army, 184
  see also Defense Department (U.S.)
Developing countries, 7, 272, 316
Dominican Republic, 37, 86

Embassies (U.S.), 87
  role of, 19–20, 220, 222, 225
Ethics, v, 121, 122
  of scientific research, 157, 174
  of social science research, 8, 35–41, 42, 78, 79–80, 81, 83, 84, 89, 90, 93, 94, 95, 96, 97, 98, 110, 111, 112, 113, 117, 120, 121, 122, 123, 124, 125, 126, 127, 154, 156, 166, 268, 274–278, 285–288, 290–295, 296–302, 303–311, 317–319, 320–321, 366
Executive Reorganization Act of 1939, 371

FLACSO, *see* Latin American Faculty of Social Sciences (FLACSO)
Fascell Subcommittee, 204, 206, 214, 223
Federal Bureau of Investigation (FBI), 19, 271
Fidelistas, 326
Ford Foundation, 101, 112
Foreign Affairs Research Council (RC) (Department of State), 179, 218, 219, 220, 224, 326–327
Foreign Area Research Coordination Group (FAR), 179, 190–191, 192, 213, 226, 227, 228
Foreign area research projects, 15–17, 207, 208, 210, 326, 332, 333–334, 335–337
  see also Foreign policy (U.S.), related research
Foreign policy (U.S.), 87, 119–120, 177, 180, 186, 189, 193, 199, 200, 232
  and developing countries, 194, 195
  related research, 178, 179, 180, 188, 211, 215, 216, 217
  see also Foreign area research projects

INDEX

Funds, source of, *see* Sponsorship (of research)

Game (theory), 135, 140, 141, 151, 263
  mixed-motive, 137, 139, 140, 151
  zero-sum, 137–139, 140, 151
  see also Conflict
Government (U.S.)
  approach to the social sciences, 180–181, 183, 189, 192–193, 211–213, 240–242, 244–260, 302, 313, 324, 327, 330–331, 333, 344, 369–370
  and foreign policy research, 180, 186, 190, 192–194, 207–208, 211–212, 215–216, 228, 240–242, 271, 272, 278–280, 323, 325–326, 328, 332, 334
  see also Foreign policy (U.S.), related research

Harlem, 277
Harvard University, 90n
Hitlerism, 31
  see also Nazism
House Foreign Affairs Committee, 15
  Subcommittee on International Organizations and Movements, 177, 214, 314, 315, 321
  see also Fascell Subcommittee
House of Representatives, 180

Ideology, 197, 198, 341, 359, 375
  Communist, 197, 200
  elitist, 353–354
  Marxist, 354
Imperialism
  anti-, 230
  Communist, 197, 200
  U.S., 13, 231, 234
Inductive approach, 150, 151
Insurgency, 51, 52, 53, 74, 143, 145, 146, 150, 151, 197, 199, 200, 201
  counter-, 13, 48, 49, 51, 52, 53, 74, 83, 143, 197, 200, 263, 288
  see also Internal war (potential)
Internal war (potential), 5, 50, 54, 55, 61, 62, 64, 149, 205
  see also Insurgency
International Security Affairs (ISA) (Defense Department), 219
International Sociological Association, 293
Intervention, -ism,
  U.S., 13–14, 86, 232–236, 327
  counter-, 13
Itamarati, 234

King Arthur's Court, v

Laissez faire consensus system, 344–347
Latin America, -ns, 37, 80, 81, 93, 96, 119
  area studies, 82, 92, 93, 94, 95, 96, 97, 98, 99, 100–106, 318
  U.S. policy toward, 199, 232–236
Latin American Faculty of Social Sciences (FLACSO), vi, 13, 86
Ligue d'Action Française, La, v

McCarthyism, 87
  neo-, 277
Malthusianism, 336
Marxism-Leninism, 338–339, 340
  see also Ideology
Methodology, and ideology, 44, 365
Military (the), *see* Army (U.S.)

National Academy of Science, 331
National Aeronautics and Space Agency (NASA), 40
National Institutes of Health, 40, 215, 327
National Research Council, 208

National Science Foundation (NSF), 40, 124, 208, 215, 327, 330
National Social Science Foundation (NSSF), 155, 182, 183, 328, 329, 330, 337
Nazism, 268
see also Hitlerism
Norodnism, 272
North Atlantic Treaty Organization (NATO), 255

Office of Education, 40
Office of External Research (XR) (Bureau of Intelligence and Research), 218, 219, 224
Office of Science and Technology (Executive Office of the U.S. President), 181, 214
Office of Social Sciences (Executive Office of the U.S. President), 181, 193, 328
Operations research, 146–147, 148, 149
Organization of American States (OAS), 37, 38

Peace Corps (U.S.), 298
Pentagon, 7, 76, 87, 217, 291–292
see also Armed Forces (U.S.)
Policy makers, -ing, 198, 210, 212, 260, 361–362, 369
versus social science, -tists, 340–341, 344, 345–347, 354, 356–358, 362, 365–376
see also Foreign policy (U.S.)
President's Research Committee on Social Trends, The, 370
Project Michelson, 16
Project Revolt, 16
Project Simpático, 16
Pure versus applied social science, 6, 129, 130, 256, 341, 367, 368

RAND Corporation, 6, 9, 108, 249, 263, 269
Research design of Project Camelot, objections to, 28–29, 30, 31, 32–35, 288, 289, 290–295, 296–302, 313, 318
Revolution, counter-, *see* Insurgency, counter-; Internal war (potential)

Science
and agency-directed research, 154, 157, 158, 173, 319
and colonialism, 295–302, 305–311
versus policy, 356
see also Agency-directed research; Policy (makers, -ing), versus social science
Simulation, 151
Smithsonian Institution, 49, 208
Social problems (approach), 10
Social science, -tist
definition of, 110–114, 116, 118
role of, 113, 115, 117, 212, 243, 244, 260–266, 272, 294, 317, 327, 375–376
role of, abroad, 20, 94–98, 102–103, 228, 274–280, 285–287, 290–302, 311–312, 316–318, 332, 334–335
role of, in government, 8, 41–43, 76–77, 89–94, 114, 123–124, 209–210, 212, 228, 243–260, 265, 267–280, 285, 303–311, 316, 319, 320–321, 325, 330–331, 375–376
and values, 117–118, 126–127, 301, 339–340, 357
see also Pure versus applied social science
Social Science Research Council, 370
Social systems (model), 10, 63, 64–65, 144, 145, 146, 149
and insurgency, 144
Sovereignty, 359–360, 365–366
Soviet Union, and social science, 290, 341–342
Special Operations Research Office (SORO), at American Uni-

versity, 4, 9, 16, 17, 24, 25, 47, 49, 50, 207, 332–333
Spelman Fund, 370
Sponsorship (of research), 71
 international, 311
 source of, 72, 73, 209–210, 211, 217–218, 275, 288, 303, 318, 332, 359, 360, 365–366
Stability, 144
 versus instability, 144
State Department (U.S.), 7, 9–10, 14, 15, 17, 20, 40, 41, 191, 215, 325
 versus Defense Department (U.S.), 18–19, 21–22, 190
 and social science projects, 42, 43, 44, 215–228, 279, 280, 323–325, 367
Strategy, 136–137, 140, 142, 263

Toryism, 343
Transitional societies, 145

United States Information Agency, 128
Universities
 and policy making, 361–362, 365, 366–376
 and values, 360–361
University of Chile, 13
 School of Sociology of, 229
 Vice-Chancellor of, 13

Values, *see* Ethics, of social science research; Social science, -tist, and values; Universities, and values
Vietnam (War), 197–198, 199, 250, 252, 253, 254, 257, 263
Violence, 136, 137, 150

Welfare system, and social science, 342–344, 346
White House Conference on the Social and Behavioral Sciences, 180, 181, 193, 328

Name Index

Allessandri Rodríguez, Jorge, 231
Almond, Gabriel, 323
Alsop, Joseph, 136n
American Psychological Association, 327
American Soldier, The (S. A. Stouffer and others), 290
America's Sixty Families (Andrew Carnegie), 112
Anderson, Hurst R., 24
Angell, Robert, 281n
Apter, David, 298
Archibald, Kathleen, 148, 148n
Ashby, Eric, 343n
Ávila, Manuel, 151
Aylwin, Andrés, 291, 301

Barber, Richard J., 358n
"Behavioral Sciences and the National Security" (Fascell Committee), 179, 180, 204
Belaúnde, Fernando, 288
Berelson, Bernard, 355n
Berle, Adolf A., 100, 337
Bernard, Jessie, 131n, 282n, 284n, 286n, 287, 292n
Boguslaw, Robert, 118n, 151, 369n
Boulding, Kenneth, 281n
Boys in White (H. S. Becker and others), 33
Braithwaite, R. B., 152, 152n

Branco, Castelo, 234
Brownlow, Louis, 370
"Buddhism and Politics in South Viet Nam" (Adam Roberts), 253
Bunster, Álvaro, 85n, 89, 229
Burdick, Eugene, 299n

Caesar, Julius, 317
Caplow, Theodore, 114n
Capone, Al, 117, 124, 125
Cardwell, D. S. L., 343n
Carnegie, Andrew, 112
Carver, George A., 252
Castro, Fidel, 326
Centurions, The (Jean Lartéguy), 250
Chamberlain, John, 128, 128n, 130
Charles I (of England), 315
Christian Science Monitor, The, 92
Coleman, James, 151
Conflict (periodical), 15

Davis, Kingsley, 85n
DeGrazia, Alfred, 282n, 283n, 295n
Deitchman, Seymour J., 187, 322
Demerath III, N. J., 375n
Denney, Jr., George C., 278, 279
DeWitt, Nicholas, 341n
Dick, William, 314, 315, 320, 322

Diderot, Denis, 7
Dulles, John F., 370
Dungan, Ralph A., 13, 14, 15, 16, 20, 315

Eisenhower, Dwight D., 308, 371
Ercilla (newspaper, Santiago de Chile), 85, 86, 88, 89, 92

Fascell, Dante B., 16, 204, 329
Fischer, John, 136n
Ford, Henry, 112
Foreign Affairs (periodical), 101, 252, 262
Frank, Andrew G., 233
Fraser, Donald M., 16, 322
Frei, Eduardo, 87, 231, 288
Frelinghuysen, Peter H. B., 324
Freud, Sigmund, 7
Fuenzalida, Edmundo, 13
Fulbright, J. W., 15, 77, 289n, 314

Galtung, Johan, 12, 13, 30, 86, 283n, 306n,
Gerver, Israel, 113n
Glazer, Myron, 282n, 286n
Glazer, Penina, 282n, 286n
Gold Coast in Transition (David Apter), 298
Goode, W. J., 144, 144n, 145, 281n
Gordon, Lincoln, 20
Graciarena, Jorge, 296, 296n
Greenfield, M., 348n
Gross, H. R., 193
Guiterman, Arthur, 323
Gulick, Luther, 370
Guns of August (Barbara Tuchman), 260
Guzardi, Walter, 233

Hagstrom, Warren O., 345n
Halle, Louis J., 324
Hamuy, Eduardo, 229, 235
Hao, Ch'en, 136n
Hefner, Robert, 150
Hill, Thomas M., 371n
Himmelstrand, Ulf, 304
Hitler, Adolf, 108, 109

Hoover, Herbert, 369, 370, 371
Hopper, Rex, 12, 13, 39, 89, 232, 295n
Horowitz, Irving Louis, 154n, 171, 204, 206, 207, 209, 282n, 283n, 284n, 285n, 289n, 291n, 292n, 312n, 320, 342n, 353n, 372n, 375n
Howton, F. William, 113n

"Ideological Operations and Foreign Policy" (House Report 1352), 179
Inkeles, Alex, 281n
"International Relations, 1960–1964" (Hans J. Morgenthau), 100
Intervention and Dollar Diplomacy in the Caribbean, 1900–1921 (Dana G. Munro), 101
Ireland, Thomas, 151

James, William, 136n
Johnson, John J., 102n
Johnson, Lyndon B., 16, 41, 92, 191, 211, 230, 235, 315, 325
Jourard, Sidney M., 132n

Kahn, Herman, 269
Kant, Immanuel, 40
Kaplan, Norman, 341n, 348n
Karl, Barry Dean, 371n
Kassof, Allen, 342n
Kaufmann, William W., 269
Keenan, B. R., 343n
Kennedy, John F., 78, 199, 301, 371
Kennedy, Mark C., 289n
Khrushchev, Nikita S., 186
Klausner, Samuel Z., 144n
Kling, Merle, 98, 100
Knights of the Round Table, v
Kornhauser, William, 137, 137n, 139
Kraft, Joseph, 135n

Lartéguy, Jean, 250, 261, 262
Lasswell, Harold, 372, 373n

Latin America Between the Eagle and the Bear (Salvador de Madariaga), 100
Latin America: Diplomacy and Reality (Adolf A. Berle), 100
Lazarsfeld, Paul F., 353n, 355n
Lederer, William, 299n
Lenin, Vladimir I., 338–339
Leoni, Raúl, 288
Lerner, Daniel, 373n
Levy, Sheldon, 150
Lewin, Kurt, 150
Lipset, Seymour M., 85n, 372n
López, José Pablo, 283n
Lowe, George E., 282n
Lundberg, Ferdinand, 112
Lundberg, George A., 117, 117n, 118, 124, 124n
Lynd, Robert, 372

McCarthy, Joseph, 15
Mace, David, 133n
Mace, Vera, 133n
McGee, Reece J., 114n
McNamara, Robert S., 16, 18, 268, 269, 315, 316
Madariaga, Salvador de, 100, 101
Making of the Good Neighbor Policy, The (Bryce Wood), 101
Malthus, Thomas Robert, 336
Mao Tse-tung, 197, 250, 261
Marder, Murrey, 136n
Marshall, George, 245
Martineau, Harriet, 366
Marx, Karl, 338–339
Means, G. C., 337
Mecham, J. Lloyd, 101
Mercurio, El (Santiago de Chile), 88
Merriam, Charles, 370
Merton, Robert K., 85n
Mills, D. L., 372n
Modern Warfare (Roger Trinquier), 250
Molina, Sergio, 233
Morgenthau, Hans J., 100, 101
Munro, Dana G., 101

Murrow, Edward R., 177
Mussolini, Benito, 108, 109
Myrdal, Gunnar, 309

New York Times, The, 73, 92
Nkrumah, Kwame, 298, 299
Nuttini, Hugo G., 11, 12, 13, 85, 85n, 86, 94, 95, 229, 232, 233, 293, 293n

Ortiz, Miguel, 14
Ostrogorskii, M., 366
Owens, Henry, 262

Parsons, Talcott, 89, 342n
Peterson, R. A., 375n
Piao, Lin, 136n
Pike, Douglas, 136n
Pincus, Walter, 313
Politics as a Vocation (Max Weber), 268
Polk, William R., 114, 114n
Pool, Ithiel de Sola, 49
Praetorians, The (Jean Lartéguy), 261, 262
Presthus, Robert, 353n
Price, Don K., 321, 345n

Redfield, Robert, 131n
Roberts, Adam, 253
Rockefeller, John D., 112
Rokeach, Milton, 119, 119n
Roosevelt, Franklin D., 370, 371
Rosenberg, Bernard, 113n
Rosenthal, Benjamin S., 16
Rostow, Walt W., 98, 261
Roybal, Edward R., 16, 321, 322
Rummel, Rudolf, 137n, 150, 150n
Rusk, Dean, 16, 17, 189, 191, 214, 223, 314, 315, 316, 324, 326

Sandino, Augusto C., 230, 231
Schelling, Thomas C., 137, 137n, 138, 139, 139n, 141, 141n, 142, 263, 269
Schwartz, Mildred A., 372n
Schwartzman, Simon, 281n
Science (periodical), 323, 324, 327

Scientific Estate, The (Don K. Price), 321
Seitz, Frederick, 331
Shaw, George Bernard, 42
Shils, Edward, 101
Siglo, El (newspaper, Santiago de Chile), 87–88, 232
Silvert, Kalman, 112, 112n, 113, 122, 123, 282n, 285n, 375n
Smith, Adam, 337
"Social Science Research and National Security" (Ithiel de Sola Pool, ed.), 49
Somit, Albert, 99n
Stages of Economic Growth (Walt W. Rostow), 261
Stalin, Joseph, 197
Strategy of Conflict, The (Thomas C. Schelling), 263
Stroessner, Alfredo, 31
Stycos, J. Mayone, 289n
Swift, Jonathan, 251
Swisher, Ralph, 148, 150

Tanenhaus, Joseph, 99n
Tilly, Charles, 118, 118n, 123, 124, 124n
Tocqueville, Alexis de, 309, 366
Trans-action (periodical), vi, 3n, 204
Trinquier, Roger, 250, 262
Truman, Harry S, 371
Tuchman, Barbara, 260
Tzu, Sun, 136n

Uliassi, Pio, 14
United States and Inter-American Security: 1889–1960, The (J. Lloyd Mecham), 101
"U.S. Army's Limited-War Mission and Social Science Research, The," 49
Urzúa, Raúl, 85n

Vallance, Theodore R., 16, 282n, 322, 323
Van Nort, Leighton, 131
Veblen, Thorstein, 113
Virginia Quarterly Review, The, 324
Vollmer, H. W., 372n
Voltaire, François Arouet de, 7

Wagley, Charles, 98n
Walsh, John, 282n
Washington Evening Star, The, 15, 313
Weber, Max, 40, 268, 366
Whiting, Allen, 249
Whyte, William H., 131n, 147n
Wohlstetter, Albert J., 269
Wolf, Jr., Charles, 143, 143n, 145, 145n
Wood, Bryce, 101
World Today, The (periodical), 253

LIBRARY OF DAVIDSON COLLEGE